WITH THE MASTER
in the School of
TESTED FAITH

– A Ladies' Bible Study of the Epistle of James –

Susan J. Heck

Tate Publishing, LLC

"With the Master in the School of Tested Faith" by Susan J. Heck

Copyright © 2006 by Susan J. Heck. All rights reserved.

Published in the United States of America
by Tate Publishing, LLC
127 East Trade Center Terrace
Mustang, OK 73064
(888) 361-9473

Book design copyright © 2006 by Tate Publishing, LLC. All rights reserved.

No part of this publication may be reproduced, stored in a retrieval system or transmitted in any way by any means, electronic, mechanical, photocopy, recording or otherwise without the prior permission of the author except as provided by USA copyright law.

Scripture quotations marked "NKJV" are taken from *The New King James Version* / Thomas Nelson Publishers, Nashville: Thomas Nelson Publishers. Copyright © 1982. Used by permission. All rights reserved.

This book is designed to provide accurate and authoritative information with regard to the subject matter covered. This information is given with the understanding that neither the author nor Tate Publishing, LLC is engaged in rendering legal, professional advice. Since the details of your situation are fact dependent, you should additionally seek the services of a competent professional.
09.11.19

ISBN: 1-5988655-9-5

060623 070323

To My Husband Doug
who has lived the Epistle of James
before me for 30 years.

Table of Contents

1	Counting Our Trials With Joy – James 1:1-4	9
2	Say Yes to Wisdom – No to Wavering – James 1:5-8	25
3	Rich Man, Poor Man – James 1:9-11	43
4	Temptations: Where Do They Come From? – James 1:12-15	55
5	The Greatest Gift of All – James 1:16-18	71
6	How to Respond to God's Word - James 1:19-21	85
7	Hear, Do, and Be Blessed – James 1:22-25	101
8	The Test of True Religion – James 1:26-27	117
9	Test of Brotherly Love – James 2:1-5	131
10	Fulfilling the Royal Law – James 2:6-13	147
11	Test of Good Works – James 2:14-20	163
12	Abraham and Rahab: Examples of Living Faith – James 2:21-26	177
13	The Danger of the Tongue! – James 3:1-6	193
14	Gaining Victory Over the Tongue! – James 3:7-12	209
15	Wisdom – From Above or From Below? – James 3:13-18	223
16	Wars and Worldliness – James 4:1-4	237
17	The Remedy for Worldliness – James 4:5-10	251
18	The Danger of Slander! – James 4:11-12	267
19	To Plan or Not to Plan? – James 4:13-17	279
20	Warnings to the Rich – James 5:1-6	293
21	The Patience of Job – James 5:7-11	307
22	Being a Woman of Your Word – James 5:12	321
23	Becoming a Woman of Prayer – James 5:13-18	333
24	A Call to Salvation – Conclusion – James 5:19-20	351
	Postscript	362

Foreword

Dear Ladies,

Several years ago the Lord gave me a pastor who used to say, "There is no substitute for verse-by-verse teaching of the Scriptures." How very right he was! There is no better way for a Christian to "study to show themselves approved" (2 Timothy 2:15), to "grow in His grace and knowledge" (2 Peter 3:18), or to "discipline themselves for the purpose of godliness" (1 Timothy 4:7).

With the Master in the School of Tested Faith is an excellent verse-by-verse Bible Study tool. Susan Heck's study of the book of James is refreshingly solid and thought provoking. It is obvious that Susan has a wonderful command of Scripture (which I happen to know is due to her many years of Scripture memory). The illustrations are clear and she does not side-step or water down the extremely convicting exhortations of James. Two outstanding features of this book are the "evaluate your faith" questions and the study questions.

I thank God for the gifts He has given Susan and her faithfulness to teach her ladies and now (through this book) to teach you. This book has been a blessing to me and will be to you, too. Study hard and seek God's glory.

In His Grace,

Martha Peace
Biblical Counselor and author of *The Excellent Wife*

Introduction

Perhaps you have just picked up this book in a bookstore and are saying to yourself, "Oh good, another book by another woman author. Honestly, don't these women have anything else better to do with their time than to write emotionally charged books for women?" Well, hold on there "Podner" (an Okie saying). This is not another emotionally charged, felt-needs book written by a woman.

Several years ago after my conversion, the Lord placed within me a deep hunger for the Word of God. My desire was to understand the Word more thoroughly. My husband encouraged me to begin memorizing the Word of God, chapter by chapter, book by book. The Lord used that in my life to whet my appetite to know and to understand what I was memorizing. I began to study the Bible for myself and that led to a deep desire to pass on to other women what I was learning. Writing Ladies Bible Studies, along with homework, and teaching the women in my church, then became my spiritual mission.

A few years ago, a friend of mine suggested I have my material published. I really didn't give a lot of thought to it, but decided to mention it to an author friend of mine, Martha Peace. After reading the study, she encouraged me to indeed pursue publication of what the Lord had taught me. Thus began an adventure, which now has culminated in the book you hold in your hand.

It is my deepest desire to equip women to be women of The Word. To be women who will not be led away by the false teachers of our day, but women who are discerning and able to study and apply truth for themselves.

My Bible Studies are not the typical "warm fuzzy" material, but are written to reveal the truth of God's Word as it is written. I have endeavored to be true expositionally, and have studied hard to be accurate to the Word's original meaning. Many of my observations and principles are born from my own love of the Word of God.

With the Master in the School of Tested Faith will be the first of what I hope to be a series entitled *With the Master*. Future studies that are to come, the Lord willing, are, *With the Master in the Upper Room* (John

13-17); *With the Master in the Fiery Furnace* (I Peter); *With the Master On Our Knees* (Prayers of the Bible), *With the Master Before the Mirror* (I John); and Colossians and Philippians yet to be named!

Won't you join me on the exciting journey *With the Master*? Oh come on, go ahead and buy the book. I promise you it won't be another book by another emotionally charged author!

1

Counting Our Trials With Joy

James 1:1-4

Throughout the years my husband and I have been in the ministry, I have seen a grievous attitude that prevails among many who call themselves "Christians." This attitude says, "I can be a Christian and live my life as I please." There is no deep consideration for what the Word of God says: "Now by this we know that we know Him, *if* we keep His commandments. He who says, 'I know Him,' and does not keep His commandments, is a liar, and the truth is not in him."[1] Few meditate on Jesus' words in the Sermon on the Mount: "Enter by the narrow gate; for wide is the gate and broad is the way that leads to destruction, and there are many who go in by it. Because narrow is the gate and difficult is the way which leads to life, and there are *few* who find it" (Matthew 7:13-14, emphasis mine). Still more sobering words to consider are "But be doers of the word, and not hearers only, deceiving yourselves" (James 1:22).

Because my ministry is mainly geared to women, I have a deep desire to make sure that the women whose lives the Lord allows me to touch are one hundred percent accurate on the issue of the gospel and how it should affect their daily living. How does one know for sure if she is redeemed? What are the evidences of a genuine faith? One of the books in the Word of God that deals with the genuineness of one's salvation, is the Epistle of James, giving us a series of tests to see if our faith is truly working. It is a practical book, relevant for the twenty-first century believer.

---

[1] 1 John 2:3-4, emphasis added. This study in the Epistle of James will use the *New King James Version* (NKJV) unless otherwise noted. *The New King James Bible,* 1980, Thomas Nelson, Inc.

The Background of the Epistle of James

Before we examine the first four verses of James, let's consider five questions which will help us to understand the background of the book and its truths.

First of all, *who* wrote the book of James? James, who was the presiding elder, the senior pastor, of the Christian community in Jerusalem, wrote this book. We will take a closer look at him later in this chapter.

Where was this book written? James probably wrote this book while he was in Jerusalem, about one year before he died.

When was this book written? The Epistle of James is probably one of the earliest New Testament books, written around A.D. 45-50. This was about twenty five years before the destruction of Jerusalem in A.D. 70. Many scholars believe it to be the oldest book in the New Testament, but there is nothing out-of-date about the message. It is timely and relevant for today.

To whom was the book written? The Epistle of James was written "to the twelve tribes, which are scattered abroad" (James 1:1). We will deal more with these twelve tribes later in this chapter.

Why did James write this epistle? James wrote this epistle to a group of Jews to get them to examine their faith. James wanted his readers to be perfect and entire, lacking nothing (James 1:4). This means that James wanted them to be complete in all their parts, with no part being wanting or inadequate in any area of their lives. By the way, this was also the desire of the Apostle Paul for the churches at Colossae and Thessalonica (Colossians 1:28 and 1 Thessalonians 3:10).

As presiding elder and senior pastor of the Christian community in Jerusalem, James had the opportunity to observe the Christians' behavior, especially during the religious feasts. He saw that it fell far short of the standard that their profession of faith demanded; therefore, he decided to write them a letter.

As we look into this book, we will see that some of these Christians were not being victorious in their Christian walk, and some, perhaps, were not genuine Christians, even though they may have thought they were. They had problems in their churches and problems in their personal lives. Some were going through difficult testing. Some were facing temptations to sin. Some were catering to the rich, while others were being robbed by the rich. Church members were competing for offices in the church, particularly teaching offices. Some of them just couldn't control that tongue. James knew that their faith was not working, and yet he knew that genuine faith does work! Yes, true faith works.

The dominant theme in the book of James is that genuine faith works practically in a Christian's life. James knew that genuine faith works when receiving trials from the Lord, as well as when receiving temptations from the devil. It's a faith that causes us to be doers of the Word as well as hearers! True faith works when it comes to loving the unlovely, those who are different from us. Having control over our tongue can only come from a faith that works. Genuine faith allows us to have wisdom from above and not from the world. True faith helps us resist the devil and submit ourselves to God in humility. Saving faith keeps us from being presumptuous about tomorrow. It is a faith that brings us to our knees in confession of our sins and dependence upon God. Genuine faith waits patiently for the coming of the Lord. True faith is so imbedded within our souls that we deeply desire to be used as a vessel by God to convert others, saving their souls from death. As you will see, James desired that their faith work, and these are just some of the issues that concerned him as he wrote this letter. As you study this short epistle, I trust you will examine your own faith in light of the evidence that James will give and ask yourself, "Do I measure up?" "Is my faith working?"

Here are some more interesting facts about the Epistle of James. This book is known as the Proverbs of the New Testament, and it is also closely related to the Sermon on the Mount. It is an example of wisdom literature, which means that the emphasis is on principles of actions applied to life situations. For example, James did not just tell us to pray, but he instructed us how to pray. He did not just tell us to be wise, but he told us how to discern true wisdom from earthly wisdom. He didn't just say to resist Satan, but he told us how to do that. It is practical.² This book is also exhortative as it contains fifty-four commands. That's one command for every two verses!

The Epistle of James, like the Epistle of Hebrews, is a very Jewish book. Of course, that makes sense since James was a Jew writing to Jews. James' writings are also very different from Paul's writings, in that there are no personal greetings or references to individuals in James' letter. James was also unusual in that he spoke often of nature: the billows of the sea, the wind, the sun, the grass and flowers, horses and other animals, birds, creatures of the sea, springs, figs, olives, grapevines, agriculture and rain. So if you like the outdoors, then you will appreciate his references and illustrations of nature. With all that in mind, let's now look at the first four verses.

> James, a bondservant of God and of the Lord Jesus Christ, to the twelve tribes which are scattered abroad: Greetings. ²My brethren, count it all joy when you fall into various trials, ³knowing that the testing of your faith produces patience. ⁴But let patience have its perfect work, that you may be perfect and complete, lacking nothing. (James 1:1-4)

James 1:1. James the Author

Notice that James began this letter with his name, James. That is not the way we would begin a letter today if we were writing someone. We usually begin our letters with the person's name to whom we are writing, "Dear Friend," and then we sign our name at the end of the letter, for example, "Love, Susan." But writing the author's name at the beginning of a letter was the custom of that day.

So, who was this James? What do we know about him? His name is the Hebrew form of Jacob. There are four men named James mentioned in the New Testament, but history tells us that the James who wrote this epistle was the brother of our Lord Jesus Christ

---

[2] Jay Adams helpfully points out: "There are more than 50 imperatives in the 108 verses of this letter! James teaches only indirectly. In James, truth is applied. Here you find truth aimed at life. That fact also means that the Book is invaluable for counselors. It meets the counseling issues head on. As a Book for counselors, James is unparalleled." Jay E. Adams, *The Christian Counselor's Commentary: Hebrews, James, 1 and 2 Peter, Jude* (Timeless Texts, 1996), p. 147.

(Matthew 13:54-56). In this passage some were commenting on Christ's teaching, and they said, "Is this not the carpenter's son? Is not His mother called Mary? And His brethren, *James*, and Joseph, and Simon, and Judas?" (Italics mine). Yet apparently, James was an unbeliever at first, because John 7:5 says, "for even his brothers did not believe in him." Let me point out that this man lived with the very Son of God, and yet at first he did not have a personal saving faith in Him. James is a prime example of how some of us have grossly erred; that is, just because you or I might have godly parents, godly mates, or godly friends, *that* does not make us a Christian. None of us will enter into the kingdom of God without personally repenting of our sins and embracing Christ as Lord and Savior. None of us will enter into the kingdom of heaven holding on to the coattails of another.

We don't have a written account of James' conversion like we do of the Apostle Paul's on the road to Damascus, but we can conclude that his former skepticism had passed away. As recorded in Acts 1:14, "His brothers" continued with the Apostles and others in the "upper room" after the ascension. He later became the leader of the Jerusalem church when Peter was released from prison (Acts 12:17), and eventually he chaired the Council of Jerusalem (Acts 15:13). Paul said in Galatians 1:19 that he saw none of the Apostles except James, the Lord's brother; and then in Galatians 2:9, Paul mentioned *James*, Cephas, and John, who seemed to be pillars of the church. James was a man of great stature in the church, and yet we don't speak much of him like we do of the Apostle Paul. History tells us he was known as "James the Just" because of his piety and integrity. Commentator D. Edmond Hiebert refers to a second century historian Hegesippus who relates how James "used to enter alone into the temple and be found kneeling and praying for forgiveness for the people, so that his knees grew hard like a camel's because of his constant worship of God, kneeling and asking forgiveness for the people."[3] James knew as he later wrote in James 5:16 that "the

---

[3] D. Edmond Hiebert, *The Epistle of James: Tests of a Living Faith* (Moody Press, 1979), p. 36. Hegesippus (between A.D. 150 and 180) was one of the earlier church historians. He wrote his *Memorials of the Christian Church,* which covered the birth of Jesus Christ to about A.D. 170. Unfortunately his work has been lost in antiquity and only quoted by Eusebius, where the piety of James the Just is mentioned. Eusebius, *Ecclesiastical History*, 2.23.

effective fervent prayer of a righteous man avails much!" Evidently a lesson he learned through lots of practice!

History also tells us that James died a martyr's death. His persecutors attempted to stone him, but he knelt down praying, "I beseech thee, Lord God Father, forgive them, for they know not what they do." Worthy of noting is that these words are almost identical to those of our Lord spoken from the cross: "Father, forgive them; for they do not know what they do" (Luke 23:34). After that, one of the fullers took a club with which he pounded clothing, and brought it down on the head of the James, and so he died.[4] This is the man who by the moving of the Holy Spirit wrote this wonderful epistle.

James 1:1. A servant of the Lord Jesus Christ

After James introduced himself, what did he say next? "Hey guys, take note! I am the very brother of the Lord Jesus Christ!" Did he say, "I'm the pastor of the church at Jerusalem"? No, he did not say either one of those things, did he? He said that he was a servant of the Lord Jesus Christ. *Servant* in the Greek text is *doulos*, which means something more than just being a servant. It denotes a person who is deprived of his personal freedom, fully becoming an instrument in the hands of his master. To his master he can never say no. And who did James say his master was? The Lord Jesus Christ. *Lord* is another name for Savior, Master, or Owner. *Christ* means Messiah or Anointed, and *Jesus* was His human name. From this introduction, we infer that James showed absolute obedience, absolute humility, and absolute loyalty to the Lord Jesus Christ. James was confessing that his earthly, older half-brother Jesus was

---

[4] Two different views of the death of James have been passed down by church tradition. Josephus records a newly appointed Jewish high priest (i.e., Ananus) who accused James before the Sanhedrin which resulted in the sentence of death by stoning. Josephus, *Antiquities of the Jews*, 20.9.1. Hegesippus however, said that Jewish priests forced him to the Temple, threw him off and because he wasn't yet dead, beat him with clubs. Eusebius, *Ecclesiastical History*, 2.23. Both traditions could be true, for Josephus also records how the people revolted against the Sanhedrin sentence against James, which might have postponed his death until later.

his Lord and deserved equal devotion with Jehovah God of the Old Testament!

James 1:1. To the twelve tribes scattered abroad

To whom was James writing? He was writing to the "twelve tribes, which are scattered abroad." These were Jewish Christians scattered outside of Palestine. The period of time during which this epistle was written seems to have been somewhere between the martyrdom of Stephen in A.D. 35 and the apostolic conference held in Jerusalem in A.D. 52, at which James acted as chairman. During this time a great persecution broke out against the Christian Church at Jerusalem with Saul of Tarsus, (who later became the Apostle Paul) as its main instigator. Acts 8:1 states: "Now Saul was consenting to his death. At that time a great persecution arose against the church which was at Jerusalem; and they were all scattered throughout the regions of Judea and Samaria, except the Apostles." So these Christians were forced to leave their homes and flee to other towns.

In the Greek, this was called the *Diaspora* of the twelve tribes. The *Diaspora* conveyed the picture of the scattering abroad of the Jews as seed. Tragically, these Jewish Christians were not taken in by their kinsmen, but rather rejected and persecuted. They became homeless, robbed of their possessions, and many hauled into court. Some say that if we want to get a feeling for what they really went through, we should read about the Holocaust of the twentieth century. History tells us that when James wrote this book, there were perhaps four million Jews scattered in the Roman world. It was probably one scattered group in particular to whom James wrote this letter.

We want to stop and consider this question: Why would a loving God do such a thing to His people? Why does God permit persecution? Why would He scatter His people? Look at Acts 8 again, this time noting verse four. It says, "Therefore they that were scattered abroad went everywhere preaching the word." One of the reasons God allows persecution is that He wants to accomplish some higher purpose than sometimes we are able to see. Sometimes that purpose is to be able to sow the seed of the Gospel in the hearts of men and women, as seen in Acts 8:4. Sometimes God has to divide His people in order to multiply His kingdom. We become too comfortable in our Christian cliques, and sometimes God intervenes to scatter his people to become witnesses for His kingdom. Sometimes God's interventions in our lives seem unpleasant and unwelcome, but they may well be "sowing" appointments in the midst of a sinful and wicked world.

James 1:1. James' Greeting

James began his letter to these persecuted and scattered believers with one simple word—*greeting*. *Greeting* means to rejoice, be glad, to be satisfied. Remember James was writing to believers who could very well have said, "We have believed in this Jesus and now look, our homes and some of our loved ones' lives have been taken away." I am confident that one of their greatest temptations would be to grumble and complain. James intended his form of greeting to prepare the readers for his admonitions that would follow on how to respond to trials. By the way, how do you start a phone call or a letter to someone, especially someone who is going through persecution or trials? "Snap out of it!" "Get with it!" "Shape up or ship out!" Hopefully not. When dealing with people who are hurting, we need to remember to be gracious, friendly, warm, and compassionate. We need to remind ourselves of what Paul said in 1Thessalonians 5:14, that we are to "comfort the fainthearted, uphold the weak, be patient with all."

After the greeting, the opening word of godly James centers in on the subject of trials in the Christian life, mentioning the Christian *reaction* to trials (v 2) and the Christian *reward* for trials (vv 3-4).

The Christian Reaction to Trials
Considering Them Joy

James 1:2. Count it all joy when you fall into various trials

After his one-word "greeting," James then stated his first command in verse 2: "My brethren, count it all joy when you fall into various trials." The Greek word for *brethren* is *adelphos,* which denotes Christian brotherhood and fellowship. James used this term fifteen times in this little epistle.[5] The command here is to count it all joy when they fell into various trials. The verb *count* in the Greek means to consider or regard as. James was saying we should regard our trials as all joy! Joy means joy in the highest sense. This means when we have a trial, we should respond with a deliberate intelligent appraisal, not an emotional reaction. James was not saying that we must force a smile, but rather we are to look at our trials from God's perspective and recognize the trial as producing something valuable. He was not saying that we should *enjoy* our trials, but we should have joy in them. The trial itself may not be joyful, but the encounter is. Do you remember what is said about our Lord in Hebrews 12:2? "Looking unto Jesus, the author and finisher of our faith, who for the joy that was set before Him endured the cross, despising the shame, and has sat down at the right hand of the throne of God." Did Jesus encounter the cross with a smile on his face? No. Scripture tells us that he was in "great agony" and His sweat was as "great drops of blood" (Luke 22:44). However, Christ considered the joy that was set before Him. He knew His trial was producing something valuable. What did our Lord's trial produce? Salvation for mankind.

---

[5] James 1:2, 16, 19; 2:1, 5, 14; 3:1, 10, 12; 4:11; 5:7, 9, 10, 12, 19. The term *adelphos* (English, *brother*) at this stage of history was not exclusively used for Christians but at times used for those who share something in common. For example, the Apostle Peter used *adelphos* when speaking to fellow Jews, who at the time were not Christians. e.g., Acts 2:29; 3:17. Even Stephen when giving his blistering sermon against Jewish leadership, called them "brethren" (Acts 7:2). Paul calls unsaved Jews in Antioch of Pisidia "brethren" (Acts 13:26, 38). But in the Epistle of James, it seems he uses the term uniformly as a reference to those who share a common faith as believers.

When is the last time you went through a trial saying, "Great! This is a reason for nothing but joy, happiness, and thanksgiving!" Most believers unfortunately do not view these difficulties as gifts from God, but as dirty rotten deals! We fail to acknowledge what James said later in chapter 1: "Every good gift and every perfect gift is from above, and comes down from the Father of lights, with whom [there] is no variation or shadow of turning" (v 17). Those "good gifts" from the Father include trials that He gives us. They *are* gifts! We fail to live in view of eternity and how each trial can be used to prepare us to be like our Lord. By the way, in my life I have found that if I choose not to respond correctly and godly to what God allows, then usually the Lord requires me to repeat the test. Only the next time the test comes, it is a little more difficult.

So what was James conveying when he wrote about "falling" into various trials? The word *fall* in the Greek means to fall into something so that one is entirely surrounded by it. The thought is of difficult situations surrounding us unexpectedly, illustrated in the case of the man traveling from Jerusalem to Jericho in Luke 10:30. The story of the Good Samaritan told by Jesus relates the account of the traveler who *fell* among thieves and then was stripped, robbed, and wounded. Most trials come just like that. One minute we are going about our own business and *wham*! When I was writing this for the study of James, that is what happened to me. I reminded myself of 1 Peter 4:12: "Beloved, do not think it strange concerning the fiery trial which is to try you, as though some strange thing happened to you." In James 1:2, the Greek word for *trial* is *peirasmois* and has the double sense of outward trials and inward temptations. Outward trials very often become occasions of temptation to sin. However, that temptation to sin in the trial is not from God. As it is written in James 1:13, "Let no one say when he is tempted, 'I am tempted by God'; for God cannot be tempted by evil, nor does He Himself tempt anyone." Trials are sent to test our faith, not to cause us to sin. But we will investigate that truth later in James 1.

James said that these trials we fall into are "various." The word *various* derives from the adjective used to describe Joseph's coat of many colors. It doesn't necessarily mean that we will have a lot of trials, but that the trials will be varied, of different colors.

Some trials may be black like these persecuted Christians were experiencing. Dark, black trials might mean the death of a relative or a friend, a financial adversity, a wayward child, an abusive husband, a bad marriage, a job loss, or suffering persecution for righteousness' sake. Some trials may be red a move to another city or state or even another country, a long-term illness, or a difficult pregnancy. Some trials may be pale yellow spilled milk, long lines in traffic or at the grocery store, or interruptions in your day. God's grace is sufficient for the day, whatever the color of our trials.

Sometimes our trials come unannounced, suddenly. How do we respond? Do we shake our fists at God? Or bow our knees in humble submission and adoration at what we can learn through this process? Remember, these Christians had a far greater challenge than do you or I today. They were martyred because of their faith in Christ. And their reaction was one of considering it joy, as they also considered the reward.

The Christian Reward for Trials
Patience and Perfection

James 1:3. The testing of your faith produces patience

You might say, well why do I want to regard my trials with joy? What is the purpose of this suffering anyway? James stated the purpose in verse 3: "Knowing that the testing of your faith produces patience." The word *know* in the Greek is *ginosko*, which suggests a knowledge that is grounded in personal experience. As believers, we should not be ignorant of the fact that God sends trials for a purpose. As Christians, we need to be able to discern what that purpose is. We should know by experience that these trials, as James says, "produces [*worketh*, KJV] patience." The testing of our faith has a significant impact on our spiritual maturity. This testing process produces patience.

This is the first time that *faith* is mentioned in the book of James. It is interesting that James mentioned faith before he mentioned works, the work being patience. We must have faith before we can act upon it. Faith works, but we must have faith before it can work! That is why we need to ask ourselves when Christians bottom out spiritually during a trial, "Why isn't their faith working?" It should be. James says our faith worketh patience. The word *worketh* means to achieve, to accomplish. Isn't it great to know that whatever you are going through right now is accomplishing something? Many times that "something" is patience.

We might ask, "Well, what is patience?" Sometimes we lightheartedly say that patience is what most of us don't have. On a serious note, we see patience in a person who bravely remains upright and firm under adverse circumstances without collapse or cowardice. This person is steadfast. Patience also has a secondary meaning of "expecting, waiting for somebody." It presents the picture of being under a heavy load and staying there instead of trying to escape. Patience is that spirit that holds up under pressure while waiting on God's timing for reward or dismissal. Would you say that you are trying to escape right now from the trial that you are facing? Stay, abide, remain, and see what great things God has in store for you!

Sometimes we tease one another by saying, "Don't pray for patience, because you'll get it!" What we mean is that we are asking for trouble when we are asking for patience. But remember, the Lord sends trouble to produce patience. And the more tests we pass, the more steadfast we become. I'm reminded of what Paul said to the Roman Christians, "And not only that, but we also glory in tribulations, knowing that tribulation produces perseverance; and perseverance, character; and character, hope" (Romans 5:3-4).

James 1:4. But let patience have its perfect work

James continued in verse 4: "But let patience have its perfect work." In other words, let patience produce its appropriate effects without being hindered. Let God do His work. And let it be developed without murmuring or rebellion (Philippians 2:14). The word *work* in the Greek is *ergon,* which indicates that endurance should be active and not passive. James was saying that while we are bearing under that terrific load, we are not to remain stationary. We are to move about and exercise our energy. There should be no passive endurance in the Christian life. Our trials should not render us ineffective for the Lord. I have seen believers who have experienced trials, and then suddenly they vanish. They have abandoned the worship of God, His people, and active ministry. As believers, this should not be our response when subjected to trials.

Why are we to let patience have her perfect work? James said it was so that we can be perfect and complete, lacking nothing. The Greek word for *perfect* means fulfillment, goal, end. In other words, it is bringing something to a successful completion. This means everything will be complete, entire, or fully carried out. All parts should be present and none missing. All parts should be intact. Just as a person may be physically mature yet minus a leg, so a believer may be spiritually mature in some respects, but not complete if she does not remain steadfast in adversity. Trials are sent to complete us. Unfortunately, too many believers or professing believers reject their trials, stifling the potential of spiritual growth. Had these persecuted Jewish Christians responded righteously to trials, they would have been able to live victoriously, wanting nothing.

Have you ever known or been around a "seasoned saint" one who has aged not only physically, but spiritually as well? Women who have allowed the trials and sufferings of life to mature them, i.e., women like Corrie ten Boom, Elisabeth Elliot and Joni Erickson Tada. There's something very attractive about these women that makes me want to be around them and to learn from them. What is it? It is the Christ-like qualities that have been produced as a result of their suffering. We may glibly say, "I want to be conformed to the image of Jesus Christ," but do we really? If we do, then we must expect trials, and we must expect many kinds of trials. Did not Paul the Apostle say in his letter to the Philippian church that he wanted to know "the fellowship of His sufferings"? (Philippians 3:10). The only way Paul could know the fellowship of Christ's sufferings was to go through many trials; and of course, we know the Apostle Paul suffered much.

Summary

In closing our thoughts on this precious portion of God's Word, may I leave you with two major principles? Hold them in your soul from this moment on.

1. Our Reaction. The reality of the Christian life is that we will have trials. The Epistle of James tells us they will come (v 2). Job said man is full of trouble (Job 14:1). If we don't have troubles today, we will have troubles tomorrow. There must be a proper reaction to your trials. James says our reaction should be joy (v 2). This is not a forced smile, but an inner understanding and contentment that God is at work.

2. Our Rewards. Reacting to trials with an inner contentment of joy depends on a forward look at the potential for what they can produce in our lives. There are rewards to trials, great and profound. In essence, when we are able to count those trials as real joy, then they cultivate patience, steadfastness, perfection, and completion (vv 3-4). What a deal!

My dear sisters, we need women today who will allow the hardships of life to bring them to perfection and maturity in Jesus Christ. Will you respond righteously to your trials, and will you allow your trials to bring you to perfection and to the conformity of our Lord Jesus Christ and His will? I pray you will.

Questions to Consider
"Counting Our Trials With Joy"
James 1:1-4

1. What facts do you already know about the Epistle of James?

2. Read James chapter 1 every day. (a) Write down all the commands that you see. (b) Would you say you are currently obedient to each of these commands? Why or why not? (c) What do you think God would have you do, and what will you do?

3. Memorize James 1:2-3.

4. James says we are to count or consider it joy when we are facing trials (v 2). How can you use the following verses to encourage yourself or someone else to face their trials joyfully? Job 19:25-26; Psalm 119:67-68, 71-72, 75-76; Romans 8:28; 2 Corinthians 12:7-10; James 1:2-4; and 1 Peter 1:6-7.

5. Read 2 Corinthians 12:7-10. (a) What did Christ say was the answer to Paul's trial (thorn in the flesh)? (b) How did Paul respond to that particular trial? (c) What do you think Paul meant when he said he would rather *glory* in his infirmities? (d) How does this relate to what James says about being joyful in trials?

6. Think of a biblical example of someone who went through a trial, and list the ways God used it to perfect her or him.

7. Honestly answer the following questions:
   (a) What is normally your first response to a trial? (b) Do you welcome trials as opportunities to develop in maturity towards Christ? How do you welcome them? (c) Why do you think we as believers resist trials?

8. Reflect over past trials you have had. How do you think they have helped you grow in the area of patience or endurance?

9. List the trials you are currently going through. Thank God for each one. Thank God for the joy that transcends each one. Thank Him in advance for the joy and confidence and patience you'll gain when the test or tests are over. Ask God for the grace and wisdom to pass each test.

10. (a) What is the greatest trial you are facing today? (b) What is your prayer request to the Lord?

2

Say Yes to Wisdom – No to Wavering

James 1:5-8

When terrorists attacked the United States on September 11, 2001, our nation was in a state of shock. Most of us were glued to the television, watching the events unfold. The media said many things like: "We need to be protected from terrorism within." "We must take aggressive action." "We must fight back." "We need to bring all of our troops home to the United States." "We need to beef up our airports' security." But little, if anything, was mentioned about our "need" to ask God for wisdom during one of our nation's most severe trials. Many of us read the newspaper from cover to cover day after day and never ran across the word *wisdom*. Rarely, if ever, did we hear it spoken by a TV newscaster or see it published in a newspaper. The word *wisdom* seemed to have eluded the popular media. Even in the church of Jesus Christ, we heard little then and still hear little today about wisdom; even worse, it is seldom practiced.

What is wisdom, and how do we obtain it? As believers in Jesus Christ, we need wisdom to endure trials, and we need to know how to apply wisdom to the everyday circumstances of our lives. The Epistle of James has some helpful tips on this topic of wisdom and especially emphasizes the need of it during trials. We need to say "yes to wisdom and no to wavering." Let us now consider James 1:5-8.

The Christian Says "Yes" to Wisdom

If any of you lacks wisdom, let him ask of God, who gives to all liberally and without reproach, and it will be given to him. ⁶But let him ask in faith, with no doubting, for he who doubts is like a wave of the sea driven and tossed by the wind. ⁷For let not that man suppose that he will receive anything from the Lord; ⁸he is a double-minded man, unstable in all his ways. (James 1:5-8)

James 1:5. If any of you lacks wisdom, let him ask of God

Having encouraged a joyful reaction to inevitable trials because of the rewards they produce, the godly Pastor of the Jerusalem church adds: "If any of you lacks wisdom, let him ask of God." James was referring to asking for wisdom during trials.[6] The first word *if* implies that some believers were falling short of the wisdom that was needed to turn trials into triumphs. We need to remember that these believers' trials were not just spilled milk, long traffic lines, or interruptions in their day. These believers had been persecuted and forced to leave their homes. Many lost their houses, employment and family, with a few being martyred for their faith, as the very author of this epistle would be. This is similar to some of the trials of the Jews during the Holocaust of the twentieth century.

As believers in the twenty-first century, we too can come

---

[6] See James 1:2. While the *King James Version* translates *peirasmois* as *temptations*, the *New King James Version* translates *peirasmois* as *trials*. This is because there are two views about its nature: 1) some suggest this refers to both inner and outward temptations because of the adjective in verse 2 (i.e., "various") would suggest every possible source. However, the adjective (Greek, *poikilois*) speaks rather of the forms of trials and not the many sources. 2) Others suggest that James is speaking of external trials that come on a believer. This is the proper sense if we keep in mind the fact that external trials are given by the Lord to produce Christ-like character, but with them could also come internal temptation seeking to shrink our soul in evil.

short of the wisdom we need in trials. We can be in great danger of going astray when going through trials. We often complain, "Woe is me" or "Why me, Lord?" We often rebel and seek the wrong solutions. So what should we do when we need wisdom in the face of trials? Seek "professional" counseling? Check ourselves into a mental clinic? Call our best friend? Call our husband at work? No, No, No! James teaches us that our first response to trials should be to ask for the wisdom of God. In this passage, James is commanding his readers to ask for wisdom, *not to tell* God to deliver them from their trials. "Let him ask of God" is not a statement that implies granting permission to solicit wisdom, but a mandate, a command, to do so.

Here we should ask, "What is wisdom anyway?" *Webster's New Third International Dictionary* defines wisdom as (1) the effectual mediating principle or personification of God's will in the creation of the world and (2) the intelligent application of learning. So, wisdom is not just knowledge, but a practical application of the knowledge we have. Wisdom is the understanding needed to live our lives to the glory of God. And James commanded us to ask God for wisdom. After all, does not all wisdom come from Him? Consider the sufferer Job as he searches for wisdom.

> 'But where can wisdom be found? And where is the place of understanding? Man does not know its value, Nor is it found in the land of the living. The deep says, 'It is not in me'; And the sea says, 'It is not with me.' It cannot be purchased for gold, Nor can silver be weighed for its price. It cannot be valued in the gold of Ophir, In precious onyx or sapphire. Neither gold nor crystal can equal it, Nor can it be exchanged for jewelry of fine gold. No mention shall be made of coral or quartz, For the price of wisdom is above rubies. The topaz of Ethiopia cannot equal it, Nor can it be valued in pure gold. From where then does wisdom come? And where is the place of understanding? It is hidden from the eyes of all living, And concealed from the birds of the air. Destruction and Death say, 'We have heard a report about it with our ears.' God understands its way, And He knows its place. For He looks to the ends of the earth, And sees under the whole heavens, To establish a weight for the wind, And apportion out the waters by measure. When He made a law for the rain, And a path for the thunderbolt, then He saw wisdom and declared it; He prepared it, indeed, He

searched it out. And to man He said, 'Behold, the fear of the Lord, that is wisdom, And to depart from evil is understanding.' (Job 28:12-28)

In this passage of Scripture, we find Job seeking wisdom in the midst of his tremendous trials. His three friends were unable to help him find wisdom; neither was his wife able to help him. And so, Job asked in verse 12, "Where does this wisdom come from?" He answered that it does not come from the land or the ocean, nor can it be purchased at the store. The only One who knows wisdom and is the source of all wisdom is God (Job 28:23). God knows the place of it. Doesn't that make sense? After all, He is the God of Wisdom who knows the beginning and the end. He knows your needs before you ask. He is the Wonderful Counselor, and He doesn't even charge you a fee for His counseling! Psalm 16:7 says, "I will bless the LORD who has given me counsel." Proverbs 9:10 tells us that "the fear of the Lord is the beginning of wisdom."

Perhaps the best example we have in Scripture of an individual who sought God for help in a trial is Solomon.

At Gibeon the LORD appeared to Solomon in a dream by night; and God said, "Ask! What shall I give you?" And Solomon said: "You have shown great mercy to Your servant David my father, because he walked before You in truth, in righteousness, and in uprightness of heart with You; You have continued this great kindness for him, and You have given him a son to sit on his throne, as it is this day. Now, O LORD my God, You have made Your servant king instead of my father David, but I am a little child; I do not know how to go out or come in. [Solomon was probably only 20 years old at this time.] And Your servant is in the midst of Your people whom You have chosen, a great people, too numerous to be numbered or counted. Therefore give to Your servant an understanding heart to judge Your people, that I may discern between good and evil. For who is able to judge this great people of Yours?" The speech pleased the LORD, that Solomon had asked this thing. Then God said to him: "Because you have asked this thing, and have not asked long life for yourself, nor have asked riches for yourself, nor have asked the life of your enemies, but have asked for yourself understanding to discern

Say Yes to Wisdom – No to Wavering

justice, behold, I have done according to your words; see, I have given you a wise and understanding heart, so that there has not been anyone like you before you, nor shall any like you arise after you. And I have also given you what you have not asked: both riches and honor, so that there shall not be anyone like you among the kings all your days. So if you walk in My ways, to keep My statutes and My commandments, as your father David walked, then I will lengthen your days." Then Solomon awoke; and indeed it had been a dream. And he came to Jerusalem and stood before the ark of the covenant of the LORD, offered up burnt offerings, offered peace offerings, and made a feast for all his servants. Now two women who were harlots came to the king, and stood before him. And one woman said, "O my lord, this woman and I dwell in the same house; and I gave birth while she was in the house. Then it happened, the third day after I had given birth, that this woman also gave birth. And we were together; no one was with us in the house, except the two of us in the house. And this woman's son died in the night, because she lay on him. So she arose in the middle of the night and took my son from my side, while your maidservant slept, and laid him in her bosom, and laid her dead child in my bosom. And when I rose in the morning to nurse my son, there he was, dead. But when I had examined him in the morning, indeed, he was not my son whom I had borne." Then the other woman said, "No! But the living one is my son, and the dead one is your son." And the first woman said, "No! But the dead one is your son, and the living one is my son." Thus they spoke before the king. And the king said, "The one says, 'This is my son, who lives, and your son is the dead one'; and the other says, 'No! But your son is the dead one, and my son is the living one.'" Then the king said, "Bring me a sword." So they brought a sword before the king. And the king said, "Divide the living child in two, and give half to one, and half to the other." Then the woman whose son was living spoke to the king, for she yearned with compassion for her son; and she said, "O my lord, give her the living child, and by no means kill him!" But the other said, "Let him be neither mine nor yours, but divide him." So the king answered and said, "Give the first woman the living child, and by no means kill him; she is his mother." And all Israel heard of the judgment which the king had rendered; and they feared the king, for they saw that the wisdom of God was in him to administer justice. (1 Kings 3:5-28)

Do you desire that kind of wisdom? I do. I also need that kind of wisdom, not only for help in my own life, but when helping and counseling others. I know that in and of myself I have nothing to offer, but God has everything to offer, as He is the God of all wisdom. In my life when I sought the help of others first, I ultimately realized that God had the answer all the time. If I had turned to Him first, it would have saved me much time and energy.

When listening to a Christian radio program, I once heard a woman being asked what she did when suffering tremendous pain. I was intrigued by her answer. She said she would spend three to four hours in prayer. What a testimony! Here was a woman who wanted to so take hold of God and His wisdom in her pain and suffering that she was willing to spend three to four hours in prayer. I am not suggesting that the Lord requires us to spend three to four hours in prayer every time we encounter a trial, even though sometimes that may be exactly the best solution for the trial of the moment. Sometimes a quick prayer will suffice: "Oh Lord, please give me wisdom right now. I don't know what to do." Nor am I saying never turn to other godly sources for advice, because God has given us mates, friends, and pastors at times for that purpose. Even the Bible tells us that "in a multitude of counselors there is safety" (Proverbs 24:6).

My admonition, however, is that when seeking counsel from others, be sure that the Word of God can confirm the counsel you receive. Sometimes we may take someone's word for something because we respect her or him, but our final authority is the Word of God. It is the manual by which we should live our lives. The first One we should seek when encountering a trial and recognizing our need for wisdom is the Lord. By the way, I have often found in my own life that God may continue to allow the trial in my life until I seek Him instead of others.

James 1:5. Who gives to all liberally and without reproach

Next James gives us two reasons why we need to seek God first for wisdom. First of all, He "gives to all liberally"; and secondly, "He gives without reproach." I used to think that the word *liberally* meant that God would give me tons of wisdom when I asked. Actually in the Greek, the word *liberally* means simplicity, sincerity, and reality. In other words, God's gift of giving is without reservation, hesitation, or calculation for a return gift. The text implies that God gives wisdom without any secondary motive, because giving is part of His nature. We know this because He has given us the best gift of all, which is the gift of eternal life through the shed blood of His Son Jesus Christ. "He who did not spare His own Son, but delivered Him up for us all, how shall He not with Him also freely give us all things?" (Romans 8:32).

James later wrote in verse 17 that "every good gift and every perfect gift is from above, and comes down from the Father of lights, with whom there is no variation or shadow of turning." He is the giver of all gifts, and wisdom is one of His gifts to those who ask, especially when facing trying times.

God not only gives liberally but He gives "without reproach." The word *reproach* means "to cast in ones teeth."[7] *Reproach* was used to describe a practice of giving stinging words along with money. Literally it means that He doesn't reproach, rebuke, or treat us harshly. He doesn't reply, "Don't you know the answer to that? That's a simple solution," *or* "What did you do with the last gift I gave you?" *or* "You have wasted everything else, why should I help you now?" *or* "I gave you a head, why don't you use it?" *or* "Have you *ever* been thankful?" Honestly! Those phrases I sometimes hear

---

[7] William Barclay helps us understand how gifts could be spoiled by the *manner* in which they are given: There is a kind of giver who gives only with a view to getting more than he gives; who gives only to gratify his vanity and his sense of power by putting the recipient under an obligation which he will never be allowed to forget; who gives and then continuously casts up the gift that he has given" (p. 46). But God's giving is not like that. The sense here is to encourage boldness in asking God for wisdom during our trials, as many might fear to ask due to a sense of unworthiness.

spoken from a mother's mouth to her children in public. (Hopefully, none of you communicate with your children in this manner.)

Many times we come repeatedly to the Lord asking for wisdom in the same situation. Isn't it wonderful to know we can come to Him a thousand times, year after year after year? Isn't it comforting to know His response will be "I'm so glad you asked"? Matthew 7:7-11 has some encouraging words for His believers.

> Ask, and it will be given to you; seek, and you will find; knock, and it will be opened to you. For everyone who asks receives, and he who seeks finds, and to him who knocks it will be opened. Or what man is there among you who, if his son asks for bread, will give him a stone? Or if he asks for a fish, will he give him a serpent? If you then, being evil, know how to give good gifts to your children, how much more will your Father who is in heaven give good things to those who ask Him!

Aren't these words of our Lord reassuring? So when I am faced with a trial, I have the privilege of coming to God and requesting wisdom from the One who gives simply, compassionately, and gently. The wise man says:

> Yes, if you cry out for discernment, And lift up your voice for understanding, If you seek her as silver, And search for her as for hidden treasures; Then you will understand the fear of the LORD, And find the knowledge of God. For the LORD gives wisdom; From His mouth come knowledge and understanding. (Proverbs 2:3-6)

James 1:5. And it will be given to him

Observe what James says next: "And it will be given to him." This does not mean that we will be given everything we desire, but it does mean that we will be given *wisdom* to know what to do during trials. What a promise—that God does not withhold wisdom from believers during trials if we ask! We all know Christians—maybe some of us are even under this delusion—who believe that being a Christian means God is under obligation to give us whatever we want. I like the story about a lady who one day was giving her nephew some lessons. He was generally a good, attentive child, but on this occasion he could not fix his mind on his work. Suddenly he said, "Auntie, may I kneel down and ask God to help me find my marble?" His aunt consented, and the little boy knelt by his chair, closed his eyes, and prayed silently. Next day, almost afraid of inquiring in case the child had not found the toy and so might have lost his simple faith, the lady asked, "Well, dear, have you found your marble?" "No, Auntie" was the reply, "but God made me not want to." That is the attitude I believe God wants from each of us. The boy may not have found the marble but discovered some wisdom from God that is far more valuable! The Christian says "Yes" to wisdom, but further ...

The Christian Says "No" to Wavering

James 1:6. But let him ask in faith

In verse 6, James says yes—that wisdom in trials will be granted us on two conditions. The first condition is to "ask in faith." James says, "but let him ask in faith." What does *in faith* mean? Does that mean when we are facing a trial and approach God for wisdom and pray in faith that He will do whatever we ask? What if we desire the trial to be gone? Or the people who are involved out of sight? That would be absurd because that would be against the character of God. In the Upper Room Discourse (John 13-17) Jesus said, "And whatever you ask *in My name*, that I will do, that the Father may be glorified in the Son. If you ask anything *in My name*, I will do it" (John 14:13-14, emphasis mine). *In My name* includes the character of God, that which would glorify Him, and that which would be for His purpose and His kingdom. Faith is a wholehearted attitude of full and unquestioning committal to and dependence upon God as He has revealed Himself to us in Christ Jesus. When we come to God to ask for wisdom, we must not only believe in His ability to answer our requests, but also in His willingness to answer in harmony with His character and purpose. In James 1:6, we see that James is not talking about the quantity of our faith as much as he is talking about the quality of our faith, which is an unreserved dedication to God.

Trials are sent to test our faith, to see whether it is genuine, to see if our Christianity is real. Trials do not destroy us, but test us. What we are in our trials is what we are. We either believe God, or we don't believe God. Hebrews 11:6 states, "But without faith it is impossible to please Him, for he who comes to God must believe that He is, and that He is a rewarder of those who diligently seek Him." Notice it is the one who "diligently" seeks God whose faith shows an unquestioning commitment to God.

James 1:6. With no doubting

The second condition that James mentions when asking God for wisdom is "no doubting" or wavering. Doubting here means to be divided against oneself. It is a union of belief and unbelief, with the latter being the stronger of the two. This is not the picture of a genuine believer who vacillates between believing and not believing what God can do. Rather, this is the picture of the professing spurious believer who wants the world and whose heart is divided. There is no promise that God will answer the prayer of one at enmity with Him. We will see in James 4:4-10 that the divided heart is "at enmity with God." This double heart is at war with Him. God is more interested in our state of mind and heart than in the details of life. God desires our holiness over our happiness. He wants us to love Him with our heart, mind, soul, and strength; and maybe sometimes He will use the trials of life to get us to that point. Another verse bearing the same theme is 1 Timothy 2:8: "I desire therefore that the men pray everywhere, lifting up holy hands, without wrath and doubting."

James 1:6. For he who doubts is like a wave of the sea driven and tossed by the wind

James continues by saying that if we waver we are "like a wave of the sea driven and tossed by the wind." Waves of the sea have no stability, do they? They are at the mercy of every wind and are tossed about. If we come to God unsettled like a wave of the sea, every new feeling that springs up will toss us about. No doubt James and his readers had witnessed the frightful storms on the Sea of Galilee. Nazareth, where James grew up, was not far from the Sea of Galilee. Even though it was only fifteen miles long and six to eight miles wide, it was subject to violent storms and strong winds that would come up in the afternoon or evening. Remember in Luke 8 when Jesus and the disciples were in a boat together and the Lord fell asleep? The passage says "a wind storm came down on the lake and they were filling with water, and were in jeopardy." That was the Sea of Galilee.

No doubt James and his readers had seen firsthand the churning of the water, which suggests the agitation of the doubter's heart. Such persons are encouraged one minute, discouraged the next. In Ephesians 4:14, Paul used similar terms to describe immature Christians: "We should no longer be children, tossed to and fro and carried about with every wind of doctrine, by the trickery of men, in the cunning craftiness of deceitful plotting." We all know those who are up and down, then down and up. Divine wisdom cannot be given to a mind that is tossed here and there by doubting God's character. When praying in trials, we must not doubt the ability of God. To do so is to deny the very character of God. To doubt the ability of God also reveals the true character of an unregenerate heart. Too often when it comes to what we think is humanly impossible, we begin to doubt in spite of the fact that God is capable of bringing it to pass. With man things *are* impossible, but with God all things are possible (Matthew 19:26; Mark 9:23; Mark 10:27; Mark 14:36). By contrast, the woman or man of genuine faith is stable and mature. She may not possess all wisdom for every situation, but when she needs to ask, she does so in confidence and to the right source. You may say, "That's too hard, I can't do that." If that is the case, do you know what the Lord inspired James to write about you? Do you know what the result of that kind of *seasick* praying is?

James 1:7. Let not that man suppose that he will receive anything from the Lord

James warns, "For let not *that* man suppose that he will receive anything from the Lord" (emphasis mine). *That* (Greek, *ekeinos*) has a note of personal rejection to it. By its use James disassociated himself from the man and placed him at a distance. James refused to be in the same category with such a doubter. And that should not be a surprise to us, because *that* man, *that* woman, turned out to be a hypocrite. In fact, if we are hypocritical, God will not answer any of our prayers, as James subsequently tells us: "You ask and do not receive" (James 4:3). Why not? Because you ask with motives of lust to gratify self in some way.

James was contrasting the man of genuine faith going through trials with the man of spurious faith going through trials. The man of genuine faith asks for wisdom out of an obedient life, but the man of spurious faith can ask all he wants, but because his heart is divided between God and the world he doesn't receive and wilts under the hot sun of the trial. This example presents a sad picture, as all of us have witnessed men and women who were "professing believers" in the following scenario. Once a trial arrives, they deny the very Lord that bought them, proving they were never in the faith. This is the man that our Lord describes in Matthew 13:1-23 in the parable of the soils. This man received the seed, heard the word, and immediately received it with joy. "Hey," he said, "this Christianity is a good deal." But Jesus said that when "tribulation or persecution arises because of the word he stumbles." He is nowhere to be found. He has disappeared. As the Apostle John said, "They went out from us, but they were not of us; for if they had been of us, they would have continued with us; but they went out that they might be made manifest, that none of them were of us" (1 John 2:19). Our overall lives should be lives of faith and trusting God.

Maybe some of you are having a hard time accepting what James is telling us. May I encourage you to read and study Hebrews

11? This inspiring chapter on faith deals with men and women who went through horrendous trials, yet they did not doubt, but were great saints of faith. They endured the trials of cruel mockings, scourgings, bonds, imprisonment, torment, and being sawn in half. Yet, they did not doubt. They did not waver. They were not like a wave of the sea rolling to and fro. They had faith. They looked to Jesus as the author and finisher of their faith! Those saints in Hebrews 11 are excellent examples for us to follow and emulate today.

James 1:8. He is a double-minded man

James wrote even more sobering words in verse 8: "He is a double-minded man, unstable in all his ways." The man or woman who doubts will not only not receive anything from the Lord, but is double-minded, unstable, and unsettled in *all* his ways. Double-minded in the Greek literally means two-souled. This Greek word is not used anywhere else in the New Testament but in this passage. It means "with soul divided between faith and the world." John Bunyan labeled this person "Mr. Facing Both Ways," in his book, *Pilgrim's Progress*. He has one soul turned toward God and the other soul toward the world. One soul believes God, and the other soul disbelieves God. The Old Testament would have provided James with this concept of a united soul, as every day the Hebrews would repeat: "Hear, O Israel: The LORD our God, the LORD is one! You shall love the LORD your God with all your heart, with all your soul, and with all your strength" (Deuteronomy 6:4-5). James' Jewish audience would have understood this completely.

The Psalmist also records for us the gravity of being double minded: "Help, LORD, for the godly man ceases! For the faithful disappear from among the sons of men. They speak idly everyone with his neighbor; With flattering lips and a double heart they speak" (Psalm 12:1-2). Another passage to consider is: "Then you will call upon Me and go and pray to Me, and I will listen to you. And you will seek Me and find Me, when you search for Me with all your heart" (Jeremiah 29:12-13). It must be a whole heart—not a half heart. My dear sister, if your faith is halfhearted, then there is no faith, for there is no authenticity to a halfhearted faith.

James 1:8. Unstable in all his ways

Not only is that man double-minded, but James says he is "unstable in all his ways." In the original language this means one who is never able to settle down. This is a person who cannot be relied upon, for she is as ready to depart from God as to be close to Him. She isn't firmly rooted in her Christian beliefs in any way. Have you ever met a person like that? She can never seem to make up her mind. One minute she is going to do something one way, the next minute another. She almost makes you dizzy with here and there decisions. This behavior reminds me of some teenagers who one day love one girl or boy, and the next day another, and the next day another. You, too, may have a sense of unsettledness, if you do not know that God is sovereign and in control of all things and that He has made certain promises to you in His Word (*if* you are His child). Trials indeed can be frightening to those who are double-minded and unstable. There is a sense of hopelessness, panic, despair, and depression. Isn't that despair really double-mindedness?

James goes on to say that this person is not only unstable, but unstable in "all his ways." She is unstable not only in her prayers, but in every aspect of her life: her principles, her integrity, her life's plans, her emotions, and her physical life. She is unreliable in all her dealings. This person's whole life is affected to the point where she finally abandons herself to living in hypocrisy and in open sin. She loses the advantage of wisdom, which God would have given her in time of trial if only she had asked. This is someone you should probably remove yourself from. "The man who does not trust God cannot be trusted by men" (Oesterley quoted by Hiebert, p. 88). Unfortunately, many "believers" live like that by not adorning the doctrine of God and making it attractive, but instead they are blaspheming the Word of God in their lives. They are indeed unstable in all of their ways. My dear friend, I trust that this is not what people are saying about us.

Summary

Are your trials proving that your faith is genuine by producing patience, perfection, and prayer in your life? Or are your trials proving your faith is spurious by producing anger, bitterness, and doubts about God? Are you seeking God for wisdom in trials or do you quickly turn to the "Dear Abby" in your life? Do you ask in faith, or are you a doubter? Have you said "yes" to wisdom, and "no" to wavering? As wise Solomon said to his son, so I say to you, "Wisdom has built her house, She has hewn out her seven pillars; She has slaughtered her meat, She has mixed her wine, She has also furnished her table. She has sent out her maidens, She cries out from the highest places of the city, 'Whoever is simple, let him turn in here!' As for him who lacks understanding, she says to him, 'Come, eat of My bread And drink of the wine I have mixed. Forsake foolishness and live, And go in the way of understanding'" (Proverbs 9:1-6).

May I encourage you today, that if your trials are not pushing you closer to the Lord and perfecting your character to be more like Jesus Christ, to consider what Paul said to the body of believers in 2 Corinthians 13:5: "Examine yourselves as to whether you are in the faith."

Questions to Consider
"Say Yes to Wisdom – No to Wavering"
James 1:5-8

1. Read James chapter one. (a) List all of the illustrations from nature that James uses in chapter one. (b) Why do you think he does this?

2. Memorize James 1:5.

3. James tells us that we should ask for wisdom when facing trials. (a) Subsequently, what does James say regarding wisdom in James 3:13-17? Contrast the world's (man's) wisdom with godly wisdom from these verses. (b) How will this help you know what kind of wisdom you possess the next time you face a trial?

4. Other than Solomon, find one example in Scripture where someone facing a trial sought God's wisdom. (a) What was the result? (b) What principle can you glean for your life?

5. Find an example in Scripture where someone facing a trial did *not* seek God's face for wisdom. (a) What was the result? (b) Whose or what wisdom did they seek? (c) What can you learn to avoid from this example?

6. Give an example from your own life when you faced a trial and went to other sources first. What was the result of that? In contrast, give an example of when you were faced with a trial and went to Him first. What was the result of this biblical approach to trials?

7. (a) Can you name some instances in your life where God's answer to your prayer for wisdom came much later? (b) What did you learn?

8. Try to write down at least one trial that comes your way this week. Honestly evaluate the situation. (a) Did you first turn to the Lord or to other sources? (b) If to Him, did you ask for (and want) His wisdom or did you want relief from the trial? (c) If you did seek Him first for wisdom how did He answer your prayer? What situation in your life today should prompt you to seek God's wisdom? Write a prayer request to the Lord.

3

Rich Man, Poor Man

James 1:9-11

After the terrorist attacks of September 11th, 2001, Wall Street closed out a horrendous week in which the Dow Jones Industrial Average lost more than 1,365 points. At that time, it was the biggest one-week point drop in history! Analysts said the plunge in stocks would further depress consumer spending, as Americans would watch their portfolios shrink. There were massive layoffs at the airlines, empty hotels and restaurants, and disappearing customers in auto show rooms. The economic damage from the terrorist attacks virtually guaranteed a recession. One man said, "things are very uncertain and everybody is nervous. People have a deer-in-the-headlights look right now. They are not traveling. They are not going out to eat. They are not going to shopping malls." Those days were "testing days" for all Americans in the area of finances. Many of the wealthy probably lost sleep as they watched their portfolios shrink.

During that time I had a conversation with a wealthy but unsaved woman who was extremely stressed about the state of the economic world. But what about the attitudes of believers in Jesus Christ? What should our attitudes be during times of financial stress? The Word of God and specifically the Epistle of James have some answers for us. As Christians, both positions, either rich or poor, can be used by God as a test, especially during times of suffering or persecution as these believers were going through in James' day. James put it this way,

> Let the lowly brother glory in his exaltation, ¹⁰but the rich in his humiliation, because as a flower of the field he will pass away. ¹¹For no sooner has the sun risen with a burning heat than it withers the grass; its flower falls, and its beautiful appearance perishes. So the rich man also will fade away in his pursuits. (James 1:9-11)

In the previous chapter, we saw the importance of seeking God first for wisdom when facing a trial. We also saw that James contrasted the genuine believer who goes through a trial with the spurious believer who goes through a trial. The genuine believer seeks God for His wisdom and does not doubt His ability to answer, nor does He doubt God's character. The spurious believer goes through a trial and is divided. He is two-souled—one soul towards God and the other towards the world. He is unstable in every area of his life and someone you might not want for your best friend and confidant!

As we now look at verses 9-11, we may ask, "Why does James insert the issue of being rich or poor in the middle of talking about trials?" He seems to be introducing a new topic. In reality, he isn't introducing a new topic at all, because in the midst of persecution, especially the kind of persecution these Christians were experiencing, the issue of money could have certainly been a trial. Just because these believers were scattered from their homelands did not necessarily change their financial status. James was writing to poor and to rich believers. Both the poor and the rich alike go through tests that are common to every generation: the test of *plenty* and the test of *want*. James was not introducing a new topic but was moving from a discussion of trials in general to specific types of trials.

The first test on which James focused—this "test" of financial status—can be applied to both the persecuted Christian and the non-persecuted Christian. We will see the poor brother's response to his humble station in life in verse 9 and then the rich brother's response to his wealthy position in verses 10-11.

The Poor Brother's Response

James 1:9. Let the lowly brother glory in his exaltation

James starts with "let the lowly brother glory in his exaltation." To be a "lowly brother" meant to be of humble circumstances or of lowly rank or employment. Most likely some of James' readers were poverty-stricken Jewish Christians. They were economically low; they were low in the eyes of the world; and no doubt low in their own eyes. Their poverty produced a lowliness of mind. This is especially true during times of persecution when material losses are great. These Christians had been robbed of their homes and persecuted. Also, church history tells us that many Christians in the early church were from the lowest economic levels of society. It is recorded that some burial inscriptions in the Roman catacombs revealed that a huge number of slaves had also embraced Christianity.[8]

James told this brother of low degree, this brother of humble circumstances, to "rejoice." He did not say that being of lowly status gave him or her license to gripe or complain or rob a bank. *Rejoice* here means to profess loudly something of which one has a right to be proud. Yes, I repeat. It means to profess loudly something of which one has a right to be proud. When is the last time we heard someone poor saying that? What in the world did these poor persecuted Christians have to rejoice about? For one thing, they could rejoice in the fact that they possessed saving faith and that their faith was being tested!

---

[8] Generally the Roman catacombs were not built to hide from state persecution but rather the government tolerated burial clubs of the poorer classes, such as the early Christians. The wealthy would be buried in *sepulchers* but the poor and slaves in caves or tunnels built under ground. The term *katatumbos* comes from the preposition *kata* (i.e., down) and the noun *tumbos* (i.e., tomb) meaning "a tomb down in the earth" as distinct from on the surface. These were built during the first three centuries, with some even claimed during New Testament times. Philip Schaff, *History of the Christian Church*, vol. II (Eerdmans Publishing Company, 1976), pp. 285-310.

As was discussed in a previous chapter, trials should be considered welcome guests and opportunities to grow. And now the poor were getting an opportunity to have their faith tested. Rejoicing in a trial is one of the best safeguards against murmuring and rebelling. James said that their proper response in God's eyes was to rejoice in that they were "exalted." These poor people not only had the blessing of knowing the Lord while on earth, but they could also rejoice in the fact that whatever their position here on earth was, their eternal citizenship was in heaven. They were co-heirs with Christ and their names were written in heaven. That is something to rejoice about! Also, the fact that God was their companion during trials, even if they were financially destitute, should have given them a reason to rejoice. It is interesting that James used this terminology: "Let the lowly brother glory in his exaltation, but the rich in his humiliation," when we compare that to what Mary, the mother of Jesus and James, said:

> My soul magnifies the Lord, and my spirit has rejoiced in God my Savior. For He has regarded the lowly state of His maidservant; for behold, henceforth all generations will call me blessed. For He who is mighty has done great things for me, and holy is His name. And His mercy is on those who fear Him From generation to generation. He has shown strength with His arm; He has scattered the proud in the imagination of their hearts. He has put down the mighty from their thrones, and exalted the lowly. He has filled the hungry with good things, and the rich He has sent away empty. He has helped His servant Israel, In remembrance of His mercy, as He spoke to our fathers, To Abraham and to his seed forever. And Mary remained with her about three months, and returned to her house. (Luke 1:46-56)

Here we have the account of Mary's visit to Elizabeth—the account of what has become known to us as "Mary's Magnificat." Notice the terminology of Mary: "My spirit has rejoiced in God my Savior," "exalted the lowly," and "the rich He has sent away empty." These thoughts carry the same connotation as what James was saying. Remember that Mary was not only the mother of our Lord but also the mother of James, who wrote this epistle. Perhaps he repeatedly heard these words from his mother's lips, and now he was passing them on to the readers of this letter. [9]

The Rich Brother's Response

James 1:10-11. But the rich [rejoice] in his humiliation

In contrast to the poor brother's response in verse 9, the rich brother's response to his wealthy position is discussed in verses 10-11. So the poor brothers were supposed to rejoice in that they were exalted, and then James said, "But the rich in his humiliation." James was saying that, on the other hand, let the rich boast in his humility. What a stark contrast to what we would say today, which would be: "Let the brother of low degree be humble, and the rich be exalted." Obviously, there would have been some wealthy Christians then just as there are today. Three mentioned were Joseph of Arimathea, Nicodemus (John 19:38-39) and Barnabas (Acts 4:37).[10] These three men used their riches for good, for the kingdom's sake.

We know of at least one man in the Scriptures whose riches kept him from the kingdom, and that was the rich young ruler in Mark 10:17-22. Christ uses him as an example to say to his disciples: "How hard it is for those who have riches to enter the kingdom of God!" (Mark 10:23).

---

[9] James, along with his half-brother Jesus, were reared in humble circumstances. Mary and Joseph were not of the upper class or even what we would call the middle class. During New Testament times in Palestine, there wasn't much of a middle class at all. As women, we should notice Mary's example to us as mothers. Our children pick up on what we say and even our attitudes. This should be a warning to us mothers, especially since we are with our children more often than others and, thus, are in a greater position to influence them.

[10] Nicodemus was a member of the Sanhedrin and one of the three richest men of Jerusalem. Tradition tells us that following his interview with Jesus (John 3) he became a Christian and that he afterward became poor; and his daughter was seen gathering barleycorns for food from under the horses' feet. Some have said that this was the result of the persecution he received for having embraced Christianity. If tradition can be trusted, somehow he lost his possessions.

So now we know that there were rich people as well as poor people in biblical times, just as there are today. James says that these rich people were to rejoice in that they were made low, or to rejoice in their humility. The rich were to cultivate the poverty of spirit, as Jesus taught in the Sermon on the Mount. "Blessed are the poor in spirit, For theirs is the kingdom of heaven" (Matthew 5:3). The rich man was to work at this lowliness, focus on it, and make that his boast—not his wealth. Faith in Christ produces true humility in those who are rich believers, because they fully realize that they are like the grass, that they are here today and gone tomorrow. The rich man, just like the poor man, is totally depraved; and like the poor man without God, he too would be destined for an eternity without Christ. Both the rich and the poor are brothers (Proverbs 22:2), and it is the Lord Jesus Christ that you should boast about. Jeremiah puts it well:

> Thus says the LORD: Let not the wise man glory in his wisdom, Let not the mighty man glory in his might, Nor let the rich man glory in his riches; But let him who glories glory in this, That he understands and knows Me, That I am the LORD, exercising lovingkindness, judgment, and righteousness in the earth. For in these I delight," says the LORD. (Jeremiah 9:23-24)

James 1:10. As a flower of the field he will pass away

James now uses the graphic picture of the field to encourage the rich brother to look beyond the temporal to the spiritual. He says: "Because as a flower of the field he will pass away." James draws his readers' attention to the almost instantaneous wilting of the grass in the field when the sun rose with its burning heat. The Greek word that was translated into burning heat was also used for the southeast wind, which brought the heat and caused vegetation so often to perish. This south wind came from the desert and burst on Palestine like a blast of hot air when an oven door is opened. It is said that this heat could wipe out all vegetation in an hour. Jesus commented on this hot wind when he said, "And when you see the south wind blow, you say, 'There will be hot weather'; and there is" (Luke 12:55). This was a weather pattern that was very familiar to the reader in James' day. This example of the burning grass would not have been a new concept to his readers, and they understood how this represented the brevity of life. Perhaps now is a good time to reacquaint ourselves with a few passages dealing with the shortness of life.

> As for man, his days are like grass; As a flower of the field, so he flourishes. For the wind passes over it, and it is gone, And its place remembers it no more. (Psalm 103:15-16)

> The voice said, "Cry out!" And he said, "What shall I cry?" "All flesh is grass, And all its loveliness is like the flower of the field. The grass withers, the flower fades, Because the breath of the LORD blows upon it; Surely the people are grass. The grass withers, the flower fades, But the word of our God stands forever. (Isaiah 40:6-8)

> Having been born again, not of corruptible seed but incorruptible, through the word of God which lives and abides forever, because "All flesh is as grass, And all the glory of man as the flower of the grass. The grass withers, And its flower falls away, But the word of the LORD endures forever." (1 Peter 1:23-25)

If we stop and think about this, what are we anyway, regardless of whether we are rich or poor? All of us are like wild grass and flowers that come up in the springtime only to fade away. Isaiah and Peter both said that people come and go, but the "Word of the Lord stands forever." James later reminded them how temporary life was when he wrote, "For what is your life? It is even a vapor that appears for a little time and then vanishes away" (James 4:14).

The Greek word translated as *grass* in James 1:10 means a feeding place or farmyard which was primarily used for the feeding of the cattle. It was like a pasture. It took a rich man to have such a field in those days, as other land would be used for crops. So the admonition to the rich would be well illustrated by the particular Greek word for grass that James used. He said that when the blast of the south wind came, then the flower of the field, of the grass, of the rich pastureland would fall. The flower is not a literal flower, but the grass that has been allowed to reach its full maturity. It is at its height, its brilliancy, just like the rich. The rich were at their height, their brilliancy, as their riches had grown immensely, but they didn't retain that brilliancy for long. James said they were like that grass, which falls, meaning that it degenerates. The brilliance of the rich man's wealth would degenerate. That is no longer humility, but it is humiliation. James said "its beautiful appearance perishes"—its beauty disappears. The rich man will fade away. His splendor and all he prides himself in will vanish. The rich man is seen here as feverishly traveling. There is no time for God or His word and to be in His house. What will happen to such a man? He will wither away; he will wear out.

I remember how clear this became to me when my father-in-law, who was extremely wealthy, was facing death. By God's grace, he embraced the Lordship of Christ before his death, and at the end of his life, he said: "I'd rather have Jesus than anything." Here was a man who had it all according to the world's standards, but when coming to the end of his life, he had nothing by God's standards. As Jesus would say, "For what will it profit a man if he gains the whole world, and loses his own soul?" (Mark 8:36).

Even wise King Solomon called the love of money futile or meaningless in Ecclesiastes 5:10. He also stated in verse 11-14 of that same chapter that wealth can bring about grievous evil, or disaster, or misfortune, and then he will have nothing to leave his son. Solomon closed his thoughts in Ecclesiastes 5:15 by saying that even if wealth were not lost but kept throughout life that we still can't take it with us to eternity. I have personally never seen a hearse with a U-Haul trailer behind it! Have you? The Lord warned the Israelites of this same danger of loving money and denying the Lord after their deliverance from Egypt:

> Then you say in your heart, 'My power and the might of my hand have gained me this wealth.' And you shall remember the LORD your God, for it is He who gives you power to get wealth, that He

may establish His covenant which He swore to your fathers, as it is this day. (Deuteronomy 8:17-18)

We should consider these passages very seriously before the Lord, as there is a dangerous temptation in our American Christianity to be very materialistic. Without a godly perspective of wealth, we are in danger of "temptations, snares, lusts, destruction and perdition" (1 Timothy 6:9). Money cannot buy you happiness, and it cannot buy you out of your trials.

James 1:11. For no sooner has the sun risen with a burning heat than it withers the grass; its flower falls, and its beautiful appearance perishes.

As we close this chapter by considering verse 11, we see that James described the fate of the rich. He used four verbs: *to arise, to wither, to fall,* and *to perish,* which suggest a rapid succession of events. At first, the rich are beautiful. Then they lose their beauty, they drop their petals, and they fade away. This is a picture of what a life dependent on riches can be. Riches rise, and they wither; they fall, and then they perish. Life is uncertain, and the woman or man who puts their trust in riches is trusting in things which the vicissitudes of life can take from him at any moment. David said, "Do not trust in oppression, nor vainly hope in robbery; If riches increase, Do not set your heart on them. God has spoken once, twice I have heard this: That power belongs to God" (Psalm 62:10-11). The Psalmist was saying that whether you are rich or poor doesn't matter; what does matter is that power belongs to the Lord. Jesus gave us yet another reminder of the danger of loving money: "And He said to them, 'Take heed and beware of covetousness, for one's life does not consist in the abundance of the things he possesses'" (Luke 12:15).

I know miserable rich people who do not possess that inner peace and joy, and happy poor people who possess the peace of God that passes all understanding. One lie of our culture today is that our contentment in life depends upon material possessions. The going expression is "if I only had just a little more." One of the important lessons we should learn early in life as well as pass on to our children is this: "If I am not satisfied with what I have, I will never be satisfied with what I want."

Contentment is an attitude that must be learned and developed. The Apostle Paul was perhaps imprisoned in Nero's dungeon or at least under house arrest, when he wrote these words:

> For I have learned in whatever state I am, to be content: I know how to be abased, and I know how to abound. Everywhere and in all things I have learned both to be full and to be hungry, both to abound and to suffer need. (Philippians 4:11-12)

Paul's contentment was because of his personal relationship with the Lord, not due to his material possessions or even the normal comforts of life. Money can buy wonderful things, but it can never buy peace with God, and it can never buy your way out of a trial.

Summary

What is your financial status this day? Are you wealthy? If so, does money occupy your thoughts and your time? Do you "shop till you drop"? Or are you poor? Are you uncertain how you are going to pay the rent, buy the groceries, or obtain medical insurance? Or would you say that you have just the right amount of money, not too much, not too little?

Whatever financial state you find yourself in today, it doesn't really matter in the long run. What does matter is how you are responding to whatever level of wealth God has ordained for you in a way that honors Him. Whatever your financial circumstances, they should not distract you from seeking God and developing that intimacy in a relationship with Him. For only an intimate daily relationship with our Creator can truly satisfy the human heart.

Questions to Consider
"Rich Man, Poor Man"
James 1:9–11

1. Read James 1:9-11. (a) Skim the rest of the book of James and note how many other references there are to the rich and the poor. (b) Why do you think this is so?

2. Memorize James 1:9-10.

3. Read 1 Timothy 6:6-19. (a) What is God's standard for contentment? (b) What pitfalls await those who desire wealth? (c) What constitutes true riches?

4. (a) Read Proverbs 10:15; 13:7; 14:20; 22:2; 22:7; 28:11. Contrast the rich and the poor. (b) What principles can you glean from these verses?

5. (a) In reading the story in Luke 16:19-31, what things stand out to you as warnings to the wealthy? (b) What principles or observations have you gleaned from reading this account?

6. Honestly evaluate where you are financially. (a) Do you believe before God that you are being a good steward of what God has given you? (b) How can you improve? (You might record your spending this week!)

7. Are you rich? Are you poor? Regardless of your financial status, what are some things you can rejoice in today?

8. (a) In what ways either now, or in the past, has money been a trial in your life? (b) Did you pass the test(s)?

9. (a) Are you or anyone you know going through a financial trial? (b) What is your prayer to God through this trial?

4

Temptations: Where Do They Come From?

James 1:12-15

In the 1970's, comedian Flip Wilson popularized the phrase "The devil made me do it." Whenever Flip Wilson said it, many of us laughed; but even worse, we used that phrase as an excuse to sin and still do. Satan does attack us, that is true. But to use him and all his evil companions to excuse our sin reveals a wrong attitude. Whose fault is it anyway when you or I are tempted to sin? Is it Satan's fault? Is it God's fault? Does the blame belong to our husbands? Our children? Just who is to blame for our sinful behavior? In this chapter we will answer those questions in light of James 1:12-15, and some of you may be a little surprised with the answer.

In the past three chapters, we have been looking at trials and their benefits, as well as how to endure them. In this chapter we are going to see how our trials, our difficulties in life, can become temptations to sin if we do not respond correctly. Every trial becomes a test to pass. Passing the test keeps it a trial; failing the test turns it into a temptation. To help us endure trials and resist temptation, James wrote:

> Blessed is the man who endures temptation; for when he has been approved, he will receive the crown of life which the Lord has promised to those who love Him. 13Let no one say when he is tempted, "I am tempted by God"; for God cannot be tempted by evil, nor does He Himself tempt anyone. 14But each one is tempted when he is drawn away by his own desires and enticed. 15Then, when desire has conceived, it gives birth to sin; and sin, when it is full-grown, brings forth death. (James 1:12-15)

In this passage of Scripture we will examine three themes regarding trials: (1) the *reward* of enduring trials in verse 12; (2) the *reasons* not to blame God in verse 13; and (3) the *risk* of entertaining temptations in verses 14-15.

The Reward of Enduring Trials

James 1:12. Blessed is the man who endures temptation

James introduced the first theme with: "Blessed is the man who endures temptation." *Blessed* here means happy, fortunate, denoting an inner quality of life, a joy and happiness not dependent upon favorable external circumstances. This is the state of a believer's soul who has experienced joy in this life regardless of her circumstances. Hasn't James already stated this in James 1:2: "My brethren, count it all joy when you fall into various trials"? This state of blessedness portrays this man or woman as enduring the various trials and refusing to give up or give in. In verse 12, James was still talking about trials because one does not endure temptation but rather resists it, as we will see in a moment. Such perseverance during trials is another sign of genuine faith. To not endure proves a spurious faith, as we studied in the last chapter.

Who is blessed? Who is happy? James says it is the man who endures temptation. The man who is indeed blessed is the one who remains steadfast, abides, or stays under testing. Why is he blessed? Because when he has been tried, he will receive the crown of life which the Lord has promised to those who love Him. These words are similar to those spoken by our Lord in the Sermon on the Mount in Matthew 5, where He gave us the eight beatitudes.[11]

---

[11] Jesus said, "Blessed are the poor in spirit, for theirs is the kingdom of heaven. Blessed are those who mourn, for they shall be comforted. Blessed are the meek, for they shall inherit the earth. Blessed are those who hunger and thirst for righteousness, for they shall be filled. Blessed are the merciful, for they shall obtain mercy. Blessed are the pure in heart, for they shall see God. Blessed are the peacemakers, for they shall be called sons of God. Blessed are those who are persecuted for righteousness' sake, for theirs is the kingdom of heaven" (Matthew 5:3-10).

James 1:12. For when he has been approved, he will receive the crown of life which the Lord has promised to those who love Him.

Pastor James says when this man is approved, or tried, "he will receive the crown of life." This verb translated *approved* is the same word used when testing coins and metals to see if they are genuine. Coins were tried, or tested, by fire and, thus, purified. This would also apply to being approved as acceptable men and women in the furnace of adversity. In order to be rewarded the believer must prove himself as genuine. As previously mentioned, such perseverance is a sign of genuine faith.

Sometimes this is referred to as the doctrine of the perseverance of the saints. Hebrews 3:6 states, "But Christ as a Son over His own house, whose house we are if we hold fast the confidence and the rejoicing of the hope firm to the end" (see also Hebrews 3:14; 6:11-12; 10:23; 10:35-39). So why should the Christian consider herself blessed during trials? Because of the crown of life which she will receive. *Crown of life* in the Greek means that which surrounds or encompasses, usually meaning the head. The Greek word *stephanos* was often used instead of the term reward. (The name Stephen comes from this Greek noun.) The *crown of life* here belongs to those who win their battle against temptation, thus proving they are victors!

In Revelation 2:10, we see this same idea. Jesus examined the church at Smyrna undergoing persecution, and told them to not fear the events to come. They would be tried and have tribulation for ten days. "But be faithful unto death," the Lord said, "and I will give you a crown of life" (Revelation 2:10). The same word *tried* is used here in James in the same way. This crown, this reward, James said, is "promised to those who love God." It is not for those who loved God for a season, but for those who love Him until the end. James indicated here that it is our love for God that is our motive for persevering when tempted. This love is *agapao,* which denotes a love of understanding and purpose, which prompts a believer to implicit obedience to God's commands. Jesus told the disciples, "If you love me, keep my commandments" (John 14:15). How often do you say that you love God but deny Him in your actions? We persevere and "hang in there" because we have a love relationship with God, just as in a marriage. You don't bail out of a marriage, or you shouldn't, just because times are tough. You hang in there because you love your spouse and have made a commitment before God to him.

A story is told of a young man who spent an evening telling a girl how much he loved her. He said that he couldn't live without her and that he would go to the ends of the earth for her, and, yes, even through fire for her. But as he was leaving, he said, "I'll see you tomorrow night, if it doesn't rain." Unfortunately, that is how it is with some of us in our relationship with God. Do you love God only when it is convenient? Do you love Him in times of testing as well as times of blessing? Do your actions show it? The crown of life will only be given to those who love him in deed and truth. Isn't it good to know that whatever trials you are facing today, if you endure, you are not only called blessed, but you will one day receive the crown of life? However, for some of us those trials can become temptations to sin. And that is why James shifts gears from trials in verse 12 to temptations in verse 13.

Every trial can be a temptation depending on how we respond. For example, if the doctor told me that one of my children had a short time to live due to an illness, this would certainly be a trial, but it could also be a temptation for me to sin. I could doubt God. I could question God in a rebellious way. I could cease from ministry or even try to abandon the Christian faith. Just as is illustrated in this example, every trial can be a temptation to sin. We need to understand the source of temptation, because it is not of God.

The Reasons Not to Blame God

James 1:13. Let no one say when he is tempted, "I am tempted by God."

In case you might be tempted to blame that trial on God, which He has allowed for your good, James warns, "Let no one say when he is tempted, 'I am tempted by God.'" That statement forbidding blaming one's temptations on God reminds me of the proverb that says, "A man's own folly ruins his life, yet his heart rages against the LORD" (Proverbs 19:3 NIV). The man mentioned here was destroyed by his own foolishness, and yet he blamed God! James says when we are tempted that we cannot blame God. The testimony of God's holy integrity cannot be challenged, even when we are faced with hot Tabasco-like trials. A cool mind will result in a cool faith.

"When he is tempted" means while one is in the process of being tempted. The tense here suggests that the one being tempted is on the verge of yielding to the temptation.[12] The excuse given for yielding to temptation is that "I am tempted of God." James warned that we are not to rationalize by saying that God is doing the tempting. In contrast to the previous chapters where we discussed the trials we encounter, this passage of Scripture now shifts to those situations in which we are enticed to do evil things. Because of a wrong inner reaction to the testings or trials that God does allow—and allows for our good—we may use them as an occasion to sin.

When going through trials, some of us are prone to think unfairly about God. "God, why did you allow this to happen? Where are you? Where was God on September 11th? It's God's fault! It's their fault! If only …" We blame God or others or both for our trials. We blame God by blaming our circumstances, our family, our weaknesses, our surroundings, our friends, and our economic situation. We may hear about a student who gets caught cheating and blames it on the teacher who is too difficult, or a thief who steals blames God for his poverty. Or the drunk blames it on his partying friends. The wife who is irritated with her husband blames it on "the time of the month." These excuses for our sinful reactions are as old as Adam and Eve, who were questioned by God in the garden.

The popular reaction nowadays is to blame our upbringing—"I come from a *dysfunctional* family." Who doesn't come from a dysfunctional family in this age? We are all sinners—we are all

---

[12] The Greek term *peirazomenos* (English, "when he is tempted") is a present passive participle and evidently refers to the temptation to sin and not just to the external trial. Remember our footnote in chapter two, that *peirasmois* can refer to either *trials* or *temptations*, according to the context. External trials are given by the Lord to produce Christ-like character but with them, could also come internal temptation which can cause our soul to seek evil.

dysfunctional—but does that excuse our sin? Absolutely not! James said let no man—not one single person—say that God is tempting him. God cannot be the source of man's temptation to sin. That is the evil within us.

James 1:13. For God cannot be tempted by evil, nor does He Himself tempt anyone.

James gives us two reasons why it is impossible for God to tempt us. First of all, "God cannot be tempted by evil." God's nature cannot be tempted by anything evil. God is not experienced in evil, and He has no capacity for evil. He is absolutely holy. John spoke of this in Revelation 4:8, when he said, "Holy, holy, holy, Lord God Almighty." Sin cannot penetrate holiness. Habakkuk wrote, "You are of purer eyes than to behold evil, and cannot look on wickedness" (Habakkuk 1:13). And John said, "God is light and in Him is no darkness at all" (1 John 1:5).

The second reason we cannot blame God James says, "nor does He Himself tempt anyone." Tempting us is not His activity; that is not what God is about. God has better things to do with His time than to be about causing us to sin. Job is a prime example of someone who could have blamed God for being behind the trials in his life. Job lost all of his children, his immense possessions, and his good health. He had three "miserable" counselors and a wife who told him to curse God and die. Yet Job realized that this was a trial from God. "In all of this Job did not sin nor charge God with wrong" (Job 1:22). Instead Job said, "He knows the way I take and when He has tried me, I shall come forth as gold" (Job 23:10).

So we've discovered the *reward* of enduring trials, the crown of life (v 12); and the *reasons* not to blame God, because He can't be tempted by evil nor does He Himself tempt to evil (v 13). This brings us to the *risk* of entertaining temptations (vv 14-15).

The Risk of Entertaining Temptations

By now you may be saying, "Well, if God doesn't tempt me to sin, then where does the temptation come from?" It is interesting that James doesn't say every temptation we encounter is from the devil. That would get each of us off the hook, and then we could say, "The devil made me do it." We cannot blame our sin on someone else, not even Satan. Everyone is prone to temptation—none of us can escape it—just like everyone is going to have trials (1 Corinthians 10:13). But how we respond to the temptations will prove if our faith is genuine or not. Listen to how Pastor James explains this:

James 1:14. But each one is tempted when he is drawn away by his own desires and enticed.

James says that every man is tempted when he is "drawn away." This is a fisherman's term. I don't know anything about fishing, but they tell me you put a worm on the hook and cast the line out into the sea. The fish sees the worm, lusts to eat the worm, and then is hooked and caught. The language here suggests a fish swimming in a straight course and then drawn off towards something that seems attractive, only to discover that the bait has a deadly hook in it. He doesn't see the hook, only the bait. He is deceived and caught. Instead of enjoying the anticipated pleasure, he is snagged by the hook.

Isn't that true of sin? We are going about our way on the straight and narrow, and then something or someone off the beaten path allures us, and we are caught away by our evil desires and then we are trapped. The bait is so attractive on the outside, and then we are caught as we pursue it. In effect, James was saying, "We are drawn away and enticed by our own lust." The word for *lust* here simply means desire. The term *epithumia,* is used mostly for evil desires in the Bible, but it can be used for good desires as well, as in Luke 22:15. Here Christ told His disciples that He desired to eat the Passover with them before His crucifixion.

Desire is not wrong per se, but it is what we do with that desire that can get us into trouble. Notice James says it is our *own* lust. Each of us has our "own" lust. We all have our own "baited hooks" which allure us. Your "baited hook" may be sexual sin—it is your *own* lust. It may be lying—it is your *own* lust. It may be soap operas—it is your *own* lust! It may be gossip—it is your *own* lust. Maybe it is laziness or a lack of submission to your husband. But again, it is your *own* lust. Some baited hooks are more alluring to us than others.

The word *enticed* means to be entrapped or caught. When we take the bait, we are surprised that we have been caught and cannot escape. Sin promises satisfaction and excitement. It lures and captures us and we are caught. You might wonder how you can resist temptation. The Apostle Paul promises us:

> No temptation has overtaken you except such as is common to man; but God is faithful, who will not allow you to be tempted beyond what you are able, but with the temptation will also make the way of escape, that you may be able to bear it. (1 Corinthians 10:13)

And what does the very next verse say? "Therefore, my beloved, flee from idolatry" (1 Corinthians 10:14), which is the real point I believe Paul is trying to get us to see, relative to overcoming temptation. There is a way of escape—just flee. The problem is that some of us refuse to take the escape route. We dabble just long enough to be enticed, and the results are disastrous. You might ask, "Well, how can I resist temptation?"

In Genesis 39 there are six principles that we can glean from Joseph and his example to us on resisting temptation. By the way, it is interesting to note that in the previous chapter, Genesis 38, Joseph's brother Judah consciously planned to sin by committing adultery with his daughter-in-law, who, unbeknownst to him, was pretending to be a harlot. But in Genesis 39, we see Joseph, this man of faith, fleeing this serious sin of adultery. Read Genesis 39:7-12 and notice the six principles of resisting temptation.

1. Joseph refused Potiphar's wife. Just say no! (v 8).
2. Joseph knew adultery was a great wickedness (sin). Know the Word of God (v 9).
3. Joseph knew adultery was a sin against God. Set your heart on pleasing God in all things (v 9).
4. Joseph said "no" repeatedly, yet his resolve did not

weaken. Never give up (v 10).
5. Joseph fled. Remove yourself from the place of temptation (v 12).
6. Joseph mistakenly allowed unnecessary temptation in his life when he entered Potiphar's house while no othermen of the house were present. Do not flirt with the potential of temptation (v 11).

If you're struggling with a certain area of sin, don't expose yourself to that temptation. If you are trying to lose weight, you might not want to go to an all-you-can-eat restaurant where you might be tempted to gorge yourself. If you struggle with lust, make sure you have protection installed on your computer. If television is a struggle, then turn it off. If you spend too much money, don't window shop at the mall or browse through magazines and catalogs. Joseph paid a price for resisting temptation; he was put in prison. But as Peter said, "It is better, if it is the will of God, to suffer for doing good than for doing evil" (1 Peter 3:17).

James 1:15. Then, when desire has conceived, it gives birth to sin

So, what happens to us if we refuse to say no to sin but instead say yes to that baited hook? Pastor James said that something very sobering will happen. "Then, when desire has conceived, it gives birth to sin; and sin, when it is full-grown, brings forth death." James switched to the metaphor to a pregnant female who gives birth to a child. This familiar language of childbirth is simple to understand. We conceive and then bring forth a child, except in this Scripture verse two births occur.

The moment of conception is evil desire, which then gives birth to *sin*. And the second birth is sin giving birth to *death*. The root idea of "gives birth" is "ceases to be pregnant," which emphasizes the inevitability of the process running its course. The idea is that sin grows rapidly, just as an embryo grows to maturity; and when sin is full-grown, the state of pregnancy must end. But the horror here is that sin does not give birth to *life* here as we expect in the physical realm, but instead gives birth to *death*. Sin produces a monstrous offspring, which is death. An interesting contrast exists between the death mentioned in verse 15 and the crown of life in verse 12. The woman that endures or perseveres is blessed with life; the woman who surrenders to sin is cursed with death. What a contrast!

So what is sin? Sin is missing the mark, knowingly being disobedient to the will of God. Sin usually starts with the desire or the emotion. "That looks good," or "I want that." Then deception takes place in the mind. "It won't be so bad," you tell yourself, and so you rationalize and decide in your mind, "I will do that; I will have that." And then follows the behavior, the act of disobedience. And so you sin. The deed is done. The sin has been committed.

As believers in Jesus Christ we must deal with the sin at the very moment it arises within us. Do not let your emotions and thoughts govern your life. The spiritually seasoned, tested Apostle encouraged the carnal Corinthians:

> For though we walk in the flesh, we do not war according to the flesh. For the weapons of our warfare are not carnal but mighty in God for pulling down strongholds, casting down arguments and every high thing that exalts itself against the knowledge of God, bringing every thought into captivity to the obedience of Christ, and being ready to punish all disobedience when your obedience is fulfilled. (2 Corinthians 10:3-6)

Paul told us to bring *every* thought captive to the obedience of Christ. We must guard our thought life. What happens if you don't guard your heart and your thoughts? What happens if you take the bait?

James 1:15. And sin, when it is full-grown, brings forth death.

James continues his warning, "And sin, when it is full-grown, brings forth death." After desire has brought forth *sin*, then sin brings forth *death*. When sin is born, it is born a murderer. Sin is a killer. We know that "the wages of sin is death" (Romans 6:23). In Proverbs 7:5-27, Solomon warned us to stay away from that strange woman, that adulterous woman, and he ended his caution with a sobering thought: "Her house is the way to hell, descending to the chambers of death" (Proverbs 7:27). Solomon is of course speaking to his son regarding women, but dear ladies we must also heed the warning when it comes to men who would also love to seduce women in the same way. You may be scoffing and saying, "that would never happen to me." Adultery may not be your sin—your baited hook. Maybe it is another sin, but perhaps you are saying, "I can just dabble in this sin—God would never take me home to heaven." If that is your response to dabbling in sin, then the Apostle Paul cautions you, as he did the Corinthian church:

> But let a man examine himself, and so let him eat of the bread and drink of the cup. For he who eats and drinks in an unworthy manner eats and drinks judgment to himself, not discerning the Lord's body. For this reason many are weak and sick among you, and many sleep.[13] (1 Corinthians 11:28-30)

How and when God judges one who has sinned a sin unto death, I do not know. In my lifetime I believe I have known of two people who sinned unto death, and it is a tragic way to end one's earthly life. How God decides when He has had enough is a mystery to me. But we all should live in "reverence and godly fear. For our God is a consuming fire" (Hebrews 12:28-29). God will not allow you to continue in sin. He will either take you home or discipline

---

[13] 1 Corinthians 11:28-30. Obviously that *sleep* is not referring to falling asleep on the back row at church, but death. The aged Apostle John gave us another warning. "If anyone sees his brother sinning a sin which does not lead to death, he will ask, and He will give him life for those who commit sin not leading to death. There is sin leading to death. I do not say that he should pray about that. All unrighteousness is sin, and there is sin not leading to death" (1 John 5:16-17). There is sin unto death. Ananias and Sapphira are sobering examples of those who committed the sin unto death in Acts 5. Together they agreed to lie to the Holy Spirit by keeping a portion of the money they earned by selling some of their land. Both were immediately struck dead, and great fear came upon all the church.

you. As it is written, "For whom the Lord loveth He chastens, and scourges *every* son whom he receives" (Hebrews 12:6, KJV, emphasis mine).

If you are His and playing with sin, He will chasten you. Being chastened by our Holy Lord is not a pleasant experience. When we reflect on this passage that sin brings forth death, it should cause us to check every evil thought and desire at the beginning of temptation. Not for one moment should we indulge in it, for soon sin may master us, and we may end up in the grave.

Summary

Now that we've unpacked these verses, let's put them back together. The *reward* of enduring trials is the crown of life (v 12). There are two *reasons* not to blame God, because He can't be tempted by evil nor does He Himself tempt to evil (v 13). And we need to keep ever before us the *risk* of entertaining temptations; it conceives sin, which gives birth to death (vv 14-15).

Someone said, "We have met the enemy and the enemy is us." We don't need Satan or the world to tempt us; the passion of our flesh is enough. We must never say, "the devil made me do it" or "my friends made me do it" or "my circumstances made me do it" or even worse "God made me do it." The fact is that you and only you made you do it!

What is your baited hook this day? Is it clothes? Food? Sleep? Material possessions? New house? Sex? Wasting time? Soap operas? A wrong response to PMS or menopause? Gossip? Anger? Idolatry? Pride? Resentment? Unforgiveness? Jealousy? Lying? Cheating? Stealing?

If you are in the grip of temptation this day, then take the first step by admitting that you are to blame and no one else. Then confess and repent of your sin before God and others if need be. Then appropriate the grace that God has given you to be victorious over sin by the power of His Son Jesus Christ!

Questions to Consider
"Temptations: Where Do They Come From?"
James 1:12-15

1. Read James 1:1-15 and list any comparisons or contrasts you see between trials and temptations.

2. Memorize James 1:13-14.

3. Read Matthew 6:13. According to James 1:13, God doesn't tempt anyone to commit sin, so why do we need to ask Him to protect us from something He apparently wouldn't lead us into in the first place? Prove your answer biblically.

4. Read Psalm 119:11, Matthew 26:41, Ephesians 6:10-18, and James 4:7. (a) How can you use these verses to help yourself and others when dealing with temptation? (b) What advice could you give?

5. Read 2 Samuel 24:1. (a) Who is tempting David to sin? (b) Read the same account in 1 Chronicles 21:1. (c) Who is tempting David to sin in this account? (d) How do you reconcile these two accounts? (e) How does this relate to James 1:13? (f) What does this teach you about comparing Scripture with Scripture? (g) Why is it dangerous to try and prove doctrine on one verse alone?

6. Hebrews 2:18 says, "For in that He Himself has suffered, being tempted, He is able to aid those who are tempted." When has God come to your aid in the hour of temptation?

7. Is there an area of temptation that you are facing today? Confess it to the Lord, and determine to change (repent). If necessary, share with someone who will hold you accountable! Don't dabble with sin!

8. What is your prayer request as you reflect on Question 7?

5

The Greatest Gift of All

James 1:16-18

When summer ends and fall begins, some of us begin to think about Christmas. If you're not thinking along those lines, then believe me, the stores and advertisements will make sure you are. I couldn't believe it when I recently saw a house already adorned with Christmas lights, and there were still three months to go before Christmas. In addition to decorating our homes, Christmas is, of course the time of year when we also start thinking about buying gifts. We ask ourselves, "What should I buy for my family and friends? What would they like?" We want to buy just the right gift, don't we? Something that will really meet the person's need or please them in some way. We want to buy a good gift, a perfect gift. I don't know about you, but I enjoy buying gifts for others, because it brings me pleasure and joy. And yet, there is One who has more pleasure and more joy than you or I do in giving gifts to those He loves. He is the giver of every good and perfect gift, and He is the giver of the best gift of all.

As we study James 1:16-18, I want to warn you ahead of time that God's gifts may not come in beautiful packages like the ones we receive at Christmastime, but they are far more valuable! In the previous chapter we already saw that trials are indeed a gift from God used to perfect us to His image. We have also seen that temptations to sin come from our own evil desires and lust. We learned that God has nothing to do with delivering temptations, as James said, "Let no one say when he is tempted, I am tempted by God; for God cannot be tempted by evil, nor does He Himself tempt anyone" (James 1:13). We can say this for two reasons. First of all, it is totally against His nature; and secondly, God is not in the business of tempting us to sin! We saw that each of us is tempted by our own lust; and when we decide to take the bait and sin, we are trapped. Many have sinned to the point of death—sometimes physical, sometimes spiritual. Now, in contrast to the death that sin brings forth, James is now going to teach us about God who brings forth life. In contrast to lust, sin, and death stands God who cannot be company in this terrible family of darkness. That is why James then said:

> Do not be deceived, my beloved brethren. [17]Every good gift and every perfect gift is from above, and comes down from the Father of lights, with whom there is no variation or shadow of turning. [18]Of His own will He brought us forth by the word of truth, that we might be a kind of firstfruits of His creatures. (James 1:16-18)

In this chapter, we will see the error of man in verses 16-17 contrasted with the will of God in verse 18.

The Error of Man: Being Deceived by Perceived Trials

James 1:16. Do not be deceived, my beloved brethren

The wise Pastor of the Jerusalem church says, "Do not be deceived." The verb *to deceive* here means to lead astray, to cause to wander. It is in the passive voice, which means to go astray by letting oneself be misled; to be deceived. The present imperative demands that the readers must not allow this danger of being led astray to continue. What was James saying here? It could be that he was saying do not be deceived about what he had just mentioned, that God does not tempt us to sin in trials (v 13). If we would all be honest with ourselves, we would have to admit that sometimes we think evil of God when we are faced with trials. Some of James' readers were probably having these same thoughts as well. Their miserable flight from Jerusalem and the ongoing persecution as Christians at the hands of fellow Jews had left them not only saying, "God is tempting me," but even left them thinking that God is not good. James was saying, "Stop it! Stop thinking that way!"

James could also have meant a transition to his next point, i.e., do not be deceived in the matter that every good and perfect gift comes from above. This term *do not be deceived* is commonly used to call attention to some truth just spoken about or to one about to be stated. So either view is correct and the author could even have used it to refer to both.

Until now James had called them *brethren*, but now he switches to the term *beloved brethren*, suggesting a sense of urgency and endearment. A good point to remember here when confronting or exhorting others is that you can soften the rebuke with loving words. We should use terms of endearment, and yet we should not shy away when a brother or sister in Christ needs to be exhorted. As Paul would command the Galatian believers, "Brethren, if a man is overtaken in any trespass, you who are spiritual restore such a one in a *spirit of gentleness*, considering yourself lest you also be tempted" (Galatians 6:1, emphasis mine). Sometimes we have to say hard things to others, but when we do, we should say them in a kind and gentle way.

James 1:17. Every good gift and every perfect gift is from above

My beloved sisters, rather than blaming God for the mess you may be in and thinking that God is the source of all evil, believe what James has told us: "Every good gift and every perfect gift is from above, and comes down from the Father of lights, with whom is no variation or shadow of turning" (James 1:17). James told his readers to focus on the fact that God is the author of all good. That every good and perfect gift is from above, and that everything that God gives us is for our benefit. In this statement, James was negating any claim from them that temptation to sin originates from God. This reminds me of what Paul says in Romans 8:28: "And we know that all things work together for *good* to those who love God, to those who are the called according to His purpose" (emphasis mine).

Two different Greek words in verse 17 are used for gifts. The first one means the "act of giving," and the second one means the "result of that act, the gift itself."[14] The *good* describes the giving as useful and beneficial. The *perfect* marks the gift as complete and lacking nothing to meet the needs of the recipient. Those gifts that God gives us are good; they are useful. Those gifts are also perfect, complete. *Perfect* has the meaning of completion, the end, or the purpose. In other words, that which God gives us has a purpose, a goal. Remember what James said in 1:4, that we should be made perfect by our trials. All of God's gifts have as their end the accomplishment of God's purpose in our lives, which is perfection.

Those good things that God gives us can even come in the form of afflictions and trials as we have seen in previous chapters. As the psalmist aptly put it in Psalm 119:71: "It is good for me that I have been afflicted, that I may learn Your statutes." The psalmist also said in verse 67 of the same chapter, "Before I was afflicted I went astray, but now I keep Your word." The Psalmist recognized what you and I should recognize today, that God's goodness can come in the form of afflictions and that there are spiritual benefits from them.

There are other good gifts that God gives us. James already mentioned one in verse 5—the gift of wisdom needed in trials when we ask God for it. Other gifts that God has given us include: the Word of God, our salvation, the Holy Spirit, the local church family, friendships, homes, families, food, touch, sight, smell, taste, good health, and so on and so on.

---

[14] The noun (Greek, *dosis*) translated "gift" (NKJV) is only used elsewhere in the New Testament in Philippians 4:15 – "Now you Philippians know also that in the beginning of the gospel, when I departed from Macedonia, no church shared with me concerning *giving* and receiving but you only." Notice the translators there consider the noun a reference to *the act of giving*. Although there are usages of this term in extra-Biblical literature referring to the gift itself, it is better because of Philippians 4:15 to refer to this as *the act of giving*. We might say James is saying, "God gives in a good way, good gifts." It is not only the gifts that are good but also the way in which He gives them, which indeed is the mental challenge when we are going through various trials.

James 1:17. And comes down from the Father of lights

Where do those gifts come from? James says they *come down* from the "Father of lights." Here James wants to give us a glimpse into the character of God. Before we fix our attention on the gift, he wants us to look at the Giver and know His nature and His action toward us. The good gifts and perfect gifts come from above! Not from your husband, your friends, or your children, but from God who is in heaven. Everything you have comes from Him and Him alone. As Paul said in Acts 17:28: "For in Him we live and move and have our being." We need to look to Him in gratitude as we think of those good and perfect gifts. Someone once said "Look to self and be depressed, look to others and be distressed, Look to Jesus and be blessed." And I say Amen!

Those good and perfect gifts that are from above *come down*; the present participle "coming down" describes an unending succession of good gifts. Sometimes I stand in awe at God's continual pouring out of gifts in my life. Sometimes it seems like they keep coming and coming, like the Energizer® bunny. As I reflect over my life just in the past few years, I stand in awe of God's goodness to me, not only in the gift of my salvation, but my family, my children, my husband, my church and the many new friends I meet as I speak to ladies' groups. The list goes on and on; it doesn't stop. Great is His faithfulness! God continues to pour out gift after gift after gift, so why would we go after those "baited hooks" when He has given us so much that is good?

The reason why the gifts from above are good and perfect is because they come from the Father of lights. Why does James call God the "Father of lights" here? This epithet is not used elsewhere in Scripture, but it was known in Jewish circles. James' audience would have recognized this title since they quoted it in the benediction "Blessed be the Lord our God who hath formed the lights."[15]

---

[15] Alfred Edersheim, *Sketches of Jewish Social Life in the Days of Christ* (Grand Rapids, Eerdmans, 1964), p. 268. Philo writes, "Every created thing must necessarily undergo change, for this is its property, even as unchangeableness is the property of God. *Allegorical. Interpretation*, 2:33.

This title describes who God is—Genesis 1:16 says, "Then God made two great lights: the greater light to rule the day, and the lesser light to rule the night. He made the stars also." He is the Father of lights. He created all the light in the galaxies. He is the Father of all the lights.

James 1:17. With whom there is no variation or shadow of turning

Then James qualified the nature of the Father of lights to show that He and the lights are not one in the same. These lights (the sun, moon, and stars) vary. Sometimes they are brighter than at other times, yet God, the Creator, is always the same. James said that there is no variation—this describes His immutability. Appearing to the human eye, the stars twinkle, and the sun and moon rotate. These all display varying intensities, but there is no variableness with Him. What James is stressing is the unchanging nature of God. While God is the Creator and Sustainer of the variable lights, as the Giver of good gifts to men there is no variation in Him. The goodness of His character changes not. God is good all the time, even when those gifts are disguised in packages labeled "trials." This verse speaks of a central aspect of His immutability, His goodness in what He gives. Hence, the trials that God sends, although difficult and at times wrapped in unattractive packages, are nevertheless good for us. God doesn't cease being good when He sends us a trial. We need to have the discernment to realize all things work together for our good (Romans 8:28).

James also said there is no *shadow of turning*—there is no eclipse. In our lives we seem to have eclipses of God just as we observe eclipses of the sun. At times we feel Him close to us, and then at other times He seems to be far removed. He is such light that not even a shadow can be cast on Him. That's why James uses the phrase *shadow of turning*. There are dark days when the sun is in the shadow, but not with the Father of lights. There is no night so dark that His light cannot shine upon you. He remains the same. Malachi 3:6 states: "For I am the LORD, I do not change." Hebrews 13:8 tells us: "Jesus Christ is the same yesterday, today, and forever." Things change in our world from day to day, don't they? The stock market bounces from bear to bull, wars and rumors of wars punctuate nightly news, international conflicts, personal health fears, financial reverses, our mood swings, and our every day lives change all the time, but not God. That's so good to know. Just as today we need to be reminded of His unchanging nature, so James' readers also needed to be reminded of this attribute of God in their time of distress. They needed to be reminded that God doesn't change. They also needed to be reminded of the good gifts, which are from Him, too. During trials, we sometimes focus on fixing the situation and how bad it is, but, oh, how we need to be reminded to praise and thank God—to focus on all that He has done.

So not only is God the Creator and the Father of all the lights but He doesn't change. He knows no turning, like the lights He created which do turn. His immutability guarantees that He always will give good gifts in a good way, regardless of our outward perception of various trials. Commentator Albert Barnes affirms this truth:

> He is always the same, at all seasons of the year and in all ages, there is no change in his character, his mode of being, his purposes and plans. What He was millions of ages before the worlds were made, he is now; what He is now, He will be countless millions of ages hence. We may be sure that whatever changes there may be in human affairs; whatever reverses we may undergo; whatever oceans we may cross, or whatever mountains we may climb, or in whatever worlds we may hereafter take up our abode, God is the same. (Barnes, p. 28)

James goes on in verse 18 to describe the most wonderful gift that the Father of lights has bestowed upon us, that is the gift of eternal life.

The Will of God: Giving Us Life by His Determined Grace

James 1:18. Of His own will

James put it this way: "Of His own will He brought us forth by the word of truth, that we might be a kind of firstfruits of His creatures" (James 1:18). As we saw in James 1:13, God does not give birth to temptation, but he does give birth to regeneration as we see in verse 18. How does He do that? James says of His own will—God *willed* it. The Greek term *boulee* was a word which was used in ancient times to express the will and determination of the gods of ancient Greece. In biblical terminology it refers to the counsel and the purpose of God as distinguished from His consequent action. This "will of God" is not a whim, but it presupposes logical thought. *Bouletheis* stands emphatically at the beginning of the sentence which stresses that the new birth is rooted in the fact that "the resolute will of God is the motivating force which gives new life."[16] God willed your salvation and mine after considerable thought about the cost it would involve for Himself. He knew it would mean the sacrifice of His own Son. He knew His Son Jesus Christ would have to forsake His heavenly glory to come down to earth, so that we would have the possibility of being a partaker of the heavenly glory. This reminds me of what the Apostle Paul says in Romans 8:32: "He who did not spare His own Son, but delivered Him up for us all, how shall He not with Him also freely give us all things?"

Perhaps this idea of God willing our salvation is a new concept to some of you. If so, perhaps further reading and study will be of great help to you.[17] God determines the salvation of those whom

---

[16] Article on *boulomai* by Gottlob Schrenk, Editor Gerhard Kittel, *Theological Dictionary of the New Testament* trans. and ed. Geoffrey W. Bromiley (Grand Rapids: Wm. B. Eerdmans Publishing Co., 1964), I p. 632.

[17] Passages relative to God's sovereign determination in salvation include: John 1:13; Romans 8:29-32; Romans 9:9-18; Ephesians 1:4-5; 2 Thessalonians 2:13-14. R. C. Sproul, *Chosen by God* (Tyndale, 1986); John Piper, *The Justification of God: An Exegetical and Theological Study of Romans 9:1-23* (Baker, 1983); B. B. Warfield, *The Plan of Salvation* (Eerdmans, 1942); Lorraine Boettner, *The Reformed Doctrine of Predestination* (Eerdmans, 1951).

He chooses. You and I had nothing to do with our salvation. Just like you had nothing to do with your physical birth, you also had nothing to do with your spiritual birth.

James 1:18. He brought us forth by the word of truth

James continued the thought with "He brought us forth." It is interesting that the Greek word here is the same one used in verse 15, which said that sin *brings forth* death. Sin brings forth death, and yet God brings forth spiritual life. James may have used this word to contrast what God really does—He brings forth life—with what some charged Him with, that is, tempting them to sin! This word *begat* (KJV) is in the past tense aorist, which indicates the completeness and the permanence of this birth. In the physical world, we are born once, and so it is in the spiritual world—you can only be born again once! God gave us this birth from above, once and for all. How does He will that? How are we born again?

James says it is with the *word of truth*, the gospel message. Jesus says, "I am the way, the truth, and the life. No one comes to the Father except through Me" (John 14:6). Other passages to consider are Ephesians 1:13, Colossians 1:5, and Romans 10:14-17. We are converted: we repent, exercise faith, and are justified by responding to the Gospel but we are regenerated by the will of God alone. No one can be saved apart from the gospel message, the word of truth. The fact that God willed our salvation before the world began should cause each of us to bow in humility. You might be asking, "Why did He do that?" "Why does Christ save me?" James says ...

James 1:18. That we might be a kind of firstfruits of His creatures

The term *firstfruits* is not one we often use, but to James' Jewish audience this term would have been quite familiar. Consider Exodus 23:19, Leviticus 23:9-10, and Deuteronomy 18:4. Here we see that laws were established so that all firstfruits were sacred to God and were offered in grateful service to God because they belonged to Him. In the Old Testament, the Israelites offered the first part of their crops as an acknowledgement that the whole harvest belonged to God. Numbers 18:12 describes this: "All the best of the oil, all the best of the new wine and the grain, their *firstfruits* which they offer to the LORD, I have given them to you" (Numbers 18:12, emphasis mine).

So, when we are reborn by the true word of the gospel, we become the property of God, even as the firstfruits of the harvest did. We have been saved, we have been consecrated, and we are the firstfruits of His creation. We are consecrated to God from the rest of mankind, from the rest of creation. We are the firstfruits of His creation. We are not to give Him our leftovers, but our very best. Our first fruit! Look at Revelation 14:1-5, for some interesting observations regarding those who are the firstfruits unto God:

> Then I looked, and behold, a Lamb standing on Mount Zion, and with Him one hundred and forty-four thousand, having His Father's name written on their foreheads. And I heard a voice from heaven, like the voice of many waters, and like the voice of loud thunder. And I heard the sound of harpists playing their harps. They sang as it were a new song before the throne, before the four living creatures, and the elders; and no one could learn that song except the hundred and forty-four thousand who were redeemed from the earth. These are the ones who were not defiled with women, for they are virgins. These are the ones who follow the Lamb wherever He goes. These were redeemed from among men, being firstfruits to God and to the Lamb. And in their mouth was found no deceit, for they are without fault before the throne of God. (Revelation 14:1-5)

In verse 4, John was talking about the 144,000 who are standing on Mt. Zion with the Lamb after His second coming. The vision mentioned here anticipates the triumph of the 144,000 still intact at the time of Jesus Christ's return from heaven to earth. We see three characteristics about these firstfruits from verse 4.

1. They are blameless, without fault (not defiled with women).

2. They are redeemed.
3. They follow the Lamb *wherever He goes*.

Christ did not save us just to sit around and twiddle our thumbs. Christ saved us so that we would be the firstfruits of his creatures. He saved us to be holy and blameless and obedient to Him. By right we belong to Him. He made us and purchased us with the blood of His Son, Jesus Christ. The truth is God gave us life by His determined grace for a purpose!

Summary

A common error is being deceived by a wrong perception of our trials, but the truth of God affirms that He always gives good gifts in a good way, without changing. This is due to another foundational truth, that truth is that God has given us eternal life by His determined grace, for a definite purpose.

What are you doing for the One who gave His very life for you? Is your life just passing you by? Do you just exist from day to day? If so, that is not the mindset of a firstfruit of God's creation! Paul wrote, "Who gave Himself for us, that He might redeem us from every lawless deed and purify for Himself His own special people, zealous for good works" (Titus 2:14). In the very next chapter of Titus we are instructed "to maintain good works" (Titus 3:8). We are born again to serve and glorify the Lord by our good works. God gives us good and perfect gifts, and the best gift is the gift of His Son. What we give back is our gift to Him.

Do you doubt God's goodness this day? Don't be deceived, dear sister! In contrast to those evil things that come from your own lusts, good and perfect gifts come from the Father above, who is unchanging. Remember the best gift of all that He has given you is your salvation. Have you been born again by the Word of truth? If so, you have been saved from the wrath to come, and yet, saved for service, saved to follow the Lamb wherever He goes. This again is an evidence of your faith. What are you doing to serve the Father of lights?

Questions to Consider
"The Greatest Gift of All"
James 1:16-18

1. Read the whole book of James. (a) Record each occurrence, chapter and verse, when James used the words *brethren* or *beloved brethren*. (b) Why do you think James uses those terms?

2. Memorize James 1:17.

3. Read 2 Chronicles 20:1-30. (a) What was Jehoshapat's particular trial? (b) How did he choose to focus on God's goodness? (c) What was the result?

4. Read Moses' rehearsal of Israel's failure at Kadesh-Barnea in Deuteronomy chapter 1. (a) What were the good gift(s) God was giving them? (b) What was the Israelite's response? (c) How did God respond to their ingratitude? (d) What principle(s) can you glean from this account?

5. (a) Why did God save you? See the following verses. (Each one should produce a different answer.) John 15:16; 1 Thessalonians 2:12; 1 Peter 1:15-16; and 1 Peter 2:9. (b) Would you say that these are the qualities that exemplify your life? Why or why not?

6. Everyday this week write down at least ten "good and perfect gifts" that the Lord has blessed you with. (You should end up with a total of 70.) Praise and thank Him for each one!

7. We are the "firstfruits" of His creation. We are born again to serve Him. How are you serving the Lord? What are you giving back to Him? Is there some area of ministry that He is calling you to? Pray and then OBEY!

8. Write a praise of thanksgiving to God for your salvation!

6

How to Respond to God's Word

James 1:19-21

One of the fun things about teaching is not only having the privilege of studying the Word of God and passing on what I have learned to others, but also the fact that I get to watch everyone's face as I teach. I can observe your expressions: smiles, frowns, boredom, confusion, yawns, etc. I am sure that one of the things all of us have seen at one time or another is people who fall asleep in church. We know from Acts 20:9 that Eutychus fell asleep while Paul was preaching and fell out of a window! I have read stories of people falling asleep and bumping their heads on the pew in front of them, people who were sitting on the platform and dozing off and dropping their hymnal, people snorting and snoring in church, a husband and wife who fell asleep with their heads propped one against the other, an elder who fell asleep—his wife nudged him—and he stood up and pronounced the benediction. I really feel sorry for them; either they aren't getting the rest they need, or perhaps they are on medication, or they are too warm, or perhaps they are bored.

However, as much as that concerns me, of greater concern to me is another type of sleep. It is not a physical sleep, but a spiritual sleep. I am more concerned today about peoples' hearts, minds, and souls that have fallen asleep. They are unreceptive to the Word of God. This also was James' pastoral concern as he wrote to his dispersed Jewish flock. In the last chapter of this study we learned that everything God gives us is good and perfect, even when He sends us trials. It is useful for us and accomplishes a goal. This God, who is the Father of lights, is different from the lights He created in that He never changes and there are not eclipses with Him as there are with the lights He created. The best gift He has given to us is our eternal salvation. But with that gift comes responsibility. We are born again to serve Him—we are the firstfruits of His creation. With the privilege of being a child, an heir, a firstfruit, comes responsibility. Part of that responsibility is our response to God and to His Word. James had already addressed what our proper response should be to trials and temptations, and now he is going to deal with a proper response to the Word of God. A genuine faith will relate rightly to the Word of God, especially as it relates to our responses towards God in a trial and what He is trying to teach us. Thus, James wrote:

> So then, my beloved brethren, let every man be swift to hear, slow to speak, slow to wrath; [20]for the wrath of man does not produce the righteousness of God. [21]Therefore lay aside all filthiness and overflow of wickedness, and receive with meekness the implanted word, which is able to save your souls. (James 1:19-21)

In these three verses, we will see what should be our response to God's Word (v 19), the reason for this response to God's Word (v 20), and the actual receiving of God's Word (v 21).

Our Response to the Word

James 1:19. So then, my beloved brethren

While the *New King James Version* translates the transitional adverb as *so then*, the *King James Version* translates it as *wherefore*. Anytime *wherefore, therefore,* or *so then* occurs in the Bible, it is there for a reason. *Wherefore* means *because of this*. Since God is the only source of good, because He tempts no man, and because we have the honor of being made the firstfruits of His creatures, then we are to respond to God in a proper way. Again note that James calls them *beloved brethren*, just as we saw in verse 16.

James softened the hard words he was about to write with

a reminder that he loved them by using the salutation *beloved brethren*. Nevertheless, he did not allow his love for them to keep him from telling the truth. We too, should never allow our love for one another to keep us from exhorting and admonishing each other, "and so much the more as [we] see the Day approaching" (Hebrews 10:25).

James 1:19. Let every man be swift to hear

Now James uses an imperative, a command, in these verses. These verses are not optional for a believer. Too often this verse is taken out of context to prove that in human relationships we are to be swift to hear, slow to speak, and slow to wrath (although in and of itself that is good advice). But what James is commanding here is how we should respond to God's Word of truth especially during a trial. As believers in Jesus Christ our response to God's Word should be drastically different from the world and its response.

There are four responses we should make to God's Word. Three are mentioned here in verse 19, and the other in verse 21. First of all we are to be *swift to hear*, which means we are to be quick to listen. James was saying that their attitude should be one of eagerness and attentiveness to what God says. In the day in which James was writing, most readers were not as privileged as we are to have a copy of the Bible, let alone multiple copies in multiple translations. They were dependent on listening to someone else read a portion of Scripture. They would have needed to be especially attentive to the hearing of the Scripture thus they were to be swift to hear the spoken Word.

Today we as believers not only have the wonderful privilege of owning our very own copy (or copies) of God's Word, but we have Christian radio, Christian television, tapes, conferences, seminars, films, books, not to mention church services and women's Bible studies, all spreading God's Word. And yet I am afraid that sometimes we are not listening. We have lost the art of listening due to excessive entertainment, which unfortunately has carried over into our church, bringing us to the point where we have difficulty listening intently to the Word. We have amused ourselves to a spiritual death.[18]

In contrast to modern-day preachers, we see that when Eutychus fell asleep and out of a window, Paul had been preaching all night and then on until daybreak. Can you imagine what would be a congregation's response today if their preacher went past noon? Our churches might find that their attendance would drastically drop. Today Ezra would never have gotten away with reading God's Word four to six hours a day, day after day (Nehemiah 8:1-8). Maybe this would be a good idea to implement, as it would certainly purify our churches, as those disinterested in a passionate pursuit of God would melt away, under the convicting impact of long exposure to the Bible.

James said that *every man* should be swift to hear, not just some men, but all men and of course all women, even the ones who may already have great knowledge of the Word. Even the person you may most respect, even John MacArthur, even Elizabeth Elliott, and even Billy Graham—even he or she should sit down and listen to the Word of God, the Word of truth, and grow in it.

Our appropriate attitude should be one of wanting to learn rather than instruct. We should listen to the Word as if for the first time. Someone once said, "Men have two ears, but one tongue, that

---

[18] Neil Postman's excellent cultural commentary, *Amusing Ourselves to Death: Public Discourse in the Age of Show Business* (Penguin Books, 1985) is summarized by the author: "This book is an inquiry into and a lamentation about the most significant cultural fact of the second half of the twentieth century, the decline of the Age of Typography and the ascendancy of the Age of Television. This change-over has dramatically and irreversibly shifted the content and meaning of public discourse, since two media so vastly different cannot accommodate the same ideas. As the influence of print wanes, the content of politics, religion, education and anything else that comprises business must change and be recast in terms that are most suitable to television" (p. 8). Media in general and television in particular is conditioning even believers to think in sound-bites, removing from many the ability to listen or read attentively God's Word. Obviously, this conditioning has become one of the greatest competitors to spiritual growth in America.

they should hear more than they speak."[19] I would like to encourage you to work at truly listening to God, to His Word. Slow down and take time to listen. This may mean that you need to limit your exposure to visual media if that is a problem for you, because it has been proven to be a hindrance to our listening. And by the way, it would be a good idea, if you don't already, to limit your children's viewing time as well. It may also mean you need to adjust your hectic schedule so that your mind and body aren't going in various directions preventing you from sitting still and listening. All believers are supposed to be quick to hear the Word because it will provide nourishment for our spiritual lives and is our weapon against all spiritual adversaries (Ephesians 6:17). It is the means by which you are strengthened and equipped for every good work (2 Timothy 3:17). It delivers you from trials and temptations and engages you in communion with the living God. The Word should be your most welcome friend!

James 1:19. Slow to speak

The second response we should have to God's Word is to be *slow to speak*. The sense is that the readers or listeners were to be slow to speak back to the Word of God or to the one proclaiming it. We should give thoughtful evaluation to what is being taught before reacting. In the Jewish churches to which Pastor James was writing, their services were less structured than ours today, and so this custom invited personal participation, and therefore the speaker could be easily interrupted. Argument and debate was accepted, so too often the Word of God was eclipsed by a heated discussion of interpretation. This would possibly have encouraged people to

---

[19] John Blanchard, Truth for Life (West Sussex, England: H. E. Walter Ltd, 1982), p. 73. The Epistle of James has often been likened to the Proverbs of the New Testament, as pithy sayings are sprinkled throughout the letter. "Let everyone be swift to hear, slow to speak and slow to wrath," contains a world of inspired instruction all compressed into a short well-phrased verse.

speak with hasty and ill-formed comments.[20] Ecclesiastes 5:2 says regarding our words in the house of God: "Do not be rash with your mouth and let not your heart utter anything hastily before God. For God is in heaven, and you on earth; therefore let your words be few."

There are similar warnings about rash words in Scripture. e.g., "Do you see a man hasty in his words? There is more hope for a fool than for him" (Proverbs 29:20). "In the multitude of words sin is not lacking, But he who restrains his lips is wise" (Proverbs 10:19). Or Proverbs 13:3 which says, "He who guards his mouth preserves his life, But he who opens wide his lips shall have destruction." But the precise command of our passage under consideration isn't really dealing with speaking in general but in a quick speaking while hearing the Word of God, which could eclipse its meaning or punch. Later in James 3:1, the Pastor of the Jerusalem church examines the broader issue of speaking itself.

James 1:19. And slow to wrath

---

[20] The Apostle Paul corrected the Corinthian abuses of their public worship, one of which involved women who evidently would enter into interpretive public debates. Notice he first called for an ordered interpreting and evaluating process of what was spoken "How is it then, brethren? Whenever you come together, each of you has a psalm, has a teaching, has a tongue, has a revelation, has an interpretation. Let all things be done for edification. If anyone speaks in a tongue, let there be two or at the most three, each in turn, and let one interpret. But if there is no interpreter, let him keep silent in church, and let him speak to himself and to God. Let two or three prophets speak, and let the others judge. But if anything is revealed to another who sits by, let the first keep silent. For you can all prophesy one by one, that all may learn and all may be encouraged. And the spirits of the prophets are subject to the prophets. For God is not the author of confusion but of peace, as in all the churches of the saints." And then, Paul forbids women from involvement in the interpreting and public evaluating process. "Let your women keep silent in the churches, for they are not permitted to speak; but they are to be submissive, as the law also says. And if they want to learn something, let them ask their own husbands at home; for it is shameful for women to speak in church" (1 Corinthians 14:26-35). If women would enter into public debate on interpretive points it was showing a lack of humble submission. This doesn't mean of course that women are not to train themselves to be discerning in what they hear or read but they cannot enter into interpretive debates in the assembly of a mixed audience. John Piper and Wayne Grudem, Editors, recovering *Biblical Manhood and Womanhood: A Response to Evangelical Feminism* (Crossway Books, 1991), article by D. A. Carson on "Silent in the Churches: On the Role of Women in 1 Corinthians 14:33b-36," pp. 140-153.

According to James 1:19, our third response to the Word of God should mean that we are *slow to wrath*. This would suggest that we should not to be angry at God's Word. The anger here is a deep internal resentment accompanied by an attitude of rejection. It denotes a strong and persistent feeling of indignation and active anger. I imagine this was a real temptation to these readers who were undergoing great persecution. Not only did the temptation exist to be angry with the Word, but also to be resentful and angry towards those who were persecuting them. An angry spirit towards the Word of God is never right and responding in this manner demonstrates an unteachable spirit. It is interesting that James says we are to be *slow* to wrath. He does not say don't ever be wrathful or angry, because there is a time when we should get angry, and that is with sin. There *is* a righteous anger. In fact, Psalm 7:11 tells us that "God is angry with the wicked every day." Ephesians 4:26 says, "Be angry, and do not sin."

But to be angry with the Word of God is never a righteous response for the believer in Jesus Christ. What would you say your response is to the Word of God and to its proclamation? Do you come to church eagerly on Sundays and Wednesdays? Are you eager to hear what God has to say in His Word? What about your daily time with Him? Is it a mere formality? Or do you eagerly come with anticipation of what He has to say to you? Then, once you hear or read His Word, do you find yourself wanting to constantly challenge what you have read or challenge the person who has proclaimed the truth? Does God's Word make you angry? Do you welcome the Word's reproofs and heed its warnings, or do you secretly resent it? When a Christian brother or sister confronts a sin in your life, do you accept or reject their counsel?

I may never forget the following experience as long as I live. My husband, Doug, had been asked to preach at a large church in Oklahoma City. In fact, it was the church that he attended after coming to Christ. He preached a wonderful sermon, and I was so proud of him. I thought he had proclaimed the truth and proclaimed it powerfully. After the service the pastor had asked us to stay at the front of the auditorium in order to shake hands with the members.

Keeping in mind that this was a large church, I was perplexed when only about twenty people came up to shake our hands. One woman approached him enraged wagging her finger and said, "I hate you and I hate what you said, and you don't understand."[21] We were flabbergasted. I never wanted to vacate a place so quickly in all my life. When we finally reached the hallway, I felt like we must have had leprosy, because no one spoke to us, not even the pastor. My husband was more encouraged and went away rejoicing, realizing that they had gotten the implications of what he was saying.

This woman with the wagging finger was a prime example of someone who was responding in anger to the Word of God. The Bible has given us a very sobering example of another angry crowd's response to the Word in Acts 7:54-60. This is the account of the crowd to which Stephen had preached confronting their sin. The Scriptures say that they covered their ears, drove him out of the city, and stoned him to death. God's truth can sometimes result in hatred for His people. But for a true believer in Jesus Christ, anger should never be the response to God's Word! James goes on to tell us the reason in verse 20.

The Reason for the Response

James 1:20. For the wrath of man

Being wrathful does not promote righteousness, and anger

---

[21] It was Mother's Day and my husband preached on "The Biblical Alternative to the Mommy Track," following the release of the Harvard Business Review secular article of a similar title, in 1986. Doug selected Titus 2:3-5 and faithfully explained the passage, which certainly contradicts the career oriented woman that Harvard Business Review was extolling. Especially the phrase, "the aged women are to teach the younger women ... [to be] keepers at home," which rattled the thinking of many. I realize there is some textual debate on which term Paul used either *oikourous* ("keepers at home") or *oikourgous* ("workers at home") but the sense is the same and forbids a career centered life, at least for a married mother. I realize it is not popular to teach that and Doug even graciously mentioned various short-term extenuating circumstances but kept faithful to the Bible. I've also spent lots of time appealing to wives to consider this phrase and be domestically oriented, with the same angry reactions we received that day.

keeps us from receiving the Word of God. Attributes usually associated with a wrathful spirit are ambition, revenge, jealousy, and egotism, just to name a few. The wrath that James was speaking of here is a wicked wrath in which the genuine believer should have no part. For example, you hear the Word of God taught at church and leave saying—maybe not as blatantly as that woman with the wagging finger, but perhaps in the privacy of your heart, or to your husband, or to your friend—"that preacher really made me angry by what he said today." And yet all that was proclaimed was the Word of Truth. That is a wicked anger. This angry reaction can happen with unbelievers as well. They can hear the gospel message and feel uncomfortable. This discomfort may turn into real anger like it did in the account of Stephen in Acts, when it was ultimately transformed into a wicked anger, a wrong anger. The result of a wicked wrath is that it does not produce the righteousness of God.

James 1:20. Does not produce the righteousness of God

What is the righteousness of God? The word *righteous* in the Greek means justice. *Righteous* presents God as a great Judge whose work is to render justice—punishment where punishment is due and reward where reward is deserved. What James was saying here is that he wants us to know that in our anger we can never render justice in any situation as God would have rendered it. Man's anger is contrary to the character of God. Even through the trials of life you do not have license to be angry with God. "Whenever man gives way to anger, he never furthers the righteousness he professedly strives for; anger blocks his goal of fostering righteousness."[22] James 1:20 surfaces in my mind when I am tempted to become angry with someone or in a situation. I know that my anger will not incur God's favor upon me, and many times the remembrance of this verse has kept me from sinning. By the way, this is a great verse to commit to memory if you have not already done so! Then the transition is made to verse 21 with *wherefore* once again in the *King James Version* and *therefore* in the *New King James Version*.

---

[22] D. Edmond Hiebert, *The Epistle of James: Tests of a Living Faith* (Moody Press, 1979), p. 127.

The Receiving of the Word

James 1:21. Therefore lay aside all filthiness

Therefore looks back to verse 20 and indicates that a different response is needed from the believer. Instead of anger, there must be meekness. There may be a reason we are not responding appropriately to the Word of God. Apparently some of James' readers were allowing sin to keep them from receiving the Word as they should, (just like some today), so James told them to put away that sin: "lay aside all filthiness and overflow of wickedness."

To *lay aside* or *put away*, as it is translated in the *King James Version*—is a term indicating a stripping off of clothes: "having put off from yourselves." The aorist tense in the Greek calls for a definite break with these things. People who are careful about their appearance quickly remove a soiled garment, don't they? I remember when our son was living at home and took a roofing job for the summer. He would come home from work with tar and all kinds of material stuck to his skin and clothing. I wouldn't let him in the house until he removed those filthy clothes! That is what James is saying in verse 20. Take off those filthy clothes—those filthy sins—so that you can receive the Word of God. James says to change clothes immediately, not later. Put off all—not some, but all. God is never satisfied with partial purity or partial holiness. There is no half-heartedness with God. He wants your all! This idea of putting off is not only found here, but also in Ezekiel 18:31, Romans 13:12, Ephesians 4:22-29, Colossians 3:8-14, and 1 Peter 2:1.

This is the fourth response that we are to have to God's Word. Remember, the first three are in verse 19—swift to hear, slow to speak, slow to wrath—and now we are told to receive the Word with meekness. But before we can receive the word with meekness, we have to put away some sins. We must first put off filthiness, disgusting things, and offensive things. Actually this word in the Greek is used to speak of wax in the ear, a disgusting sight. Sin in our lives is like having wax in our ears. It prevents the Word of truth from reaching our hearts, for if it cannot penetrate through the ear, it will not come down to the heart. As Christians, we must remove the wax from our ears so that the Word is able to influence our lives. When wax accumulates in one's ear, it can make her deaf. And a woman's sins can make her deaf to God. If we leave such filth in our ears, it plugs up our spiritual ears so that God's Word cannot enter. Paul tells us, "Therefore, having these promises, beloved, let us cleanse ourselves from all filthiness of the flesh and spirit, perfecting holiness in the fear of God" (2 Corinthians 7:1).

James 1:21. And overflow of wickedness

Not only are we to put away all filthiness, but we are also to put away the *overflow of wickedness*. Overflow of wickedness means abounding in evil, an overflowing of malignity. An abundance of malice and ill will create the desire to injure another. This notion suggests the dangerous capacity of malicious wickedness to overflow the banks of self-control. It is important to take note here that James did not call these two character attributes of filthiness and overflowing of wickedness a "human weakness" or a "psychological complex." Instead he calls them *sins*. James says we must put away these filthy and wicked sins. We must lay them aside.

You might wonder why I am making such a big deal about this *putting off*? Because so often I hear, "Oh, you see, I just have so much to work on in my life, I can only fight one area at a time." Nonsense! Where is that notion confirmed in the Bible? God's Word is clear—we are to put away A-L-L. All! Not some, but all. After we put off the filth and wickedness in our lives, then we can receive with meekness the engrafted Word, which is able to save our souls.

James 1:21. And receive with meekness

How are we to receive the Word? *With meekness*. This is in contrast to the anger which blocks us from hearing God's Word. Meekness indicates an attitude of gentle considerateness. This receptivity is the opposite of angry self-assertion. It fosters humility and teachability. If your heart is pure and humble, you will be teachable and will set aside all resentment, anger, and pride so you can learn God's truth and apply it to your life. Spiritual pride is one of the worst things we as the children of God can possess, especially pride towards the receiving of God's Holy Word. You may say, "Oh, I know that already" or "I don't need that sermon, I already have that area whipped in my life." Or "that sure is a good lesson for *her*, I hope *she* is listening. *I* have already studied that!" Is that a spirit of meekness? Is that receiving God's Word in meekness? No, it is not. So, exactly what are we to receive with meekness?

James 1:21. Receive ... the implanted word, which is able to save your souls

We are to receive the *implanted word* or the *engrafted word*, as it is translated in the *King James Version*. The word *receive* is in the aorist imperative which conveys a sense of urgency. This reception of the Word is a duty that cannot be put off—do not neglect receiving the engrafted word. *Engrafted* and *implanted* come from two words—"*in*" and "*to plant*." In other words, it means to plant in.

This idea may have been derived from Jesus' parable of the sower in Matthew 13. The word of God here is described as "implanted" because when it falls in the human heart upon soil that has been prepared by the Holy Spirit to receive it, it is welcomed. It takes root, and so transforms the soil. James speaks of the Word, which has been planted once and for all in our hearts, as we saw in verse 18, which discussed believers as the firstfruits of His creatures. The Word rooted in our hearts is then able to save our souls. This saving is simply the function of God's Word, saving us from the destructive consequences of sin. Scripture speaks of a past, present, and future aspect of salvation. You have been saved from the penalty of sin (salvation), are being saved from the power of sin (sanctification), and will ultimately be saved from the presence of sin (glorification).

The phrase "save your souls" carries the idea that the

implanted Word has the ongoing power to continually save one's soul. It is a reference to the present and ongoing process of sanctification, which is nurtured by the Spirit and energized by the Word of God. The Holy Spirit implanted the Word within you at the time of your salvation. God's Word is the source of power and growth for your new life in Christ. Your responsibility is to receive the Word in purity and humility so it can do its sanctifying work. If and only if you respond to the Word in these ways, will you then be able to be saved from the destructive consequences of your sin.

Summary

James was challenging his contemporary and future readers to examine themselves in light of their responses to the Word of God. How you and I respond to the Word of God is another evidence of our faith. Have you received with meekness the Word of God, which is able to save your soul? Has it been implanted in your heart? Have you put away all filthiness in your life? Would you say you are eager to hear God's Word? Can you not wait to get to church? Are you slow to speak back when God speaks to you? Do you become angry with God's Word when it is proclaimed? Is there anything in your spiritual ears that is preventing you from clearly hearing the Word of truth? Are your soul and heart asleep when it comes to responding to God's Word? Wake up! Cleanse and unplug your spiritual ears! Be swift to hear, slow to speak, slow to wrath. And then receive with meekness the implanted word, which is able to save your soul!

Questions to Consider
"How to Respond to God's Word"
James 1:19-21

1. Read James 1. (a) What are the terms that James uses for the Word? (b) What is the significance of these words in their context? (c) Also, make note of all the responses we are to have towards God and His Word. (d) Are these your responses?

2. Memorize James 1:19-20.

3. What do you think James means in verse 20?

4. Read Numbers 20:7-13. (a) What did God tell Moses to do? (b) What did he do instead? (c) What was the sin that Moses committed? (d) What was the result of his sin? (e) How does this relate to what James says in 1:19-21? (f) What advice found in the Epistle of James did Moses fail to heed? (g) What principles can you learn for your own life when facing the temptation to go against what God has told you to do?

5. Recall a time when you did not respond to God's Word in a proper way. What was the result?

6. Honestly answer the following questions: (a) Are you eagerly listening to God and His Word? (b) Are you slow to speak back to Him? (c) Are you slow to get angry at His Word? (d) Are you meekly receiving the Word?

7. In what area of your life is God speaking to you as a result of this chapter? What is your prayer to God?

7

Hear, Do, and Be Blessed

James 1:22-25

Imagine with me that I am the owner of a rapidly growing company and that you are my executive assistant. I am interested in expanding overseas, but in order to do this, I must travel abroad and stay there until the new branch of the office is established. I make all the arrangements to take my family in this move to Europe for six to eight months, and I leave you in charge of the company at home while I go abroad. I tell you that I will write you regularly to give you directions and instructions. I leave and you stay. Months pass. A flow of letters are mailed from Europe and received by you at the national headquarters. I spell out all of my expectations. Finally, I return. Soon after my arrival I drive down to the office, and as I approach the office, I am stunned! Grass and weeds have grown up high. A few windows along the street are broken. I walk into the receptionist's room and she is doing her nails, chewing gum, and listening to her favorite radio station. I look around and notice the wastebaskets are overflowing, the carpet hasn't been vacuumed for weeks, and nobody seems concerned about the fact that the owner has returned. I ask around about where you are and someone in the crowded lounge area points down the hall and yells, "I think she's down there." Disturbed, I move in that direction and bump into you as you are finishing a chess game with our sales manager. I ask you to step into my office (which has been temporarily turned into a television room for watching afternoon soap operas).

"What in the world is going on?" I ask.
"What do ya' mean?" you reply.
"Just look at this place! Didn't you get any of my letters?"

"Letters? Oh, yeah, sure, I got every one of them. As a matter of fact ... we have had a *letter study* every Friday night since you left. We even divided all the personnel into small groups and discussed many of the things you wrote. Some of those things were very interesting. You'll be pleased to know that a few of us have actually committed to memory some of your sentences and paragraphs. One or two memorized an entire letter or two! Great stuff in those letters!

I reply, "Ok, ok. So you got my letters. You studied them and meditated on them and discussed them and even memorized them. BUT WHAT DID YOU DO ABOUT THEM?

"Do? Uh, we didn't *do* anything about them."[23]

Such behavior would be professionally absurd. In fact, it would be professional suicide. But we are just as absurd spiritually when we hear God's Word without the slightest inclination to obey the letters He has written to us. That would be spiritual suicide. James says:

> But be doers of the word, and not hearers only, deceiving yourselves. [23]For if anyone is a hearer of the word and not a doer, he is like a man observing his natural face in a mirror; [24]for he observes himself, goes away, and immediately forgets what kind of man he was. [25]But he who looks into the perfect law of liberty and continues in it, and is not a forgetful hearer but a doer of the work, this one will be blessed in what he does. (James 1:22-25)

In the last chapter we noted that we should have four responses to God's Word. We should be swift to hear, slow to speak, slow to wrath, and receive the Word with meekness. We saw that some of us have not responded to the Word in these ways because we have not put off filthiness and wickedness; and, therefore, we cannot receive the Word properly. In this chapter we are going to see that we should have two more responses to the Word of God: we are to hear and obey the Word (vv 22-24), and we are to look and continue in the Word (v 25).

---

[23] Reworded paraphrase of an illustration by Charles R. Swindoll, *Improving Your Serve* (Waco, TX: Word, 1983), pp. 170-171.

Hear and Obey the Word

James 1:22. But be doers of the word

As we learned in the last chapter, the genuine believer has been implanted with the Word or has had the Word engrafted within his heart. The true believer continually strives for more and more practical obedience to the Word that already has been implanted, and that's why James says: "But be doers." In the Greek the sense reads "make sure that you are." This indicates that some were regularly listening to God's Word but were never real disciples. They were interested in hearing the Old Testament Scriptures and the New Testament Apostles' doctrine preached but they lacked obedience. This would not be a new idea to the Jewish reader nor should it be to us.[24] For example, the Lord had warned the nation of Israel through Moses:

> If you do not carefully observe all the words of this law that are written in this book, that you may fear this glorious and awesome name, THE LORD YOUR GOD, then the LORD will bring upon you and your descendants extraordinary plagues--great and prolonged plagues--and serious and prolonged sicknesses. Moreover He will bring back on you all the diseases of Egypt, of which you were afraid, and they shall cling to you. Also every sickness and every plague, which is not written in the Book of the Law, will the LORD bring upon you until you are destroyed. You shall be left few in number, whereas you were as the stars of heaven in multitude, because you would not obey the voice of the LORD your God. And it shall be, that just as the LORD rejoiced over

---

[24] The appeal to obedience to the Word of God is anchored to reward: "Therefore keep the words of this covenant, and do them, that you may prosper in all that you do" (Deuteronomy 29:9). Again, it is a multi-generational command: "The secret things belong to the LORD our God, but those things which are revealed belong to us and to our children forever, that we may do all the words of this law" (Deuteronomy 29:29).

you to do you good and multiply you, so the LORD will rejoice over you to destroy you and bring you to nothing; and you shall be plucked from off the land which you go to possess. (Deuteronomy 28:58-63)

Doers of the word does not refer to the person who sporadically obeys, but the one who does so habitually, regularly and characteristically. Obviously this doing of the Word of God will not be in perfection but certainly it will resemble a genuine level of consistent desired obedience. The way James states it, *doer of the Word* instead of *do the word,* puts the emphasis on the kind of person a Christian should be, not just some act she performs. She is a "doer of the Word"—that's just what she does! Paul mentioned this idea in his letter to the Romans: "For not the *hearers* of the law are just in the sight of God, but the *doers* of the law will be justified" (Romans 2:13, emphasis mine).[25] Our Lord said it this way, "My sheep *hear* My voice, and I know them, and they *follow* Me" (John 10:27, emphasis mine). It's one thing to run in a race; it's something else to be a runner. It's one thing to teach a class; it's another thing to be a teacher. It's one thing to bake a cake, but it is another thing to be a baker. Runners are known for their running. Teachers are known for their teaching. Bakers are known for their baking. Likewise, doers of the Word are known for their obedience to biblical truth. The direction of the life is one of real obedience to God's revealed will, not a sporadic obedience nor a partial obedience. Would others say about you, "Now, she is a doer of the Word"?

James 1:22. And not hearers only

James continued his warning that we should not be "hear-

---

[25] Robert L. Thomas of The Master's Seminary comments on the term "hearer" (Greek, *akoatai*): "This occurs only in Romans 2:13. It is in close similarity to passages which suggest that Paul had seen James or James had seen Paul's letter to Romans. The word in classical Greek referred to attentive listening; it was used of those who attended lectures or philosophers and public speakers." *Exegetical Digest of the Epistle of James,* Edited by Robert L. Thomas (1976, Robert L. Thomas), p. L. 14.

ers only." In the Greek text, a hearer refers to one auditing a class. Auditing students attend class and listen to the instructor but don't do any work or receive credits. People who listen to God's Word but never obey it are spiritual auditors who delude themselves by thinking that hearing the Word is all God requires of them. Yes, hearing the Word is essential, but our obligation does not stop there. I fear many are just auditing the hearing of the Word in our churches today, but are not acting upon what they hear. These people can listen attentively and show a real interest in what they are hearing but possess no desire or intent to obey what they have heard. Unfortunately, many churches today are full of "hearers only." They attend church, but their lives never seem to change. My husband and I see them all the time, and many of them come to church faithfully. But their lives seldom really change. It is grievous to witness! I once heard a story—perhaps apocryphal—about a new pastor who preached a wonderful sermon his first time in the pulpit. The pulpit committee knew they had done well by calling this man to their church, until the next Sunday when he preached the same sermon again. They were somewhat perplexed. So when some members of the congregation asked the new pastor why he preached the same sermon again, he replied, "When you start living the first message, then we will go on to the next one." Perhaps that would be a good rule for our churches.

James 1:22. Deceiving yourselves

Those who hear the Word only but do not obey it, James said, are "deceiving themselves." The Greek here means they are beside themselves. They have miscalculated, reckoned wrongly. What have they deceived themselves about? According to the larger context of the epistle, they are deceiving themselves about their salvation. This man or woman has deluded themselves into thinking that they have received the Word, when all they have done is had a superficial encounter with it. This statement of James is frightening! You're not deceiving God, my friend, and you're probably not deceiving the people that are around you all the time either—your husband, your children, your friends. They know if you are just a hearer of the Word and not a doer. In His Sermon on the Mount Jesus affirmed, "You will know them by their fruits" (Matthew 7:16). In other words, we will know true believers by what they do. Notice it is not what they claim (e.g., "I'm a Christian" or "I've been saved"), it is what the life actually does. The new nature from God manifests in a new life of obedience. People will know—you can't fool them for long. If you are producing fruit, then you are a doer of the Word. Not only will people know, but God also knows—you will never fool Him, not even for a minute. This idea of deceiving yourself was familiar not only to James. Look at 1 Corinthians 3:18, 1 Corinthians 6:9, 1 Corinthians 15:33, and Galatians 6:3-4, 7. These are just a few of the warning passages we have in the Word of God about self-deception. Look also at the words of Jesus:

> Not everyone *who says to Me*, 'Lord, Lord,' shall enter the kingdom of heaven, but he who does the will of My Father in heaven. Many will say to Me in that day, 'Lord, Lord, have we not prophesied in Your name, cast out demons in Your name, and done many wonders in Your name?' And then I will declare to them, 'I never knew you; depart from Me, you who practice lawlessness!' (Matthew 7:21-23)

As the Lord Jesus concluded His sermon, He warned His audience and us today about *two unacceptable responses* to His commands. First, Jesus began by warning about a mere *verbal* profession. He said, *"Not every one* who says to me, Lord, Lord, shall *enter* the kingdom of heaven, but *he who does the will of my Father in heaven"* (Matthew 7:21 emphasis mine). Notice the determining factor concerning who enters into the kingdom of heaven is *obedience* to the Father's will! It's not simply a verbal profession of Jesus Christ's Lordship but a real obedience to God. And we would add, that doing the Father's will and doing the will of Jesus is the same thing. Then secondly, the Lord gives one of the most chilling warnings He ever uttered: *"Many* will say to me in *that day,* [i.e., the great Day of Judgment] 'Lord, Lord, have we not prophesied in Your name, cast out demons in Your name, and done many wonders in Your name?'" (Matthew 7:22). You see, the issue is not what we *profess* or *say* to the Lord today, or even what we will say to the

Lord at the great Day of Judgment, but whether our verbal profession is matched by moral obedience! Some on the Day of Judgment will claim extraordinary service to the Lord as a basis for entering the kingdom, but Jesus will not accept orthodox professions of faith nor Christian service as a substitute for obedience! And so He explains, "And then I will declare to them, '*I never knew you; depart from me, you who practice lawlessness*'" (v 23). Those deceived worked iniquity in their lives instead of obediently submitting to His sovereign Lordship, and so He issues their eternal doom in judgment! Remember, James was the half-brother of Jesus who gave this initial warning, which echoed in his pastoral heart as a burden needing repeating to others.

By the way, it is interesting to note that the word *many* in verse 22 of Jesus' warning was translated from the Greek word *polloi*, which is synonymous with the word *most*. So in this passage, we see Jesus in the Sermon on the Mount warning us that *most* would be deceived during their lives and even deceived on the Day of Judgment. *Most* have deceived themselves right into hell. Frightening indeed! After telling us not to deceive ourselves by being hearers of the Word only, James then gave us an unflattering description of the person who hears only but does not obey what he hears.

James 1:23. For if anyone is a hearer and not a doer, he is like a man observing

The *King James Version* translated the Greek participle *katanoont i* as "beholding," and the New King James as "observing." *Katanoont i* means to observe fully. Both translations mean that the man is not glancing at himself in a casual way but is engaging in a careful, cautious, observant stare. Here we see a man taking a good long look at himself, examining himself with careful scrutiny. Hearers of the Word are not necessarily superficial or casual in their approach to Scripture, for they can be serious students of the Word. And yet, the fact is that some Sunday school teachers and even some pastors are not true believers. Some even write biblical commentaries and books. Your *response* to the Word, not your depth of study alone, is the issue with God.

Read Ezekiel 33:31-33, which is a very sobering passage. Ezekiel had developed a popular following among the people, who recognized him as a prophet. They frequently gathered to hear his messages. They liked to hear the Word, but neglected to obey it and put it into practice. They were paying lip service to God, but harboring sin in their heart. Ezekiel's words were like beautiful love songs, but the message never penetrated their heart. There would come a day when they would realize what Ezekiel had said was true, but it would be too late. That is what James was saying here—"You listen and you like it, but you do not heed it."

James 1:23. His natural face in a mirror

Mirrors in biblical times were different from the ones we use today. They usually consisted of bronze, copper, tin, and sometimes silver polished to reflect the light. Such a mirror certainly gave an inferior reflection, but nonetheless, it did reflect light. Just like a mirror gives a physical reflection of our faces, the Word, the spiritual mirror gives us a reflection of our hearts. Then in verse 24, James tells us that after this man finished observing himself, he went away and immediately forgot what he looked like.

James 1:24. He observes himself

Despite the hearer's lingering look in the mirror, he failed to respond, and the image reflected in the mirror soon faded. Here James was referring to what we all experience, the fact that we do not retain a distinct impression of ourselves after we have looked in a mirror. While we are actually looking in the mirror, we see all our features. When we turn away, the image and impression both vanish. While looking in the mirror, we see all our blemishes, defects, gray hairs, sags, etc., but when we turn away, those defects are out of sight, out of mind!

So it is when we hear the Word of God. It is like a mirror that is held up before us. We see our sins, our defects, and perhaps we think we should correct them. We might even become emotionally aroused during a sermon, but afterwards, some of us will immediately turn away only to forget every word we heard. If however, we are doers of the Word, we will endeavor to remove all these defects, these sins, to bring ourselves to conformity with what God requires.

For example, let's say that after my morning walk, I came in and went to the mirror and realized that I needed to shower then change my clothes in order to get ready for the day. But instead, I went away from the mirror and went about my day forgetting what manner of woman I was, a mess. This behavior would be foolish. And yet that is precisely what we do when we hear the Word and do nothing about what we hear.

I am afraid that too many church members deal with God's Word in the same way. In fact, how many of you can even remember last Sunday's sermon or the last message you heard in a ladies' Bible Study? If you can remember, was your conscience stirred? What did you do about it? Have you made any changes? By the way, just as my showering and dressing benefit those around me, so does my hearing and doing God's Word—it benefits those around me.

James 1:24. Goes away, and immediately forgets what kind of man he was

James continues his thoughts in verse 24 saying that this person "goes away," which implies that the departure was a settled condition. He did not return to the mirror for a second look nor follow up with repeated inspections. The look into the mirror produced no result, so it was a waste of time and effort. If you don't take action on what you see in the mirror, then why bother looking in the first place? Sometimes our physical appearance is so bad that we don't even want to go back for a second look. Spiritually, too, we may not like what the Word reveals about our heart condition, so we depart and don't return to look. Or maybe we say, "I will take care of that sin or that problem tomorrow or next week. What's the rush?" Some of us may turn on the television or get involved in busy work to drown out our convictions.

Completing the metaphor of the mirror, James then turned from the unflattering picture of a "hearer only" gazing into the mirror of the Word to a positive illustration of a doer looking into the perfect law of liberty.

Look and Continue in the Word

James 1:25. But he who looks into

In verse 25 the Greek verb *parakps as*, translated in the *New King James Version* as "looks into," conveys the idea of bending down, leaning over so as to peer within, and examining something with care and precision. It is a penetrating look. It is the same idea we see in John 20:5, when Peter was looking into Jesus' empty tomb. He stooped down and *looked intently*, no doubt examining every corner of the empty tomb. In his first epistle, Peter used this same word in this passage: "To them it was revealed that, not to themselves, but to us they were ministering the things which now have been reported to you through those who have preached the gospel to you by the Holy Spirit sent from heaven—things which angels desire to *look into*" (1 Peter 1:12, emphasis mine). The woman who looks intently into the Word will go out of her way to study its pages—conceivably even bending or stooping over, looking intently at the pages.

"Looking into" also implies humility and a desire to see clearly what Scripture reveals about your own spiritual condition. It is an attitude as well as an action. It is an attitude that is accompanied by eagerness and a desire to learn and obey. James is describing the doer as one who has such an intense interest in the Word that he will go out of his way to study it (perhaps stooping or bending over its pages). Does that describe you?

James 1:25. The perfect law of liberty

James calls the Word "the *perfect* law of liberty." It is perfect because it is complete, sufficient, comprehensive, and without error. Unlike an imperfect poor metal or silver mirror, the Word is perfect. It is also perfect because it is God's law, and He is perfect. Another reason James called this the perfect law is rather interesting. Do you remember in our second lesson on trials when we learned that one of the benefits of trials was perfection? James said we are to let patience have its perfect work. We brought out that *perfection* was used to describe something that was reaching an end, or bringing something to a successful completion. That is the same word used here. So, we would say that if a man obeys the law of Christ, he will fulfill the purpose for which God sent him into the world. He will be the person he ought to be and will make the contribution to the world that he ought to make. He will be perfect in the sense that he will, by obeying the law of God, realize his God-given destiny.

James 1:25. The perfect law of liberty and continues in it

In addition to calling the law perfect, James also called it the *law of liberty*. That may sound paradoxical, because we tend to think of law and freedom as opposites. But as you look intently into the Word, the Holy Spirit enables you to apply its principles to your life, thereby freeing you from the guilt and bondage of sin, as well as sinful passions and lusts, and enabling you to live to God's glory. A doer of the Word sees God's Word as liberating, not binding. That is true freedom.

So a doer will look into the Word and "continue" in it or "abide" in it. The verb in the original Greek text is *parameno* and means to stay beside or near, to remain, and to continue. The idea is that a doer of the Word continually and habitually gazes into God's perfect law. The same idea is conveyed by the Psalmist who said, "Oh, how I love Your law, it is my meditation all the day!" (Psalm 119:97). The Psalmist was not just a Sunday learner! He was a persevering learner. The one who looks and continues to look is not a forgetful hearer.

James 1:25. And is not a forgetful hearer but a doer of the work

Don't we all forget at times? The older I get, the more I forget. But a doer of the Word determines beforehand that she will not forget what she is going to hear. The hearer-only, however, may approach the Word predetermined to forget, saying, "I will just forget what I hear." What a sad attitude that is. But not so for the doer! The doer of the Word knows that God's Word is a mirror; and unlike any natural mirror, it shows people their sin. It also shows them how they can be right with God. Doers of the Word desire conformity to Jesus Christ and want the sin rooted out of their lives and righteousness to take sin's place. A doer of the Word hears the word then does the work!

So we have seen four responses that we should have towards the Word: to be hearers of the Word, to be doers of the Word, to look intently into the Word, and to continue in the Word. Now what happens to this individual who manifests these responses to the Word?

James 1:25. This one will be blessed in what he does

James said, "He will be blessed in what he does." Blessing here is in the very act of obedience. The blessing is not in the hearing, but in the doing. Just like the blessed one who endures under a trial (v 12), you will be blessed in the very act of keeping the law. Psalm 19:11 says, "Moreover by them [i.e., the law of the Lord] Your servant is warned, And in keeping them there is great reward." Jesus said, "blessed are those who hear the word of God and keep it!" (Luke 11:28). There is a blessing in the doing, in the obeying. As believers, this truth is one of which we are well aware. Obedience always brings blessing, and disobedience always brings cursing!

Hear, Do, and Be Blessed

Summary

These verses are a clarion call to carefully examine yourself in light of God's standards. Examining yourself to see if you are in the faith is not a popular thing to do. When was the last time you examined yourself? All these lessons in James are really tests to see if we are in the faith, and it is imperative that we conduct a self-examination.

"Letters, Lord? Oh yeah, sure, I have all 66 of them. As a matter of fact, Lord, the ladies of our church participated in a letter study every Tuesday morning. We even divided all the women into small groups and discussed many of the things you wrote. Some of the things were really interesting. You'll be pleased to know that a few of us have actually committed to memory some of your sentences and paragraphs. Some of us are working on memorizing an entire letter! The one from James—there's great stuff in that letter!"

"Okay, you got My letters, you studied them and meditated on them, discussed and even memorized them. BUT WHAT DID YOU DO ABOUT THEM?"

Questions to Consider
"Hear, Do, and Be Blessed"
James 1:22-25

1. Read James 1, noting all the words that are repeated at least 3 times or more. Do you think there is any significance to the repetition?

2. Memorize James 1:22.

3. James mentions in 1:22 that those who hear the Word, but do not do it, deceive their own selves. (a) What other things can we be deceived about? Look at 1 Corinthians 3:18; 6:9-10; 15:33; Galatians 6:3-4,7; James 1:26; and 1 John 1:8. (b) After contemplating how self-deceived we can be about many things, what do you think your response should be? Use Scripture to back up your answer.

4. Read Matthew 13:1-23 noting the various soils and what they represent. Which one(s) are actually saved, i.e., actually doers? Support your findings.

5. Read Deuteronomy 28 listing all the blessings of obedience and all the curses of disobedience. What principles can you glean for your life from this chapter?

6. Why do you think a mirror is a good illustration of God's Word?

7. Think about the last few sermons you have heard. (a) Was your soul stirred? (b) How have you applied what you heard? (c) If you did not, how should you have applied it? (d) What is keeping you from being a doer?

8. Is there an area in your life where you are failing to be a doer of the Word? What is your prayer to God?

8

The Test of True Religion

James 1:26-27

The following true story took place in the 1700s, when that great preacher John Wesley was preaching a sermon. He noticed a lady in the audience who was known for her critical attitude. All through the service she just sat and stared at his new tie. When the meeting ended, she came up to him and said very sharply "Mr. Wesley, the strings on your bowtie are much too long. It's an offense to me!" He asked if any of the ladies present happened to have a pair of scissors in their purse. When the scissors were handed to him, he gave them to this critical lady and asked her to trim off the streamers to her liking. After she clipped them off near the collar, he said. "Are you sure they are all right now?" To which she replied, "Yes, that's much better." Then John Wesley asked her for the scissors and said, "I'm sure you wouldn't mind if I also give you a bit of correction. I must tell you madam, that your tongue is an offense to me—it's too long! Please stick it out ... I'd like to take some off." Now I hope that no one would ever want to cut off some of our tongues. Sad to say, some of us may need a sharp rebuke like John Wesley gave that lady in his church. Many of us have tongues that are out of control. They need to be bridled. James is just getting his foot in the door here regarding our tongue. He is brief here, but wait until we study chapter 3 of his letter! Let's now look at the last two verses of chapter 1.

> If anyone among you thinks he is religious, and does not bridle his tongue but deceives his own heart, this one's religion is useless. [27]Pure and undefiled religion before God and the Father is this: to visit orphans and widows in their trouble, and to keep oneself unspotted from the world. (James 1:26-27)

Pastor James has been dealing with the fact that being a hearer of the Word should produce a doer of the Word. James has stressed the fact that receiving the Word of God means putting it into practice, being a doer. James is now going to give his contemporary and future readers some practical ways to put the Word and our faith into practice, and so he gives three tests to let us know if we are accomplishing that: the test to *ourselves*, to control our tongue (v 26); the test to *others*, to visit those in need (v 27); and the test to *the world*, to keep ourselves unspotted from the world (v 27).

The Test to Ourselves – Control Our Tongue

James 1:26. If anyone among you thinks he is religious

The *New King James* translators used *thinks*, while the *King James* translators used *seems*. Here it means a person who has deceived his own heart by performing religious acts and supposing that this is what it means to be a doer of the Word. Perhaps a good expanded paraphrase might be: "If any woman among us seems to be religious by attending church every Sunday, by singing in the choir, by fasting and praying, by working in the nursery, by teaching a Sunday school class, by having her devotions *every* day—all outward deeds—if any woman among us does all these things, yet does not bridle her tongue, her religion is vain." The Greek word for *religious* here describes the details of formal religion, those outward acts of service to God. These are the people who have performed their religious rites of worship and feel content that they have been obedient to the Word. The noun form here in the Greek for *religious*, means, "to tremble, to be afraid of," which also suggests that ceremonial service of religion which springs not from real love for God, but from the dread of God. Our service to God should not be dread, but love. And then and only then shall we be happy in the doing of the work of God. In other words, the primary attention of the doer should not be on the external ceremonies, not on what is seen by others and commented on by oneself but what is within the heart, which can be seen by God alone. It reminds me of what Jesus said to the Pharisees, scribes, and hypocrites:

> Woe to you, scribes and Pharisees, hypocrites! For you are like whitewashed tombs which indeed appear beautiful outwardly, but inside are full of dead men's bones and all uncleanness. Even so you also outwardly appear righteous to men, but inside you are full of hypocrisy and lawlessness. (Matthew 23:27-28)

James 1:26. And does not bridle his tongue but deceives his own heart

We too, must be on guard that our religion is not merely external, but internal, changing the very fiber of who we are. Every religion has its ceremonies and practices. Catholicism, Judaism, Hinduism, Mormonism, and Christianity have religious acts that its members are expected to perform. And so we must be careful that our Christianity changes the inner man—not just display the outward acts. James was saying, "Hey, if you seem religious, if you do all the outward stuff, yet you cannot bridle your tongue, you deceive your own heart, and your religion is vain." James was comparing an unbridled tongue to a powerful, rearing horse, which will take off on a wild ride if the reins are not kept. Most of us have probably seen a living example of this at a rodeo. The bridle is the part of the harness that fits over the horse's head and is used to hold him back or control him. It is used on the horse so that he won't run ahead toward his own destruction. We are not going to dwell long on the issue of the tongue at this point because we are going to study it in-depth in James 3.

Look at James 3:1-10 for a taste of where we are going. James does not give us any particular examples of what sort of unbridled speech he is referring to. Perhaps he is referring to slander. John Calvin says: "A man will steer clear of adultery, of stealing, of drunkenness, in fact he will be a shining light of outward religious observance—and yet will revel in destroying the character of others, and this under the pretence of zeal but really through the lust of slander."[26] Slander would certainly have been a temptation for these readers due to the persecution they were undergoing. The temptation to slander their persecutors would be ever before them. And yet, that is the temptation for all of us, isn't it, even if we are not being persecuted? You might feel like you are doing this and that for the Lord, you are so religious, faithful in your devotional life, busy for God, etc. Pride swells up within you and then you begin to look at others, becoming critical because they are not like you, not as religious as you.

Sometimes we speak too freely of the achievements of ourselves, don't we? That is another area of our tongue that we need to control. We get caught up in gossip, criticism, and even foolish jesting. We all need a bridle on our tongue lest we let it run too much and too fast. Even though you may have perfect church attendance, possess knowledge of the Bible envied by others, pray much, or tithe regularly—it doesn't matter. If you don't control your tongue, then you are in trouble. Our Lord told us that when we have mouth trouble, we have heart trouble also. He put it this way: "For out of the abundance of the heart the mouth speaks" (Matthew 12:34). To control our mouths, we need to take care of the real issue, which is the condition of our hearts.

If you are guilty of an unbridled tongue, James says two things about you. First of all, "you have deceived your own heart." We saw in verse 22 that being a hearer without being a doer describes one who has deceived himself or herself. Here James is telling us again that our own heart is deceived. A woman can be very religious, and yet if her speech is evil, it reveals her self-deception. The danger here is not so much hypocrisy as it is self-deception. This term, (*apaton*) also has another meaning, which is not only to deceive but

---

[26] John Calvin, *A Harmony of the Gospels Matthew, Mark, and Luke Volume III and The Epistles of James and Jude*, tran. A.W. Morrison (Eerdmans, 1972), p. 274.

also to cheat, going beyond even being deceived by false logic. How terrible a thing it must be to cheat one's own heart of the happiness that it receives when we do the will of God.

James 1:26. This one's religion is useless

The second characteristic about this person is that her "religion is useless," vain, futile, worthless, aimless, having no object, leading to no end, especially that end being God. It is like building houses on sand, chasing the wind, shooting at stars, pursuing one's own shadow. It accomplishes nothing. It is counterfeit Christianity. If you can't control your tongue, your religion is useless. The failure to control your tongue would be just another evidence that the inner life has not been changed. Your faith would then be dead.

"Useless" (Greek *mataios*) is also the same word used to describe pagan worship or idol worship. What James is saying here is that such religion without controlled conversation might be as unprofitable as bowing before an idol. Would you and I do that? Absolutely not! Yet, we too often will gossip and speak evil of one another and speak prideful accomplishments of our self. A side note here is appropriate: When you have a difficulty with a fellow sister or brother in the Lord—don't mention that to others. This is sinful and stirs up unnecessary division in the body of Christ. You need to go to them and them alone following the principles that our Lord set for us in Matthew 18:15-20. Let us be a people who are committed to the proper steps of dealing with difficulties and sin in one another's lives.

How many of us sing "O For a Thousand Tongues to Sing" on Sunday, and yet use our tongues on Monday to have heated words with our husband or children, or gossip with our neighbor or best friend, or get into a relaxed atmosphere where we loosen our tongues to participate in foolish jesting or off-color comments? By now you may have had enough conviction for one day, but we aren't quite finished yet.

James has one more verse to zap us with as we close with the last verse of chapter one. In verse 27, James is now going to give us two more signs to tell if our religion is pure and undefiled. We can't get away from the fact that outward deeds are essential for the assurance of salvation; they are a sign that we have genuine faith, as we will soon see in chapter 2, telling us that faith without works is dead.

The Test to Others – Visit Those in Need

James 1:27. But pure and undefiled religion

James first gives us a positive description of religion, by telling us what *pure* religion is. *Pure* means genuine, free from pollution and the guilt of sin, pure in the sense of our motives for doing good works. If we do things to gain acceptance with God and others, that is not pure. If we do it out of love for God, that is pure. The main idea by *pure* is not necessarily what we do, but why we do it.

He then gives us a counter-negative description of religion, which is *undefiled*. *Undefiled* means that which hasn't been soiled and stained by contact with moral evil. It is important that our Christian service be pure in motive. What are the reasons you do what you do for the Lord? Is it for recognition—good feelings? That is not pure and undefiled religion. Many years ago, I remember examining my decision to serve the Lord in a particular area, and I was convicted once I clearly saw that my motives were to please someone else and not the Lord.

James 1:27. Before God and the Father is this

So, is this pure and undefiled religion to be before other people? No. It is to be before God and the Father. We can all perform to impress each other, but to perform before God in purity and holiness is another thing. Why does James say *God and the Father*? God is used to represent God's omnipotence and sovereignty in dealing with our religious practices. But He is also our Father, which is used to show He has His children's interests at heart. *Before God and the*

Father stresses that acceptable religion must be in harmony with the divine standard. God's eye is what counts. As Paul said, "For do I now persuade men, or God? Or do I seek to please men? For if I still pleased men, I would not be a bondservant of Christ" (Galatians 1:10). God is the one who will ultimately judge our works, as well as the intent of our hearts. We know this by 1 Corinthians 4:5 where Paul wrote: "Therefore judge nothing before the time, until the Lord comes, who will both bring to light the hidden things of darkness and reveal the counsels of the hearts. Then each one's praise will come from God."

There is coming a day in which everything hidden will be made known and the true motives of our heart will be revealed. So what are these signs of true and undefiled religion? What kinds of activities please God and the Father? The first one has to do with our sensitivity to others who are in need.

James 1:27. To visit orphans and widows in their trouble

The first sign of pure and undefiled religion before God and the Father is to visit orphans and widows in their trouble. Who were the fatherless and the widows in James' day? They were the most helpless people in Jewish society. They were the ones who were without defense, protection, or provision. In fact, the word *widow* means without. To "visit" (Greek, *episkeptesthai*) them does not mean to casually look in on or occasionally call, but to go see them with the aim of caring for and meeting their needs. You assume responsibility and support for them. That may mean you sacrifice your time. It may even mean that you sacrifice in the area of giving financially. Life for some of us has become so complex, and we are so busy that we have not been the people of God that we should be by fellowshipping in the suffering of others. I just imagine that during this time of stressful persecution the number of widows and orphans may have been greater, too. Remember they did not have social security or welfare, at least not in the sense we have it in America today. That was probably a good thing—I think the church today gets off too easy by relying on provisions from our government. The church today is not doing what she ought regarding the matter of widows and orphans.

Sensitivity to orphans and widows in their emotional and economic distress was a frequent Old Testament exhortation, as well as a New Testament one.[27] The loss of a husband or a parent often meant total disaster. Widows sometimes became prostitutes, and orphans were sold into slavery. God has just as much concern for starving children, lonely widows in nursing homes, and the homeless on the street as he does for the church and its programs (Luke 7:11-16). As one summarizes, "If we worship God who is Father and who loves His creatures, while we ourselves are heartless and merciless, we should be able ourselves to see that there is something incongruous in our worship."[28]

What are some practical ways that we can be obedient to this direction? Do you know who the widows are in your church and then do you meet their needs for companionship and friendship, while making sure that things are done around the house, such as mowing the yard and servicing the car? Do you know the children of single parents? Do you take the opportunity to help by babysitting them or taking them out to the park or to get ice cream? These are just some of the practical things we can do. There are times when my husband has to travel, and I am grateful for the reminder during these times that it can get very lonely, and this causes my sensitivity to the widows to be enhanced. The Lord gives us some sobering warnings in Isaiah 10:1-3 as well as in Matthew 25:31-43, to those of us who harden our hearts towards those in need. Jesus says, just as James says, that our religion is futile—it is not real—if we are not meeting the needs of the destitute. This is what Christ condemned

---

[27] For example, the *Old Testament* considered provision for orphans and widows as essential: Exodus 22:22-24; Deuteronomy 10:17-19; 24:17-22; Psalm 68:4-51. Then during *New Testament* times, the Apostle Paul building from the Old Testament instruction (which Timothy was well-versed in; compare with 2 Timothy 1:5; 3:14-17), added an extensive admonition about widows specifically (Timothy 5:3-8). As matter of fact the first official order of church business was to make sure that widows were cared for by godly men, in order to free the Apostles to minister the Word and give themselves to prayer (Acts 6:1).

[28] J.W. Roberts, *A Commentary on the General Epistle of James*, p. 82.

the Pharisees for. Remember?[29] How can we be believers in Jesus Christ while being indifferent to the needs of others?

The Test to the World – Keep Unspotted from the World

James 1:27. And to keep oneself unspotted from the world

The second sign of true religion is to "keep oneself unspotted from the world." This means we should strive for personal holiness and avoidance of spiritual contamination from the sinful world. "World" (Greek, *kosmos*) is a reference to the world system with its values and practices, which are under the sway of Satan. We are to avoid the world's lifestyles, its philosophies, its morals, and its ethics. This means the believer must be watchful at all times. This means that we will attend to our souls and be constantly cleansing ourselves from any defilement from the world. The Apostle John told us in 1 John 5:19 that the whole world lies in wickedness. Earlier in 1 John he stated:

> Do not love the world or the things in the world. If anyone loves the world, the love of the Father is not in him. For all that is in the world—the lust of the flesh, the lust of the eyes, and the pride of life—is not of the Father but is of the world. And the world is passing away, and the lust of it; but he who does the will of God abides forever. (1 John 2:15-17)

---

[29] Jesus warned the scribes and Pharisee, "Woe to you, scribes and Pharisees, hypocrites! For you devour widows' houses, and for a pretense make long prayers. Therefore you will receive greater condemnation." On another occasion He warned others about the scribes and Pharisees: "Then He said to them in His teaching, 'Beware of the scribes, who desire to go around in long robes, love greetings in the marketplaces, the best seats in the synagogues, and the best places at feasts, who devour widows' houses, and for a pretense make long prayers. These will receive greater condemnation.'" The Lord was indeed serious about this! Also 1 John 3:17-18 is another sobering passage to consider.

James is going to tell us in James 4:4 that those who are friends with the world are enemies of God. He tells us that you cannot be a worldly Christian—there is no such thing. Then James gives us the remedy for such worldliness in James 4:7-10.

Peter also tells us, "but as He who called you is holy, you also be holy in all your conduct, because it is written, 'Be holy, for I am holy'" (1 Peter 1:15-16). What else does the Apostle Paul have to say about this? "For God did not call us to uncleanness, but in holiness" (1 Thessalonians 4:7). If we as believers in Jesus Christ are not progressing towards Christ-likeness and looking less and less like the world, and hating sin more and more in our members, then something is amiss. The world should not impact our lifestyle or our behavior. James would say that if it does, then you might as well be worshipping an idol, because your religion is worthless.

Summary

You know, it is so easy to become self-deceived by our religiosity. But there are three tests here of true religion: (1) The test to our self. Keep a tight rein on your tongue. We must be free from gossip and slander or our religion is worthless. How is your speech today? (2) The test to others. True religion means hands-on caring for the victims of the pressures of life. Do you desire to meet the needs of others and do you do this from a caring heart? (3) The test to the world. Acceptable religion means keeping a pure life. We must be holy as He is holy! Do you desire to be part of the world? True religion involves our words, our hands, and our hearts. May God help us!

Questions to Consider
"The Test of True Religion"
James 1:26-27

1. We have now completed chapter one. Read over James 1 and write down one truth that God has impressed upon you.

2. Make two columns. Label the left column "True religion" and the right "Vain religion." (a) According to James chapter one, what things validate true religion and what things validate vain religion? Put them in the proper columns. (b) After looking over these two columns, how would you evaluate your own religion—true or vain?

3. Memorize James 1:26-27.

4. (a) What outward manifestations of religion were the rulers of Sodom and the people of Gomorrah practicing in Isaiah 1:10-17? (b) What does God say about those works? (c) What does He say is "true religion"? (d) Does James say the same thing?

5. (a) According to Zechariah 7:8-14, what happens when we refuse to be obedient in the area of being "truly" religious? (b) What lessons can you glean for your own life?

6. Read Colossians 4:14 and Philemon 24. (a) What do these verses say about Demas? (b) Now read 2 Timothy 4:10 to see what happened to Demas. (c) What warning(s) do these Scriptures send to you and me? (d) How does this coincide with James 1:27? (e) Do you think Demas was truly redeemed? Why or why not?

7. Is there someone in your neighborhood or church that you should be "visiting"? Ask God for wisdom and discernment on how you might best demonstrate His love to that person.

8. (a) What activities are you involved in that are merely external with no inner spiritual significance? (b) Which activities actually show true religion? (Examples: visiting the fatherless and widows, keeping your tongue bridled, and keeping yourself unspotted from the world.) (c) What should be added and subtracted from your weekly round of "religious" activities in order to align yourself with God's priorities?

9. Write a prayer request for either how you might better minister to those in "affliction" or how you might keep yourself "unspotted from this world."

9

Test of Brotherly Love

James 2:1-5

Discrimination has created one of the greatest social tensions of our time in American culture. Racial discrimination has fostered tension between whites and blacks. We have social discrimination between the rich and the poor. We also have religious discrimination among Christian denominations and world religions. There is also political discrimination between Republicans and Democrats; and, of course, educational discrimination exists between the educated and the uneducated.

Discrimination can also come from judging outward appearance. We discriminate against those who may not be as pretty as we are, who wear different clothes than us, or drive a different kind of car. Maybe you are only attracted to those who have it all together—whatever *all together* is. Sometimes we are judgmental of peoples' personal habits, such as their social etiquette, their English grammar, their hairstyles, the décor of their house, or the appearance of their yards. Things that seem offensive to us can trigger discriminatory responses in our actions, our words, and most of all, I think, in the privacy of our thought life. Such unkind conduct may not be too surprising in a world where selfishness and self-rights are the guiding principles. However, a higher standard is expected from those who profess the Christian faith. James puts it this way:

> My brethren, do not hold the faith of our Lord Jesus Christ, the Lord of glory, with partiality. ²For if there should come into your assembly a man with gold rings, in fine apparel, and there should also come in a poor man in filthy clothes, ³and you pay attention

to the one wearing the fine clothes and say to him, "You sit here in a good place," and say to the poor man, "You stand there," or, "Sit here at my footstool," ⁴have you not shown partiality among yourselves, and become judges with evil thoughts? ⁵Listen, my beloved brethren: Has God not chosen the poor of this world to be rich in faith and heirs of the kingdom which He promised to those who love Him? (James 2:1-5)

During this study we have been looking at tests to examine ourselves to see if we are in the faith; and now as we begin the second chapter of James, we are given another test, the test of showing partiality. In this chapter we are going to see: the statute against partiality (v 1), the scenario of partiality (vv 2-3), the sin of partiality (v 4), and the Savior of partiality (v 5).

It is possible that this event actually happened in the early church of Jerusalem, an event that James probably witnessed himself, which makes this scenario all the more disturbing.

The Statute Against Partiality

James 2:1. My brethren, do not hold the faith of our Lord Jesus Christ

James' first two words, *my brethren,* is a reminder that Christ's disciples have an intimate and sacred bond of union in the common relationship they bear to the glorious Lord. Then he told the brethren, "Do not hold the faith of our Lord Jesus Christ, the Lord of Glory, with partiality." This literally means, "Do not try to combine your faith in our glorious Lord Jesus Christ with acts of partiality, you who profess to believe in Jesus Christ and claim Him as your Lord." While practicing your faith, do you play favorites in the church? Do not be a Christian and simultaneously a hypocrite. Do not hold the faith of Jesus Christ and at the same time show partiality—that is a contradiction. And you do that with the "Lord of glory," our glorious Lord Jesus Christ? If you are going to confess Jesus Christ as the Lord of glory, then stop being partial!

James 2:1. The Lord of glory, with partiality

Glory (Greek, *doxes*) here means divine and heavenly radiance. This is really James' confession of faith concerning the true identity of Jesus Christ. He is the Sovereign One who rules over all His creation, the One in whom the fullness of God's glory is revealed. John 1:14 says, "The Word became flesh and dwelt among us, and we beheld His glory, glory as of the only begotten of the Father, full of grace and truth." James asks, "You show this faith with the Lord of glory with partiality, with respect of persons?"

The *New King James Version* uses "partiality," while the *King James Version* uses "respect of persons." *Respect of persons* (Greek, *prosopolepsis*) derives from two Greek words: (1) receiving of face and (2) to understand. Receiving of face also means to lift up the face. To lift up a person's countenance, or face, was to regard him with favor, in contrast to perhaps casting down his countenance. To understand also meant to comprehend or to seize with the mind, favoritism or partiality, or a biased judgment based on external circumstances such as race, wealth, social rank, popularity, or political status. To posses such an attitude would prompt a person to scan the features of a new face coming into the church and immediately form an opinion.

Although *prosopolempsiais* is only used in James 2:1, the two terms that combine in this compound word (i.e., *lambanein* and *prospopon*) are translated *respect of persons* affirming that Jesus does not "accept the person of *any*" (Luke 20:21). Literally translated it means, "Teacher, we know that you ... do not receive the face." Even the church's enemies and their spies recognized that Jesus did not show partiality. James in effect is saying, "My brothers, as believers in our glorious Lord Jesus Christ, who so lowered Himself in poverty and humility, don't show favoritism to the rich." We judge people so easily by the clothes they wear, by the words they speak, by their appearance, instead of taking the time to find out where they really are and whether there is a good reason for their actions. James goes on to illustrate how they were demonstrating partiality in verses 2 and 3.

The Scenario of Partiality

James 2:2. For if there should come into your assembly

The Pastor of the Jerusalem church suggests a scenario to illustrate his point: "For if there should come into your assembly a man with gold rings, in fine apparel, and there should also come in a poor man in filthy clothes." Here we have the scenario of two individuals who have come into the assembly. Important to note is the repetition of the verb *come*. This dual repetition indicates each one's arrival as a separate event. They did not come in at the same time. The "assembly" were those assembled together in the synagogue. (Today we would say the local church).

James 2:2. A man with gold rings, in fine apparel

This man was wearing gold rings and fine clothes. The gold "ring" was indicative of rank. It was said that some wore rings on every finger except the middle one. Rings in New Testament times were common ornaments of the rich, and even shops in Rome had rings that could be rented for special occasions. The "fine apparel" would indicate rich and splendid dress. It can also have meant freshness or cleanliness. (Today we might say that they smell good or are the best dressed.) So this rich and well-dressed man comes into your church, and you immediately determine that he is a fine man or woman worthy of your attention. Then in walks this poor man.

James 2:2. And there should also come in a poor man with filthy clothes

"Poor man" means he is filthy or foul. He has on filthy, vile clothes, which means they are cheap or shabby clothes. This Greek adjective *hrupara* is also used in 1 Peter 3:21 to talk about putting away the filth of the flesh, and also in Zechariah 3:4 in reference to Joshua, the High Priest's filthy garments.[30] Today we might say in comes a homeless person or a bag lady. The reference here does not seem to be limited to those who commonly attended public worship, (we might call them church members), but those who might drop in to witness the worship service of Christians. We might say today that they are the visitors, so here would be a critical moment that would reveal the hearts of the regular attendees, the members of the church.

Now before proceeding, I want to clarify that Pastor James is not criticizing the wearing of jewelry or fine clothing per se, but if doing so is designed to show off and call attention to yourself, that is not good. Remember that Paul gives women guidelines on the proper way to dress and behave in church:

> In like manner also, [I want] that the women adorn themselves in modest apparel, with propriety and moderation, not with braided hair or gold or pearls or costly clothing, but, which is proper for women professing godliness, with good works.
> (1 Timothy 2:9-10)

Notice that Paul defines his meaning of modesty, not actually dealing condemningly with short skirts or tight outfits, which is another serious issue. But rather dressing modestly refers to dressing in such a way that doesn't draw attention to yourself. Instead of making an ostentatious display, he commands a more common or humble dress. Peter gave women guidelines for their appearance as well, emphasizing the same.

---

[30] The Old Testament was primarily written in Hebrew, with a few portions in Aramaic. But with the growing Jewish population in Alexandria, Egypt who were Hellenized (trained in Greek ideas and culture, including the language of Greek as the primary one) there arose a need to translate the Old Testament from Hebrew into Greek. If the *Letter of Aristeas* is authentic then the project began as the royal librarian in Alexandria convinced King Ptolemy II Philadelphus (285-246 B.C.) that such a translation was needed. Six elders from the 12 tribes of Israel (hence, 72 in all), according to early tradition produced this first translation of the Hebrew Scriptures, known today as the LXX. This was evidently the primary Scripture used by Jesus and the Apostles who quote it most often. Zechariah 3:4 in the LXX uses *hrupara*, for the Hebrew term.

> Do not let your adornment be merely outward--arranging the hair, wearing gold, or putting on fine apparel--rather let it be the hidden person of the heart, with the incorruptible beauty of a gentle and quiet spirit, which is very precious in the sight of God. (1 Peter 3:3-4)

Neither Peter nor Paul was forbidding the wearing of jewelry, but commending women to pay more attention to the inner heart rather than external beauty. Think about it: When you dress for church, is it to draw attention to yourself? Do you judge others on their appearance, whispering to a friend, "That dress went out of style ages ago," or utter to yourself, "Where did she get that outfit?" On the other hand, I do not think these verses give us freedom to never bathe and dress like a slob. As the old saying goes, "cleanliness is next to godliness."

So these two individuals have come into the church, both rich and poor. When you contemplate it, discrimination was being practiced in the treatment of both of these individuals. Now we will see in verse 3 how the rich man as well as the poor man was being discriminated against.

James 2:3. And you pay attention to the one wearing the fine clothes and say to him, "You sit here in a good place."

Here the rich man was being discriminated against because he was being elevated above the poor man. The poor man was being discriminated against because he was humiliated when he entered the assembly. Even the speaker about whom James was writing (v 3) had a seat but didn't offer it to the poor man, although he did so to the man wearing the fine clothes. A fine example he was to his flock. James was telling the brethren that they were paying better attention to the man wearing the fine clothes.

In the *King James Version*, it is translated this way: "And ye have respect to him that weareth the fine clothing." In this verse "respect" means looking upon with favor, being impressed by his garment. James didn't specifically say, but it is possible that the rich man was looked upon with favor because of money he might have given to the church! The Greek tense indicates that the rich man immediately attracted attention, heads turned. This word *respect* also has a secondary meaning of "to eye with envy," meaning to be focused on the well-dressed man instead of being fully occupied with watching the Lord Jesus Christ and worshipping him. My dear friends, we come to church to worship the Lord, so if our clothing is distracting in any way, then it could be a hindrance to others' worship.

James 2:3. And say to the poor man, "You stand there," or, "Sit here at my footstool"

So these two individuals come in, and to the rich the speaker said, "Give him the place of honor. Sit with me!" And to the poor was said "Stand there, or sit here under my footstool." The *footstool* here was a stone bench running along the walls, with a lower tier for the feet of those sitting on the bench.[31] A modern day analogy might be pews with footrests. James may have been alluding to the Old Testament practice of placing one's enemies beneath his footstool (Psalm 110:1-2). The footstool implied the place of humiliation and subordination, where common people stood or squatted. To have someone seated at your feet would puff you up while humiliating him or her.

We may not see the exact thing happening today, but we have situations far worse. We determine the worthiness of a person by the color of her skin, her background, her upbringing, her clothes, or her political or social standing. All people should be considered equal before God, rich or poor. He is the maker of them all! I once read a story about a pastor who never ministered to an individual or family in his church without first checking a current record of their financial contributions. The more generous they were

---

[31] In Jewish synagogues where the early Jewish Christians would often meet, the *Chazzan* was the man in charge of seating people. Most of the congregation actually sat on the floor, limiting only a few to sit on chairs or footstools.

with their money, the more generous he was with his time. That's an appalling example of favoritism, but it is a good contemporary day example of what James is saying here. These readers needed to be reminded of this truth especially during their persecution, as it left many of them scattered and most of them very poor.

Maybe we should remind ourselves about the fact that even our Lord, this "Lord of glory," was poor. He was not a rich man, even though some false teachers today say he was.[32] When it came to earthly possessions, our Lord Jesus Christ was poor. He was born in a borrowed manger, preached his first sermon in a borrowed boat, rode into Jerusalem on a borrowed donkey, ate His Last Supper with the disciples in a borrowed room, and was buried in a borrowed grave. How do you think you would treat a person of that status today if he came to our church? Jesus never catered to the rich and powerful.

Now before we go on I do want to clarify that James is not prohibiting close friendships. Even Jesus spent more time with Peter, James, and John than He did with the other disciples. The favoritism that James is mentioning refers specifically to "receiving face" among the wealthy while ignoring the needs of the poor. It is perfectly acceptable to have good friends at church and have closer relationships with some more than others. This passage is not claiming that we interact socially with everyone to the same degree. My husband and I have many friends in our church in Tulsa, but we spend more time with some than others, due to a closer friendship that the Lord provides. Continuing with his discourse exposing partiality, James now asks them two questions in verse 4. Both ques-

---

[32] Oral Roberts published *How I Learned Jesus Was Not Poor* (Creation House, 1989), seeking to validate by twisting Scripture that our Lord was wealthy while on earth. Oral gives seven points: Jesus had a house enough for guests; Jesus had money, enough so that He had to have a treasurer; Jesus had a team, a large one that He had support financially from city to city; Jesus had a donor base, a faithful group of financial partners who "ministered to Him of their money; Jesus wore good clothes, clothes that many people today might call designer clothes, clothes that were costly and unique to His needs; Jesus was put in a rich man's trust to insure he had a proper burial place – actually, so that He might be buried with the rich; and it is Jesus' riches by which God said he would supply all your needs. No, Jesus wasn't wealthy on earth and false teachers rewrite the clear intent of Scriptural teaching to support their heretical health-wealth gospel.

tions are asked in a manner anticipating *yes* for the answer.

The Sin of Partiality

James 2:4. Have you not shown partiality among yourselves?

James asks in a tone of amazement, "Have you not shown partiality among yourselves?" Have you not made distinctions? Are you not divided? Are you not double-minded? James uses the same train of thought that he has been using so far in his epistle. By their attitude of partiality and double-mindedness they had denied the heart of Christianity. By their attitude of favoritism, they had denied the core of Christianity. They had become double-minded or divided, the term describing the attitudes that James had already exposed in James 1:6-8. Their "facing both ways" was comparable to a divided jury or a divided court.

James 2:4. And become judges with evil thoughts?

The second question he asks with amazement is "Aren't you become judges with evil thoughts?" This means to be evil in a moral sense, malicious. Favoritism stems from selfishness. Their conduct showed that they took it upon themselves to be judges of the character of men who were strangers. Motivated by evil intentions, they judged these men based on their dress alone. They showed that they placed more value on the soul of the well-dressed man than that of the poor. We have no right to judge men on their outward appearance, even though we do. 1 Samuel 16:7 affirms that men are guilty of judging on outward appearance. "For the LORD does not see as man sees; for man looks at the outward appearance, but the LORD looks at the heart." Jesus says, "Do not judge according to appearance, but judge with righteous judgment" (John 7:24).

Now let's suppose two different families started coming to

your church. One family is on welfare, not due to any fault of their own. The other is middle-class and well respected. Who do you think would receive the warmer welcome? Do you think the youth of both families would be as eagerly invited to the youth trips? If the men of both families were both biblically qualified for the position of elder or deacon, which one would be chosen? Our churches must be the one place in the world where discrimination is not found. There should be no distinction of any kind when we meet in the presence of the King of glory. In His presence all earthly distinctions are less than the dust and all earthly righteousness is as filthy rags. God's children and God's church must never give others the impression that God sides with those who have power, position and wealth. James continues with his rebuke in verse 5.

The Savior of Partiality

James 2:5. Listen, my beloved brethren, has God not chosen the poor of this world

"Listen, my beloved brethren" is how James begins verse 5. James is motivated by love and seeks his brethren's welfare. And now he asks them a third question in amazement, which he expects will be answered in the affirmative.[33] "Has God not chosen the poor of this world to be rich in faith?" This does not mean that God is not as willing to save the rich as well as the poor, for He has no partiality, but that there are circumstances in the condition of the poor which make it more likely that they will embrace the offers of the gospel than the rich.[34] The word *chosen* in the Greek indicates that His choice was entirely in the past. As Paul said, "Just as He chose

---

[33] The Greek begins with a rousing term, *akousate* (English, "listen"), as he speaks as one both amazed and wanting to get their attention. He used a similar method after he had heard the various debates at the famous Council of Jerusalem and acting as a summarizing moderator: "And after they had become silent, James answered, saying, 'Men and brethren, *listen* to me'" (Acts 15:13).

[34] See Matthew 11:1-6; Luke 4:16-21.

us in Him before the foundation of the world, that we should be holy and without blame before Him in love" (Ephesians 1:4). Remember that we touched on the doctrine of election when we were studying James 1:18. But if you still don't comprehend this doctrine, then maybe you will identify with a woman I once read about. She said: "I have long settled that doctrine; for if God had not chosen me before I was born, I am sure He would have seen nothing to have chosen me for afterwards!"

It is interesting that church history verifies the fact that a greater number of poor people than rich have responded to the gospel.[35] Generally speaking, God has chosen poor people to populate His kingdom. This does not mean that there is any merit in poverty, or that poverty is a reason for election, or that only the poor and not the rich will be saved. But it is saying that God has not discriminated against the poor as a class, and that more poor have responded to the gospel (as the result of divine election) than the rich and powerful. Remember when Matthew told us the story of the rich young ruler who went away sorrowful because Jesus asked him to sell all he had and give to the poor? Matthew writes, "Then Jesus said to His disciples, 'Assuredly, I say to you that it is hard for a rich man to enter the kingdom of heaven. And again I say to you, it is easier for a camel to go through the eye of a needle than for a rich man to enter the kingdom of God'" (Matthew 19:23-24).

The term "poor" (Greek, *ptochous*) refers to one who crouches or cowers for fear, the one for whom the burden of life is so great that he can only beg. The rich depend on their possessions, but the poor on their possessor. Do you remember when James referred

---

[35] This is precisely what the Apostle Paul observed in the first century: "For you see your calling, brethren, that not many wise according to the flesh, not many mighty, not many noble, are called. But God has chosen the foolish things of the world to put to shame the wise, and God has chosen the weak things of the world to put to shame the things which are mighty; and the base things of the world and the things which are despised God has chosen, and the things which are not, to bring to nothing the things that are, that no flesh should glory in His presence ... as it is written, 'He who glories, let him glory in the LORD'" (1 Corinthians 1:26-31). Both James and Paul were reflecting on past history and their present observation.

to the poor as the brother of low degree (James 1:9)? And yet the poor should have rejoiced in that they were exalted—they were to exalt in the fact that they were rich spiritually. And now James says two more things about them.

James 2:5. To be rich in faith and heirs of the kingdom which He promised to those who love Him.

First of all, the poor are "rich in faith." Faith in God their Savior is more valuable than riches. Their wealth consisted of their salvation and all the blessings that accompanied it. The world tends to "choose" those who are rich in money. God "chooses" the poor to be "rich in faith."

Secondly, the poor are "heirs of the kingdom which He promised to those who love Him." This instance is the only mention of the word *kingdom* in James. The poor may now be insignificant to the world, but they possess the glorious prospect of inheriting the kingdom of God. For example, if you are an heir of someone in this world, you may inherit money; but as God's children, someday we will all inherit the kingdom of God. This is a promise. The Greek tense looks back to the fact that God made the promise to believers. Their inheritance was not a sudden thought, but a long premeditated gift. Remember in chapter one, verse 18, we learned that when God willed our salvation, He sat down and considered the cost? That is the same idea here. James says this heirship is promised to those that love Him. What a wonderful truth! And yet, what a sad disservice this church here had done to this poor visitor. He would be far more likely to become a believer than the rich man, and yet he was the one treated with disdain, with disgust, with humiliation.

Summary

I want you to picture yourself attending a Ladies Bible Study in your church. Suddenly two women attend who have never been there before. The first woman is well dressed, obviously wealthy, as indicated by her jewelry and designer clothes. The second one obviously poor, evidenced by her musty fragrance and shabby clothes. How would you respond to each visitor? Answer honestly. Would you greet the wealthy lady first, take her to the refreshment table, introduce her to everyone, making her as comfortable as possible? No doubt that would be a nice thing to do. But if you are only trying to win her favor while avoiding the poor woman, you have committed a vicious sin. Your true motives will be revealed in your treatment of the poor woman. Would you show her equal honor, as you did the wealthy woman? Or instead ignore her and say to yourself, "Let *someone else* go greet her."

Favoritism, partiality, can be so subtle that we don't even recognize it in ourselves. In fact, I was talking to someone the other day who had gone to visit a new church. They drove into the parking lot and waited until others arrived. When they saw what kind of people got out of their cars—fat and sloppy—they drove off and went to their old church. I was shocked and disgusted at that kind of wicked attitude!

That illustration is a prime example of the attitude that James is condemning here. "My sisters, these things ought not so to be!" What is even worse is for us to smugly say, "We would *never* have that attitude." Except for the grace of God, we will, because as humans we do look on the outward appearance. That is why I believe with all my heart that we must be in prayer and in the Word constantly so that the Spirit can penetrate our deepest thoughts, our most secret motives. Then and then only, will we not be guilty of the awful sin of showing partiality.

Questions to Consider
"Test of Brotherly Love"
James 2:1-5

1. Read James Chapter 2. What are the "tests of faith" that James mentions in this chapter? In other words, what things does James say that prove the reality of one's faith?

2. Memorize James 2:1.

3. Read Deuteronomy 10:17-19; 2 Chronicles 19:7; Acts 10:34-35; Romans 2:9-11; and Colossians 3:25. What do these verses teach you about God's impartiality?

4. (a) According to 1 Corinthians 1:26-31, whom has God chosen? (b) How would you say that compares with the current "health, wealth, and prosperity" gospel?

5. After carefully looking over James 2:1-5 answer the following questions. (a) If you were a visitor in the church James was writing to, what would you have heard and seen? (b) In what ways has each person involved (rich, poor, church member, and the Lord) been dishonored? (c) How does the title that James assigns our Lord in verse 1 help put this behavior in perspective?

6. (a) What characteristics about certain people make it difficult for you to associate with them? (b) Are those personal characteristics sin, or are they just preference issues? Ask God to help you love them and determine not to be a "respecter of persons" or show partiality.

7. (a) In what ways are you showing partiality in your church to the people who attend there? (b) What changes do you need to make? (c) Is there someone whom you intentionally ignore? Why?

Determine to get out of your circle of friends, your comfort zone, and reach out to all (especially visitors), as God would have you do.

8. After looking over question number 7, especially part b, what is your prayer request?

10

Fulfilling the Royal Law

James 2:6-13

We no sooner got our foot in the door of the last chapter than James hits us again with another test, the test of partiality. In verses 1-5 of the last chapter, we saw that two visitors came to church, one well dressed and the other one in filthy rags. The well-dressed person was elevated and honored, while the poor was humiliated and disdained. Yet of the two, the poor man would have been more likely to embrace the gospel, but considering the church's reception of him, he probably departed saying, "If that is Christianity, no thanks!" Of this situation, James continues:

> But you have dishonored the poor man. Do not the rich oppress you and drag you into the courts? [7]Do they not blaspheme that noble name by which you are called? [8]If you really fulfill the royal law according to the Scripture, 'You shall love your neighbor as yourself,' you do well; [9]but if you show partiality, you commit sin, and are convicted by the law as transgressors. [10]For whoever shall keep the whole law, and yet stumble in one point, he is guilty of all. [11]For He who said, 'Do not commit adultery,' also said, 'Do not murder.' Now if you do not commit adultery, but you do murder, you have become a transgressor of the law. [12]So speak and so do as those who will be judged by the law of liberty. [13]For judgment is without mercy to the one who has shown no mercy. Mercy triumphs over judgment. (James 2:6-13)

In this chapter, we will discover the *character of the rich* (vv 6-7), the *character of the redeemed* (v 8), the *character of the rebellious* (vv 9-11), and the *character of the Redeemer* (vv 12-13).

The Character of the Rich: They are Oppressive and Blasphemous

James 2:6. But you have dishonored the poor man.

James continues by saying, "But you have dishonored the poor man." In the *King James Version*, the translators put it this way: "But you have despised the poor." To despise means to dishonor, to treat shamefully. The church members should have recognized that between the two visitors, the poor man was the more likely prospect for the kingdom of God. By their reception of him, however, the poor man could only conclude that he was not "good enough" for their Christianity. James now reminds them that their conduct is certainly ironic in light of the treatment that they themselves received from their wealthy neighbors. James goes on to tell his readers three things that the rich were doing to the poor. By the way, in the context of this Scripture passage, it is unlikely that these rich folks were genuine believers, nor is James saying that all rich people behave this way.

James 2:6. Do not the rich oppress you

First of all, these rich people were "oppressing" them. This means the rich were exercising power over those under their control in a hurtful and oppressive manner. The Greek word for oppress (*katadunasteuousin*) is used only one other place in the New Testament, Acts 10:38. Peter was preaching here to the Gentiles in the house of Cornelius, and he said: "... God anointed Jesus of Nazareth with the Holy Spirit and with power, who went about doing good and healing all who were *oppressed* by the devil, for God was with him." *Oppressed* is used to describe the devil's rule over his victims; these rich oppressors are equated with the devil. James was saying that they are hard, unrepentant, and devilish, and yet they are granted a premier place in the hour of worship.[36]

Isn't something similar happening in our churches today? We exalt wealth and influence. As a result, in many of our churches the devil has taken first place, and the fact that Christians have put him there is frightening. Oh, how our churches need to undergo self-examination in the evil days in which we live, when even in the house of God we give the devil first place. It is no wonder we fail to see an authentic spiritual awakening in the hearts of those to whom we preach the Gospel. In Proverbs 22:16 it is written, "He who oppresses the poor to increase his riches, and he who gives to the rich, will surely come to poverty."

James 2:6. And drag you into the courts

The second characteristic of the rich oppressors was that they were dragging the poor into the courts. *Draw*, as it is translated in the *King James Version*, literally means to drag the poor by force into court. The rich were using the courts to exploit the poor. In the custom of James' day, they literally would drag the poor into the courts and take what little money they had, probably to collect a debt. If a creditor met a debtor on the street, he could seize him by the neck of his robe and literally drag him into court. They had no sympathy—all they cared about was the money. James was telling the Christians, "You despise the poor, and yet look how the rich treat you!" Perhaps these church members thought that by giving him a prominent seat in the synagogue, the rich guest would return the favor. Furthermore, James said, not only are they dragging you into court, but they are doing something even worse.

---

[36] The Greek term *katadunasteuosin*, although only used twice in the New Testament (Acts 10:38 and James 2:6) was used frequently in the LXX, in reference to power against anyone to his hurt. It was used for the oppressive lawsuits. In New Testament times it was customary that if a creditor met his debtor on the street, he could seize him by the neck of the robe and literally drag him into court, e.g., Acts 4:1-3; 13:50; 16:19; 19:23-41.

James 2:7. Do they not blaspheme that noble name by which you are called?

The rich were blaspheming the noble name by which the believers were called, Christians. To "blaspheme" means to slander or revile, or show contempt or lack of reverence for God. They were blaspheming God by dishonoring speech towards Him. These blasphemous utterances against Christ may have been expressed in the court and in daily life. They were blaspheming that "noble name," the name of Jesus Christ—that glorious name, that beautiful name, that attractive name, that noble name, that good name, that name by which the believers "were called." In the Greek *called* is the word used when a wife takes her husband's name in marriage or for a child being called after his father. For example, when I got married I took on the surname of Heck, as did my children when they were born. The Christian takes the name of Christ. She is *called* after, named after, Christ. It is as if she was married to Christ, or born and then christened into the family of Christ. This term describes the believer as identifying himself with his God and therefore being known as one of His followers. This speaks of having a personal relationship with the One with that worthy name, Jesus Christ.

Typically new converts made a public proclamation of their faith in Christ at their baptism. From that moment they were called "Christians," meaning "Christ's own." They were "little Christs." So when people slandered Christians, they were slandering Christ Himself. As Jesus said, "Inasmuch as you did not do it to one of the least of these, you did not do it to Me" (Matthew 25:45). It was their identification with Christ that caused the blasphemy. James was rebuking his readers because they were showing favoritism to the very enemies of our Lord, those who were blaspheming His name. How could they let that happen? How could they participate in that?

But now James has a word of encouragement for some of them in verse 8 before he again challenges them in verse 9.

The Character of the Redeemed:

They are Loving to Others in Need

James 2:8. If you really fulfill the royal law according to the Scripture

The initial word *if* suggests that James considered the possibility that not all of the church members to whom he was writing were guilty of this partiality or favoritism, and yet from his readers James is anticipating an excuse that their favored treatment of the rich man at the expense of the poor one was in reality an expression of love for their neighbor. Indeed, if that was their true motive, then he had no objection.

"If you really fulfill" means if you perform or carry out. The *royal* law indicates the quality of the law as being truly royal or kingly in its character, a law befitting a king. Because it is excellent, it is supreme. James said that this "royal law" is "according to the Scripture." To what Scripture is James referring? Leviticus 19:18 is the first reference to the royal law; however, Jesus, who was James' half-brother, reiterated this royal law.

> You shall not hate your brother in your heart. You shall surely rebuke your neighbor, and not bear sin because of him. You shall not take vengeance, nor bear any grudge against the children of your people, but you shall love your neighbor as yourself: I am the LORD. (Leviticus 19:17-18)

> Jesus answered him, "The first of all the commandments is: 'Hear, O Israel, the LORD our God, the LORD is one. And you shall love the LORD your God with all your heart, with all your soul, with all your mind, and with all your strength.' This is the first commandment. And the second, like it, is this: 'You shall love your neighbor as yourself.' There is no other commandment greater than these. (Mark 12:29-32)

The Tuesday before the Friday that Jesus was crucified, a lawyer asked Him about the greatest commandment. Jesus' answer was that love for God and love for neighbor was preeminent among all the laws. From the very lips of Jesus came the words that if we love God and our neighbor then we fulfill the whole law. If we love God, we will not put any other gods before Him, we will not make idols, we will not misuse His name, and we will remember to keep the Sabbath holy. If we love our neighbor as ourselves, we will honor our father and mother, we will not murder, we will not commit adultery, we will not steal, we will not give false testimony, and we will not covet. That is the whole law! And Jesus says that all the law and prophets hang on these two commandments. Paul also wrote, "For all the law is fulfilled in one word, even in this: 'You shall love your neighbor as yourself'" (Galatians 5:14).

James 2:8. "You shall love your neighbor as yourself," you do well

The Greek word here for love is *agape* which calls for an intelligent and purposeful love, a love that voluntarily seeks the welfare of its neighbor. It is not a warm and fuzzy feeling towards someone. We cannot depend on that kind of love, because it changes every day, doesn't it? The world's definition of love is that shallow, emotional, self-oriented love that permeates our society, but the love called for here is a sacrificial love that places the needs of others above our own. *Agape* love is utterly incompatible with favoritism and partiality, which seeks only to further its own selfish goals.

The "neighbor" here can be anyone, not just your next-door neighbor. Jesus thoroughly defined *neighbor* in his parable of the Good Samaritan. After the traveler fell among brutal thieves, who was the true neighbor? It was the one who showed mercy (Luke 10:25-37).

James then completed the sentence by telling them that if they loved their neighbors as themselves, they did "well." *Well* here in the Greek speaks of that which is excellent. Because they were acting in a manner consistent with God's impartial, loving nature, they were doing an excellent thing. If you treat people according to their true worth, not just their net value, then you do well. If you don't judge others by their clothes or color of their skin, then you do well. I doubt that any of us have any trouble loving ourselves. In fact, we probably love ourselves too much. But do we love others as much as we love ourselves? Jesus said, "Greater love has no one than this, than to lay down one's life for his friends" (John 15:13). Guess what? The word "friend" in the Greek means neighbor. James is commanding here that we should measure our love toward others by the measure of love we have for ourselves. So James realized that while some were fulfilling the royal law, he also realized that some were not, which explains why he included the next thought in verse 9.

The Character of the Rebellious — They are Lawbreakers

James 2:9. But if you show partiality, you commit sin, and are convicted by the law as transgressors.

The connective "but" marks the sharp contrast from those who were fulfilling the royal law to those who were not. The verb tense of the clause "if you show partiality" indicates that these believers behaved this way continually, habitually. To slip once or twice in this area was one thing, but to continue in it was another. If you show partiality, James says two things about you. First of all, "you commit sin." This indicates a deliberate, premeditated action and demonstrates a decision on your part to continue in this sinful behavior. *Sin* is missing the mark, knowingly being disobedient to the will of God.

Secondly, if you show partiality, not only do you commit sin, but you are "convicted by the law as transgressors." *Convicted* means to reprove with conviction upon the offender. The effect produced by this reproof is not necessarily on the mind itself as when we are guilty of sin, but the fact that God condemns it.

What does "by the law" refer to? This is the Mosaic Law mentioned in Leviticus 19:18, the royal law that James has already mentioned in verse 8 when he said, "You shall love your neighbor as yourself." And then, if you show partiality, you are convicted as a "transgressor," one who is guilty of having passed over a forbidden boundary. We all know what trespassing means—Keep out! If you transgress in the area of showing partiality, then you have stepped over the line of rebellion against God. It is interesting that sin is missing the mark and falling short of God's holy standard, whereas transgressing refers to going beyond the accepted limits. One says you've fallen short; the other says you've gone too far. Both are equal violations of God's holy standards. Showing partiality is sin and a transgression of the law. James goes on to tell his readers exactly that. If they show partiality, they are guilty of violating the whole law.

James 2:10. For whoever shall keep the whole law, and yet stumble in one point, he is guilty of all.

"Whoever" means anyone and applies universally, no matter who you are. We know this because God is no respecter of persons and does not show partiality. It does not matter if you are the pastor's wife. It does not matter if you teach Sunday school. It does not matter who you are! If you keep the whole law and yet offend or stumble in one point, you are guilty of all.

"Offend" means to trip, to stumble, or to fall. If you offend or trip in just one point, "you are guilty of all." Now this does not mean you are guilty of violating every single law, but you have violated the law of God. For example, if you break the speed limit, then you have broken the law. You may not have committed murder, but by breaking the speed limit, you have still broken the law. If you have broken a law, then you are a lawbreaker. Our obedience to God's will cannot be on a selective basis; we cannot choose the parts that we prefer and disregard the rest—God's law is not a spiritual smorgasbord. To violate any part of the God-given law is an offense against the Divine Lawgiver. To do so shows a lack of true reverence for the Lawgiver and His law and breaks our personal relationship of obedience to Him as His disciple. For Jesus said, "Whoever therefore breaks one of the least of these commandments, and teaches men so, shall be called least in the kingdom of heaven" (Matthew 5:19).

The Jewish reader would understand that to break one law would be to break the whole law. This was not a new concept to them. The Jewish rabbis even taught this in the Torah: "If a man performs all the commandments, save one, he is guilty of all and each; to break one precept is to defy God who commanded the whole" (*Shabbath* 70.2).

Paul was referring to the Law of Moses when he said, "For as many as are of the works of the law are under the curse; for it is written, 'Cursed is everyone who does not continue in *all* things which are written in the book of the law, to do them'" (Galatians 3:10, emphasis mine). We cannot despise the poor, show partiality, and retain God's favor any more than we can commit murder or adultery and still please Him, as James pointed out in the next verse.

Before going on to verse 11, I want to emphasize that James is not saying that every sin carries with it the same consequences. Some sins are obviously more heinous in the sight of God than others. For example, adultery has a greater potential to devastate than does lust, for lust consumes only the lustful person. The act of adultery, however, involves the adulterer, the illicit partner, and the betrayed spouses of both. Adultery also defiles and weakens a community, hence the Old Testament term, "defile the land," as we see in Leviticus 18:25. In Matthew 5:28, Jesus attaches equal guilt to the sins of lust and adultery. Open adultery and hidden lust are unequal in their human consequences, but they are equal in their damning guilt before God. Sin is sin. James continues his point in verse 11.

James 2:11. For He who said, "Do not commit adultery," also said, "Do not murder." Now if you do not commit adultery, but you do murder, you have become a transgressor of the law.

The fact that a murderer may not have committed adultery

will not excuse him in a court of law. He has still broken a law. Apparently some of James' readers had some misconceptions. They thought that sins committed against the poor, such as prejudice, partiality, and indifference, were not as serious as murder and adultery. Perhaps they believed they could make up for their favoritism by keeping God's law in other areas. You might be asking, as did I, why James uses these two particular offences of the law—adultery and killing—in the context of a discussion about showing partiality. Jesus' words in Matthew 5:21-22 helps us answer this question.

> You have heard that it was said to those of old, "You shall not murder, and whoever murders will be in danger of the judgment." But I say to you that whoever is angry with his brother without a cause shall be in danger of the judgment. And whoever says to his brother, "Raca!" Shall be in danger of the council. But whoever says, "You fool!" shall be in danger of hell fire. (Matthew 5:21-22)

To call someone *Raca* meant you were calling them empty and worthless. Call them a fool, and you were calling them silly, stupid, and foolish. In fact, we get our English word *moron* from this word. Do you see the connection here? Aren't we in essence calling someone "foolish, silly, raca, worthless" when we are showing favoritism and partiality? Jesus equates those sins with murder, in the sense that they deserve the same punishment. The sin of favoritism cannot be excused, since many times it results in murder in our hearts. Now James gives us a solemn warning here about how Christians should speak and act in view of coming judgment.

The Character of the Redeemer: He is Merciful to the Merciful

James 2:12. So speak and so do as those who will be judged by the law of liberty.

"So speak and so do," indicates that Christian love is shown in both speech and action. Because both verbs are in the present tense, they are calling for habitual action. James is urging his readers to show obedience to the royal law, to love their neighbors as themselves in what they say and do. He is telling them to practice what they preach! What we say must not be inconsistent with what we do. James is saying, "Keep on speaking and keep on acting in the reality of the coming judgment."

Because we are going to be judged "by the law of liberty," we should consider our speech and our actions. The law of liberty is not part of the Ten Commandments or the Mosaic Law, but is the same as the "perfect law of liberty" which James discussed in chapter 1, verse 25. There we saw that those who look into the "perfect law of liberty" are blessed. And now here in James 2:12, we see that we will be judged by that same law of liberty. It simply refers to the Word of God as found in the gospel, centered in loving others. This law of liberty sets believers free from guilt and slavery to sin. But it also places them under obligation to obey their Lord and Master. This is the law of liberty by which we will be judged.

As Christians we live under the law of liberty, and it is by this same law of liberty that we will be judged. All of us will appear at the judgment seat of Christ where our works will be judged. Each Christian will stand before Christ and render an account of obedience to God. Second Corinthians 5:10 says, "For we must all appear before the judgment seat of Christ, that each one may receive the things done in the body, according to what he has done, whether good or bad." Even every word we have spoken in our entire lives will have to be accounted for. Jesus said, "But I say to you that for every idle word men may speak, they will give account of it in the day of judgment. For by your words you will be justified, and by your words you will be condemned" (Matthew 12:36-37). Christian conduct must be motivated by the certainty of God's future judgment. Judgment is not a popular topic these days—it's about as popular as sin—but it is a biblical doctrine and we should live and speak accordingly. The knowledge of impending judgment should cultivate personal holiness in our lives, and we should think of the coming judgment especially when we consider the sin of partiality. Now verse 13 explains why the sin of partiality will be punished with special severity.

James 2:13. For judgment is without mercy to the one who has shown no mercy. Mercy triumphs over judgment.

James is simply saying that mercy will be withheld from those of us who have shown no mercy toward others. The unmerciful will not receive mercy. What a terrifying thought! A deeper terror imbedded in James' words is this: favoritism and partiality is evidence of an unmerciful spirit. The merciful do not show favoritism. James is saying that a life characterized by discrimination and favoritism is a life characterized by a damned soul. We all know the principle. Matthew 5:7 says, "Blessed are the merciful, for they shall obtain mercy." A paraphrase would read, "If you forgive others, God will forgive you. If you don't, then He won't." Other passages to consider on the merits of granting mercy are Matthew 7:1-2 and Matthew 18:23-35. God will not call evil good, whether it is unjust favoritism or something else.

What exactly is "mercy"? Mercy (Greek, *eleos*) is the outward manifestation of pity and compassion in kindly action towards the misery of others. Notice that this definition does not say "kindly words," but "kindly action." John MacArthur says:

> A person who shows no mercy and compassion for people in need demonstrates that he has never responded to the great mercy of God, and as an unredeemed person will receive only strict, unrelieved judgment in eternal hell. The person whose life is characterized by mercy is ready for the Day of Judgment, and will escape all the charges that strict justice might bring against him

because by showing mercy to others he gives genuine evidence of having received God's mercy.[37]

What did Jesus say in the Sermon on the Mount? "Blessed are the merciful, for they shall obtain mercy" (Matthew 5:7).
Praise God, because James ends with an upside to this verse: "mercy triumphs over judgment." Mercy rejoices; it triumphs; it has no fear of judgment! Having received God's mercy, we will be able to stand in the judgment that otherwise would overwhelm us. All of us deserve hell, none of us deserve heaven.

> The merciful man, the man who showed mercy toward his fellow men down here on earth, when he appears before the judgment seat, will not be afraid of his own sin because he will have the mercy that he consistently and generously manifested to others. The mercy that he showed down here will be a cause for boasting up there.[38]

Mercy will appear to gain a victory over judgment. You know, if we all got what we deserved, what was just, what was due us on the Day of Judgment, it would be condemnation. But even though it never triumphs at the expense of justice, mercy does plead for us, for our salvation, and ultimately prevails.

---

[37] John MacArthur, Jr. *The MacArthur Study Bible* (Word Publishing, 1997), p. 1929. There are three major views about this judgment: some consider that this refers to the future judgment of the unsaved (the White Throne Judgment) but the later half of 2:13 does refer to some who show judgment are believers. Some consider this judgment as dealing with the saved only (the Judgment Seat of Bema of Christ) but that could hardly be pictured as "without mercy." The best option is to consider this judgment as a reference to all future judgments, dealing with both the saved and the lost. It is a universal principle. The lost, who didn't manifest mercy, will be treated without mercy; the saved who did manifest mercy will be shown mercy. God doesn't have one set of standards for the saved and another for the lost. Although there might be different phases of judgment, Jesus spoke of judgment without distinguishing one phase from another. John 5:28-29; Matthew 25:31-46. And the principles of judgment are clearly without partiality
[38] Spiros Zodhiates, *The Work of Faith* (AMG Publishers, 1985), p. 193.

Summary

All of us can fool each other by knowing and saying a few religious words or by quoting a few Bible verses or by repeating some evangelical clichés. We can learn to give a proper Christian testimony and deliver it with apparent conviction, but does that necessarily mean that our faith is real? James is saying that real faith is indicated not only by avoiding the big sins, like murder and adultery, but by how we treat our neighbors, particularly the needy. Being merciful towards others is another sign of genuine faith.

Where is your heart today in this matter of showing partiality? You and I have wonderful opportunities every day to put into practice these verses about showing mercy to those less fortunate, especially while those around us are practicing selfishness and greediness. Why not show mercy to someone who is suffering with a disease, such as cancer or AIDS? Why not show mercy to someone who is of a different race, a different social status, or a different denomination? Why not determine this year that you will work on a friendship with someone who is different from you, either socially or racially? Perhaps some of us need to show mercy right in our own homes, towards our husband and children. What about the elderly? Perhaps you know an elderly person who needs assistance with buying groceries. One of the biggest opportunities we have is to be merciful towards the lost. We all have a wonderful opportunity to share the gospel with those who are without Christ—that is probably the greatest act of mercy you can show! Let's not be like the Pharisees who allowed the external trappings of their religiosity to blind them to the misery of others. Let us instead choose to be blessed by God, for blessed are the merciful, for they and they alone shall obtain mercy on that day!

Questions to Consider
"Fulfilling the Royal Law"
James 2:6–13

1. (a) Read James chapter 2, noting all of the responses that we should have towards others. (b) Are these yours?

2. Memorize James 2:9-10.

3. Answer the following questions after reading James 2:6-13. (a) How does James define the royal law in verse 8? (b) How do these verses respond when you argue that showing partiality is only a small sin? (c) What responsibilities do being under a law of liberty place upon you?

4. Find an example in Scripture where someone did or did not fulfill the "royal law." What example(s) should you avoid or follow?

5. Read Matthew 18:21-35. (a) What does this passage teach us about being merciful? (b) What lessons can you learn for daily living?

6. (a) In what ways do you think you can show mercy to your husband and children? (b) In what ways are you lacking in mercy towards them? Confess, repent, and be determined to change.

7. (a) Are there some "laws" in God's Word that you are not obeying because you think they are not as essential as the "BIG ONES"? (b) Are there some "laws" of the land (government) that you are not obeying (Have you checked your speedometer lately?), thinking that they are not as essential as the "BIG ONES"?

8. (a) This week write down the ways in which you find yourself showing favoritism. (b) What did you learn about yourself and about this sin? (c) What will you do to change?

9. Think of one person you tend to ignore. What might you do to show love or mercy to this person? Put your need in the form of a prayer request.

11

Test of Good Works

James 2:14-20

The following was taken from a cartoon illustrating a conventional church building with a large billboard out front advertising its ministry. The sign read like this:

> The *Lite* Church
> 24% fewer Commitments
> Home of the 7.5% Tithe
> 15-Minute Sermons
> 45-Minute Worship Services
> We only have 8 commandments—your choice.
> We use just 3 Spiritual Laws.
> Everything you've wanted in a church ... and less![39]

Grievous, isn't it? Unfortunately, most evangelical churches in America today could easily have billboards similar to that one. There is no pricking of the conscience in our services, no feeding of our souls, no commitment—no real faith. Faith is one of the great concepts of our Christian experience, and yet few "Christians" really possess a genuine saving faith. What is saving faith?

---

[39] *Leadership Journal*, Volume 4, Number 3, Summer 1983, p. 81. If you want an outstanding help in explaining the compromising philosophy behind this trend in the evangelical world, *Word Pictures: Does the Truth Matter Anymore?* Taught by John MacArthur, Jr. This is a 5-hour video presentation published by Cross TV that deals with the shift toward pragmatic and entertainment-oriented ministry. Cross TV 370 West Camino Gardens Blvd., Boca Raton, Florida 33432.

Well, some people press faith to the extreme by implying that it makes no difference how they live their lives—faith is all that matters. They say, "I've got my fire insurance, so I can now live any way I want." They say that is saving faith! On the other end of the continuum, there are those trying to earn their way into heaven by doing good deeds. They volunteer for every good work, always making meals, attending church every Sunday, and showing kindness to their neighbor. So, which side of the camp is right? Which way produces the genuine saving faith, faith or works? Or both? I trust that after we study James 2:14-20 we will be able to marry the two together, faith and works, and see the appropriate conduct that should flow out of genuine faith. About this question James wrote:

> What does it profit, my brethren, if someone says he has faith but does not have works? Can faith save him? [15]If a brother or sister is naked and destitute of daily food, [16]and one of you says to them, 'Depart in peace, be warmed and filled,' but you do not give them the things which are needed for the body, what does it profit? [17]Thus also faith by itself, if it does not have works, is dead. [18]But someone will say, 'You have faith, and I have works.' Show me your faith without your works, and I will show you my faith by my works. [19]You believe that there is one God. You do well. Even the demons believe—and tremble! [20]But do you want to know, O foolish man, that faith without works is dead? (James 2:14-20)

James' written discourse deals with four categories of faith: a *dead* faith (vv 14-17); the *disciples* faith (v 18); the *demons* faith (v 19), and a *damning* faith (v 20).

A Dead Faith – Produces Nothing

James 2:14. What does it profit, my brethren, if someone says he has faith but does not have works? Can faith save him?

"What does it profit, my *brethren*?" Again we see James using the term *brethren*, yet another reminder of his concern for them. The verb in the clause, "if someone *says* is in the present tense, which means that this someone is repeatedly saying that his faith is all he needs. Here in verse 14 James was writing about someone who claimed to have a genuine faith, and yet had no works. The word "faith" here in the Greek is simply assent or knowledge, without that assent or knowledge producing good works. "Works" are acts in which a man proves that his faith is genuine.

Remember some of the specific works James has already mentioned? Believers bridle their tongues; they go through trials with joy; they visit the widows and orphans in their trouble; they keep themselves unspotted from the world; they don't show partiality or favoritism; and they show mercy. These are just some of the works that should be present in the life of a believer. So James says, if you have faith, but none of these works, then "can that faith save you?" Can mental assent alone to the gospel save you? Can believing that Christ died and rose from the grave save you? Can believing you are a sinner save you? Can going forward at the end of a church service save you? Can saying a prayer save you? Can saying you accept Christ in your life save you? Can raising your hand in an evangelistic service save you? Can any of those things save you? James asks the question: Can such faith save a person? The Greek grammar negative here makes it clear that the expected answer to this question was "No."

James is contrasting genuine faith, which inevitably produces action because it is alive, with a mere claim to faith, which is a verbal profession only and has no life changing power. None of those things I just mentioned mean anything without works, without fruit. What did Jesus say? "By their fruits you will know them" (Matthew 7:20). I think that people today too often make professions of faith, and we are satisfied with that. A great danger exists in telling someone that faith in Jesus Christ comes by saying a flippant "yes" without subsequently changing his or her life. The works to which James is referring here are the fruits of faith, the result of salvation, and the life of the new birth. James asks, what is the profit, what is the advantage of that kind of faith without works? He asks in verse 14 and then answers in verses 15 and 16 by giving us an example of one way to determine if someone's faith in Jesus Christ is real or not real, authentic or false, genuine or spurious.

James 2:15. If a brother or sister is naked and destitute of daily food

James is probably still reflecting on the rich to whom the believers were showing favoritism at the expense of the poor. *If a brother or sister* refers to fellow Christians. *Is naked* could have described complete nudity, although this term was also used to describe less extreme cases. For example, it describes someone without an outer garment, without which no decent person appeared in public unless he was engaged in manual labor. So we see that this brother or sister is not only naked, but is also "destitute of daily food," which would be an entire day's supply. The parable of the laborers in Matthew 20 is a good example of laborers being paid their wages at the end of each day. They were paid daily, not on the fifteenth and thirtieth of every month. So the people about whom James was writing were without food and without clothes, which would mean that they were cold and hungry.

James 2:16. And one of you says to them, 'Depart in peace, be warmed and filled,' but you do not give them the things which are needed for the body, what does it profit?

Test of Good Works

So James writes: "And one of you says to them, 'Depart in peace, be warmed and filled.'" *Depart in peace* is a farewell, which was a signal to the other person that the encounter was over and that nothing further would be done to help. In essence this phrase was saying, "Go get yourself a good meal and some warm clothes or let someone else feed and warm you." This phrase is still used to this day by people who live in Palestine in order to get rid of people. It means, "God help you, but don't expect me to do so." We do that today, don't we? For example, we might say to someone in need, "Oh, I'm really sorry about your situation. You know God is sovereign. I'll pray for you." Yet, do we pray? If possible, do we try to meet the need? If these pious words are expressed without the accompanying acts, if you do not give them the things which are needed for the body, then James says, "What does it profit?" What good does it do? What use is that? The only answer to that question is "none at all." It is of no gain to you or to them. Consider what John, the aged old Apostle wrote:

> By this we know love, because He laid down His life for us. And we also ought to lay down our lives for the brethren. But whoever has this world's goods, and sees his brother in need, and shuts up his heart from him, how does the love of God abide in him? My little children, let us not love in word or in tongue, but in deed and in truth. And by this we know that we are of the truth, and shall assure our hearts before Him. (1 John 3:16-19)

It is sad to think that if this individual were our mother, father, sister, brother or child—a member of our physical family—most of us wouldn't even think of refusing them. How then can we treat our spiritual family this way?

There is a story that illustrates the opposite of this dead faith that James has just described. A former student of Moody Bible Institute in Chicago was returning to the campus from the nearby YMCA where he had been playing basketball. He was hurrying down the street, when he noticed a poorly dressed man who stopped and asked him for some money. The student asked him why he needed the money and the man told him he was hungry. So the student took him to dinner and fed him. While eating, he noticed how bad his clothes were, and so the student gave him his shoes. In addition to sharing his shoes, the student also shared the gospel with him. As he left the restaurant, the student was stopped again by an elderly woman standing at the bus stop. She had been watching the whole ordeal and she asked the student why in the world he would help such a man. "People just don't do that anymore," she said. He shared his testimony with her. In fact they were so busy talking that the lady missed her bus. He offered to carry her bags and walk her to the next bus stop so that she wouldn't have to wait so long for the next bus. As they walked and talked the lady was so moved by everything she saw and heard, that she told the student she would like to receive Christ. Because of this student's obedience in this area of meeting others' needs, he was privileged to introduce two people to Jesus Christ. That is a prime example of real faith put into action by works. James teaches us that in the next verse.

James 2:17. Thus also faith by itself, if it does not have works, is dead.

Thus also means in the same way. In the same way, "faith by itself, if it does not have works, is dead." *Dead* means having no effect. We abound in mouth mercy, which is dead without deeds. It is like hearing without doing, which we saw in James 1:22-25. Saying without doing is words without action. Mouth mercy, which is not accompanied by works of mercy, demonstrates your faith is dead. My dear sisters, dead faith will get no one into heaven. You may have faith enough to recite all the right words, but unless works are present, it is like a dead body in a coffin. It looks as life-like as possible, but there is no life. A faith without works is no more a genuine faith than a corpse is a living person. In the *King James Version*, it reads: "faith ... is dead, being alone." In the *New King James Version*, this is translated "faith by itself ... is dead." *Faith by itself* is without accompanying fruits or results, and therefore, it is dead. As John the Baptist said, "Bear fruits worthy of repentance" (Matthew 3:8).

So now in the next verse we are going to see someone who is fighting this idea; perhaps even some of you may be struggling with this notion in your mind. You may argue with what has been said, just as James anticipated some of his readers would.

The Disciples' Faith – Produces Something

James 2:18. But someone will say, "You have faith, and I have works." Show me your faith without your works, and I will show you my faith by my works.

Here is one who claims to have faith and another who points to his deeds. You have one form or manifestation of religion and I have another. "Show me your faith" the objector says! The term *show* means bring it to light, display it; demonstrate your faith before me. You who maintain that faith is enough—I can't see your religion—prove the existence of your religion. You who maintain that faith is enough to prove the existence of your religion, you who say that all that is necessary in order to be saved is merely to believe, show me your faith! Since faith is invisible, James is saying works must manifest the faith he claims to possess. "You show me your faith without your works, and I will show you my faith by my works." James is willing to meet his own challenge, and to evidence his faith in a way in which there can be no doubt.

There is no other way to manifest our claim of faith other than by its fruit. "You will know them by their fruits" (Matthew 7:16). Whoever disconnects faith from works endeavors to walk with one foot, which is impossible. Faith and works are the two feet by which we walk in Christ, and when the Holy Spirit promotes one, He promotes the other. If you are trying to walk into heaven by works only, you are attempting the impossible. If you are trying to walk into heaven by faith alone, thinking that you don't have to manifest a changed life, then that is impossible as well. James now confronts this objector on his own ground. By the way, this is a good principle for us to follow when facing objections from people.

The Demons' Faith – Produces Dread

James 2:19. You believe that there is one God. You do well. Even the demons believe—and tremble!

"You believe that there is one God," James said. You believe, you hold a mental persuasion, but not a saving faith. James confronts the objector on his own turf, his orthodox faith. Each morning and evening all pious Jew recited the words from Deuteronomy 6:4-5. "Hear, O Israel: the Lord our God, the Lord is one! You shall love the Lord your God with all your heart, with all your soul, and with all your strength." "If you believe in one God," James said, "You do well." He is saying that orthodoxy is better than heresy. There is no irony here, but James is painfully aware that an intellectual confession alone is tragic. He finishes the sentence with "even the demons believe—and tremble." James is saying, "The demons believe the same thing you do, but at least they know to tremble, which is more than can be said for you!" In the Greek, *believe* means to have a mental persuasion. This belief, this mental persuasion, is not a saving faith. And yet, James says, these demons *tremble*. This is the only time in the New Testament when this word is used, and it means to bristle, to stand on end. It refers to a man whose hair stands on end when he is frightened out of his wits, and then shudders and quakes with fear. The present tense of *tremble* conveys this image as their reaction when they ultimately face the reality of the eternal God. They believe, my friend, but their belief, their faith, does not get them into the kingdom.

Yet the demons are aware of God's power. In this verse, the demons were fully aware of the awesome power of God, and they were smart enough to tremble, which is more than can be said for most people today, who have no fear whatsoever of God before their eyes! The demons believed in the same manner as the person who believes that there is a God but is not godly. Readers everywhere need to be reminded that the faith that saves must be more than just an intellectual assent to the truth, for even demons recognize the existence of God and yet do not possess the faith that saves. If you read national polls on this subject, you know that the great majority of Americans believe in God. Just ask the people in your neighborhood. Most will say, yes, I believe in God. Anyone with a sound mind can come to the conclusion that there must be a God behind the universe and the human body.

In fact, I always find it interesting when conversing with others that I am getting to know. Usually at some point I will ask if he or she is a Christian. "Ah yes," they will usually say, and tell me when they made a decision for Christ at church camp or a revival. But then as you probe further into their lives, you learn that they no longer attend church, they don't read their Bible, they have no fellowship with the saints, and they have no hunger for God. Where is that kind of Christianity found in the Bible? Jesus Himself taught that there would be few who are genuinely saved.

> Not everyone who says to Me, "Lord, Lord," shall enter the kingdom of heaven, but he who does the will of My Father in heaven. Many will say to Me in that day, "Lord, Lord, have we not prophesied in Your name, cast out demons in Your name, and done many wonders in Your name?" And then I will declare to them, "I never knew you; depart from Me, you who practice lawlessness!" (Matthew 7:21-23)

> And He went through the cities and villages, teaching, and journeying toward Jerusalem. Then one said to Him, "Lord, are there few who are saved?" And He said to them, "Strive to enter through the narrow gate, for many, I say to you, will seek to enter and will not be able." (Luke 13:22-24)

One of the earliest occasions where Jesus corrects the notion that somehow a spurious faith that results in no actual transformation of life results in salvation is found following some miracles done in Jerusalem.

> Now when He was in Jerusalem at the Passover, during the feast, many believed in His name when they saw the signs which He did. But Jesus did not commit Himself to them, because He knew all men, and had no need that anyone should testify of man, for He knew what was in man. (John 2:23-24)

Notice some are actually unsaved *believers*, whose faith was spurious. In fact, the next chapter (John 3) illustrates one of these spurious believers, Nicodemus, who believed but needed to be born again to start the new life. If our belief in Jesus Christ does not produce a holy life and good works, then our belief is just a mental assent. Otherwise, demons would be justified and saved by that kind of faith. Instead, their intellectual understanding of God only produced fear of doom, not the fruit of repentance toward God and trust in Jesus Christ. James ends this section repeating what he has already said in verse 17.

A Damning Faith – Produces Condemnation

James 2:20. But do you want to know, O foolish man, that faith without works is dead?

Then James asks, "But do you want to know, O foolish man, that faith without works is dead?" In other words, are you willing to know? The fact that he asks at all suggests a resistance of the objector to face the issue. "Are you willing to recognize this?" he is asking. "Do you really want a clear proof?" The vocative *O* is used sparingly in the Greek; and when it is used, it is for the purpose of extreme emphasis. *O* foolish man! *Foolish man* means empty creature, void of understanding. It may also mean one who lacks normal common sense. This person supposes himself to be very knowledgeable, and yet James tells him "faith without works is dead." Faith that doesn't produce good works is useless in the matter of salvation. It is *dead*, which means it is barren, idle, useless, and unproductive. The term *dead* is used of money to describe earning no interest, thus indicating here that faith without works is unproductive for salvation.

Genuine faith produces a changed life. Ephesians 2:10 says, "For we are His workmanship, created in Christ Jesus for *good works,* which God prepared beforehand, that we should walk in them" (emphasis mine). Faith without works does not work! There is no such thing as a "*lite* church, just like there is no such thing as a "*lite* faith. A real faith is committed. Faith wholeheartedly follows the Master and proves itself genuine by reaching out to those in need.

Summary

Is your faith a faith that works? Or is your faith dead? My dear friend, I can think of no greater blessing than to commit your life to His Lordship if you have not. I can think of no greater tragedy than to think you are redeemed when in fact you are not!

At this point I want you to consider a series of questions I have taken from the book of First John, another wonderful book that reveals areas where we can test our faith to see if it is genuine or not. I would ask you to answer these questions honestly before God. These questions are wonderful indicators to determine if you have genuine saving faith. I know of no better time than the present to make sure you are in the faith. As Paul says, "Examine yourselves as to whether you are in the faith. Test yourselves" (2 Corinthians 13:5). Paul also said, "Behold, now is the accepted time; behold, now is the day of salvation" (2 Corinthians 6:2). Are you ready to take the test?

1. Do you have fellowship with Christ and the Father? (1 John 1:3)
2. Are you sensitive to sin? (1 John 1:6)
3. Do you obey God's Word? All of it? (1 John 2:4)
4. Do you reject this evil world? (1 John 2:15)
5. Do you see a decreasing pattern of sin in your life? (1 John 3:9)
6. Do you love other Christians? (1 John 3:14)
7. Do you experience answered prayer? (1 John 3:22)
8. Do you experience the ministry of the Holy Spirit in your life, His enabling, His power, His conviction and leading? (1 John 4:13)

If you could not answer yes to these questions, please do not delay another moment to turn around from the present road you are walking—it leads to destruction. Turn away from your transgressions. Do not let iniquity be your ruin. Walk down the road that leads to eternal life. "Today if you will hear His voice, do not harden your hearts. "Behold, now is the accepted time, behold now is the day of salvation" (2 Corinthians 6:2).

Questions to Consider
"Test of Good Works"
James 2:14-20

1. (a) Read James chapter 2 noting how many times faith and works are mentioned together. (b) Why do you think James emphasizes that? (c) How does James contrast true faith and dead faith?

2. Memorize James 2:19-20.

3. (a) What is Paul saying in Galatians 2:16? (b) In Ephesians 2:8-9? (c) Are these a contradiction to James 2:14-20? (d) Why or why not?

4. Read John 15:1-8. (a) What illustration did Jesus use for spiritual fruitfulness? (b) What is the prerequisite for fruitfulness? (c) What fruit (evidences of a redeemed life) should we be bearing according to verses 9-14? (d) How does this relate to what James says in James 2:14-20?

5. Read John 8:12-47, where Christ spoke to the Pharisees regarding the characteristics of those who know Him and those who do not. (a) Make a list of those things that characterize those who know Him and those who do not, for example, dead faith versus true faith. (b) What have you learned?

6. If you were asked the question, "Of what use is your faith?" what would you say?

7. (a) From the text, how does Christian faith differ from the faith that demons have? (b) What are some ways that you as a believer can demonstrate your faith by your works?

8. Put your "faith to work" by endeavoring to share your faith with

at least one other person this week. (This may even be one who claims they have faith, but by their lack of works, they prove their faith is dead.)

9. Is your faith working? What is your prayer regarding this matter of genuine faith?

12

Abraham and Rahab: Examples of Living Faith

James 2:21-26

There is a parable from the philosopher Søren Kierkegaard, which illustrates the lack of authentic faith, an obvious problem in our churches of today. The parable is about *Duckland*. It was Sunday morning. The ducks dutifully came to church, waddling through the doors and down the isle into their pews where they comfortably squatted. After all were settled and the hymns were sung, the duck minister waddled to his pulpit, opened the Duck Bible, and read: "Ducks! You have wings, and with wings you can fly like eagles. You can soar into the sky! Use your wings!" It was a marvelous, elevating duck scripture, and thus all the ducks quacked their assent with a hearty "Amen." Then they plopped down from their pews and waddled home.[40]

That amusing yet revealing parable illustrates how some professing Christians of today respond after attending church. They hear about the victorious Christian life and how to live it, and yet they return to their homes only to live like they have been living all along, just like those ducks that listened to the message of how they could fly and yet waddled home instead. That kind of faith is dead and useless, as we discovered in the last chapter. A mental assent to the gospel without a changed life is as useless as the money we invest that earns no interest. It is as useless as a body without breath,

---

[40] Quoted from Gary Vanderet, *Discovery Papers*, Number 3989 (May 25, 1986), "The Skill of a Genuine Faith."

unproductive in the matter of salvation.

James now gives us two living illustrations from real people, Abraham and Rahab, whose actions demonstrated that their faith was alive. Indeed, their faith was working, in contrast to the dead faith that we studied in the previous chapter. James wrote:

> Was not Abraham our father justified by works when he offered Isaac his son on the altar? [22]Do you see that faith was working together with his works, and by works faith was made perfect? [23]And the Scripture was fulfilled which says, "Abraham believed God, and it was accounted to him for righteousness." And he was called the friend of God. [24]You see then that a man is justified by works, and not by faith only. [25]Likewise, was not Rahab the harlot also justified by works when she received the messengers and sent them out another way? [26]For as the body without the spirit is dead, so faith without works is dead also. (James 2:21-26)

In this lesson, we will learn from the working faith of *Abraham* (vv 21-24) and the working faith of *Rahab* (vv 25-26).

The Working Faith of Abraham

James 2:21. Was not Abraham our father

Why does James mention Abraham as an example of faith and works? Because Abraham's example carried great weight for James' readers. To the Jew, Abraham was a man of faith who enjoyed a close relationship with God and was considered to be their spiritual father. For example: "Do not think to say to yourselves, 'We have *Abraham* as our father'" (Matthew 3:9, emphasis mine) and "… the faith of *Abraham*, who is the father of us all" (Romans 4:16, emphasis mine).

In John chapter 8 a dialogue is recorded between Jesus and the Jews, which we might summarize as: Jews: "We are Abraham's seed." Jesus: "I know you are Abraham's seed." Jews: "Art thou greater than our Father Abraham who is dead?" Jesus: "Your father Abraham rejoiced to see my day, and he saw it and was glad." This illustrates the central importance of Abraham to the Jews, the immediate audience of Pastor James. To further illustrate this, if I were to use the lives of Elizabeth Elliott or Corrie ten Boom to draw examples of faith and works, that would carry great weight for most of us in the evangelical world today. We know of these women, and we know of their faith and works.

James 2:21. Also justified by works

James asks: "Was not Abraham justified by works?" *Justified* means to acquit, to pronounce and treat as righteous. It means the opposite of to condemn. It is like a judge in a court of law who pronounces a just sentence. God is the judge who pronounced a just sentence on Abraham. Men and women are justified by their works, that is, works are the evidence that they are justified and are regarded and treated as righteous by their Maker. So, what justified Abraham? "He was justified by works." Right now you might be saying, wait a minute. Aren't we justified by faith? Doesn't Romans 5:1 say that we have been justified by faith? James must be mistaken, right? Abraham wasn't justified by works, but by faith. Is James saying something to the contrary? Aren't we saved by divine power, not by human effort or human works?

The Apostle Paul helps us with this ostensible contradiction in Romans 4:2. "For if Abraham was justified by works, he has something to boast about, but not before God." *But not before God* is the key here. Paul is talking about being justified before God. James is talking about being justified before man (James 2:18).

Yes, people are justified by faith alone before God. James is saying that Abraham's faith was justified by works *before men*.[41]

---

[41] The verb *justified* (Greek, *edikaiothe*) was used in two senses: (1) It sometimes had the meaning of making or pronouncing something just. In this case someone would declare something just, e.g., God declared Abraham just. The Apostle Paul uses the verb in this way in his epistle to the Romans. (2) It sometimes had the meaning of manifesting or being shown just, e.g., James says Abraham was justified by works. There is no contradiction between Paul and James, as the Apostle Paul was looking at the inception of Abraham's faith resulting in his justification (Genesis 15:6) before God; Pastor James is considering Abraham's later manifestation of his faith before others (Genesis 22).

The whole world could see the reality of his faith when he was willing to sacrifice his son Isaac. Abraham was justified *before God* through faith; likewise, no works are involved in our salvation. In Romans, Paul is talking about our works being useless when trying to gain merit before God, and James is talking about our works as the evidence of our salvation. It was by his faith that Abraham was justified; his works did not earn his justification. His works were simply the fruit and the outward evidence of his faith. Some of us may be having difficulty understanding the distinction between Paul's words and the words of James. Perhaps the words of John Calvin will help: "Faith alone justifies, but the faith which justifies is not alone." Acts or deeds which prove the reality of one's faith are the works that James is speaking of. The works of Abraham present a crowning example of the kind that James insists must follow from a living faith. What were the works of Abraham?

James 2:21. When he offered Isaac his son on the altar

James wrote, "He offered Isaac his son on the altar." The Greek here suggests that Abraham was declared righteous when he brought his son to the sacrificial altar. In this instance, Abraham proved that his faith was not dead. Now is a good time to read Genesis 22:1-18. As you read, I want you to put yourself in Abraham's place, trying to feel with him, trying to walk in his shoes. Make a note of things that are worthy as you read: for example, unlike most of us, Abraham asks no questions. If we were in Abraham's shoes, we might say, "But God, are you sure?" or "Why *my* son?" Also note that Abraham immediately obeys. He appears not to waver, even up to the last minute of binding Isaac to the altar. Remember our first lesson on James chapter 1: "Let him ask in *faith*, with no doubting" (James 1:6). What faith! The enormity of Abraham's faith must not be treated lightly. It was Isaac, his only beloved son, that was about to be sacrificed, and yet, according to what God had promised thirty years earlier, (Genesis 15:1-6) it was to be through Isaac that his seed would be blessed, as we shall see in a moment. As parents, we must stand in awe at the trust that Abraham placed in God. No doubt

Abraham believed in God so much that he presumed that Isaac would be resurrected. Why else would Abraham have told the young men guarding the donkey that "*we* will come back to you" (Genesis 22:5, emphasis mine). Abraham may have even been a little disappointed that he didn't get to sacrificially offer Isaac so that he would get to see the first resurrection. That is unbelievable faith!

James 2:22. Do you see that faith was working together with his works?

After James highlights Abraham's great faith displayed by offering Isaac on the altar, he then asks his readers, "Do you see that faith was working together with his works, and by works faith was made perfect?" This seemed so obvious, but it appears that some could not see it. "Faith working together with his works" means that faith cooperated or worked together. Faith cooperated with Abraham enabling him to perform his acts of obedience, his works. The verb *working* is in the imperfect tense, suggesting that this cooperation was continual. This great display of faith was not just a one-time event in the life of Abraham. His whole life exemplified faith. When you ponder Abraham's faith and works, you realize they were not just limited to the example of Isaac but were characteristic of his whole life. Other examples include his willingness to move to Egypt and his obedience in circumcising himself and his family (on the very day God asked him to). This list goes on, and so it should be in our lives. People should see that our faith works in our life and is a continual practice, not just a one-time event.

James 2:22. And by works faith was made perfect?

James completes the question with the phrase: "And by works was faith made perfect?" This means that his faith was made complete, finished, or entire. Abraham's faith had its goal in the providence of God. What was Abraham's goal? Obedience to God. The goal was: through faith Abraham would be brought into such an intimate relationship with God that he would voluntarily act to please God first in every area of life. Without genuine faith, which results in obedience, that kind of work—the offering of his son Isaac—could not have been performed.

Each of us can recall times when we exercised faith in obedience to God even when perhaps it seemed crazy to others. I remember when we moved from California to Tulsa believing that it was God's will for us. I remember some people thought it rather odd that we were coming "by faith." But we have seen the hand of God in our move here, and we rejoice! Someone said: "Faith is the heart and works is the hand. The hand cannot move without the cooperation of the heart. Abraham's hands would have never lifted the knife to place it in Isaac's chest, if the heart did not lift it. By means of the hand, the obedience of the heart was proven." That is the key by which we know our faith is real, enabling us to do whatever God asks even though we don't understand the purpose and value of it. In the next verse, James discussed the effect of Abraham's sacrificial offering upon Scripture.

James 2:23. And the Scripture was fulfilled which says, "Abraham believed God."

"The Scripture was fulfilled." What Scripture? Let's look at Genesis 15:1-6 to see what Scripture was fulfilled:

> After these things the word of the LORD came to Abram in a vision, saying, "Do not be afraid, Abram. I am your shield, your exceedingly great reward." But Abram said, "Lord GOD, what will You give me, seeing I go childless, and the heir of my house is Eliezer of Damascus?" Then Abram said, "Look, You have given me no offspring; indeed one born in my house is my heir!" And behold, the word of the LORD came to him, saying, "This one shall not be your heir, but one who will come from your own body shall be your heir." Then He brought him outside and said, "Look now toward heaven, and count the stars if you are able to number them." And He said to him, "So shall your descendants be." And he believed in the LORD, and He accounted it to him for righteousness. (Genesis 15:1-6)

Fulfilled means the Scripture was demonstrated or accomplished. "Abraham believed God." What did he believe that God was going to do? He believed that God would make his descendants as numerous as the stars of heaven. Because of the faith portrayed in Genesis 15, he was able to produce works, foremost being the offering of Isaac in Genesis 22. Through Isaac his seed would be blessed, yet God said kill him! Do you know what fascinates me? God's promise in chapter 15 was made thirty years before Abraham's offering of Isaac in Genesis 22. Thirty years! Have you been waiting in faith for anything for thirty years? Some of you aren't even thirty-years-old! That example should give us great hope as we trust God and pray for things that we sense are His will. Abraham knew God would spare his son, because he knew that God could not cancel his promise.

James 2:23. And it was accounted to him for righteousness. And he was called the friend of God.

And James says, "it was accounted to him for righteousness." *Accounted* means it was counted or calculated like something being placed to one's credit. God took Abraham's faith and regarded it as sufficient grounds for receiving him into His favor, as having the value of being righteous, which he did not have of his own, being a sinner. And so he was called the "friend of God"!

Friend in the Greek comes from the word *philos*, which is a love found in two persons because of common interests and concerns. In James 2:23, it is significant that this word *philos* is used after the illustration of Abraham's willingness to sacrifice his son Isaac at the request of God, because God did exactly the same thing yet more: He sent His Son Jesus to die on Calvary! Abraham is called *the friend of God* two other places in Scripture: "Abraham Your friend" (2 Chronicles 20:7), and "Abraham My friend (Isaiah 41:8). Jesus also gave the name *friend* to his twelve disciples: "I have called you *friends*, for all things that I heard from My Father I have made known to you" (John 15:15). Just before that, Jesus said, "You are my *friends* if you do whatever I command you" (John 15:14).

By God's divine grace Abraham, the disciples, you, and I can be called friends of God. Abraham stands as a stark contrast to what James is going to tell his readers later in chapter 4, verse 4, that those who are friends of the world are enemies of God. Now we know that in order to be friends of God, we must not be friends of the world. We are either God's friends, or we are God's enemies. And if we do whatever He tells us to do, we are God's friends. Wouldn't it be great to have written on your tombstone, "She was a friend of God"? In verse 24, James continues the answer to the question he posed in verse 14: "What does it profit, my brethren, if someone says he has faith but does not have works? Can faith save him?"

James 2:24. You see then that a man is justified by works, and not by faith only.

Here James is insisting that one's works must prove any claim of justification by faith. He is demanding a working faith. In the Greek, "you see" means to take heed, beware. It is a warning to some who might still be insisting that a mere profession of faith without works is adequate. "Now that I have presented an illustration from Abraham, it must be very clear to you," James is saying, "that a man is proved to be righteous by works, and not by faith alone." Watch out, James says! Since a man is proved righteous by works and not by faith alone, you had better produce some works to back your words! James ends his thoughts on "working faith" with yet another example, this one very different from Abraham. A woman and a harlot—Rahab!

The Working Faith of Rahab

James 2:25. Likewise, was not Rahab the harlot also justified by works?

"Likewise" teaches the same truth using a different individual. James gave us this example of one so different in character to demonstrate that no one, regardless of spiritual condition, nationality, or societal class, has ever been counted righteous without works. We can understand why James used Abraham, but why Rahab? She was a Gentile, a prostitute, a woman, a liar, and a resident of the pagan city Jericho. Abraham was a Jew and a righteous man. Abraham was a godly patriarch, and Rahab was a godless prostitute. How could such a person like Rahab illustrate true faith? Well, let's see! As you read the Scripture passage describing the account of Rahab, try to walk in Rahab's shoes (Joshua 2:1-14). Unlike Abraham, Rahab knew little about the true God; but what she heard, she believed, and what she believed she acted on. Abraham had believed for thirty years; Rahab had recently come to faith when the Israelites surrounded Jericho and sent their spies into the city. In Joshua 2:8-11 we read her confession of faith.

> Now before they lay down, she came up to them on the roof, and said to the men: 'I know that the LORD has given you the land, that the terror of you has fallen on us, and that all the inhabitants of the land are fainthearted because of you. For we have heard how the LORD dried up the water of the Red Sea for you when you came out of Egypt, and what you did to the two kings of the Amorites who were on the other side of the Jordan, Sihon and Og, whom you utterly destroyed. And as soon as we heard these things, our hearts melted; neither did there remain any more courage in anyone because of you, for the LORD your God, He is God in heaven above and on earth beneath.' (Joshua 2:8-11)

There is no implication that she continued in her sin after coming to faith—a mark of a true believer. Her act of faith meant a complete turn around —repentance—in her life. If there is no such repentance in your sinful life after your conversion, then there is no conversion, no genuine faith, and no justification. In fact, she was believed by tradition to have become not only a believer, but to have married Joshua, becoming the maternal ancestor of many priests and prophets, including Jeremiah and Ezekiel. Along with Abraham, she is even mentioned in the genealogy of our Lord Jesus Christ in Matthew 1:5, and was considered to be one of the four beauties, along with Sarah, Abigail, and Esther.

James 2:25. When she received the messengers and sent them out another way

James says that Rahab was justified by her works when she "received the messengers." Joshua secretly sent these messengers to Jericho to view the land. She *received* them, which means she welcomed and entertained them as guests, because she considered them to be God's messengers rather than spies. After receiving them, she "sent them out another way." She acted with urgency, showing personal concern for their safety even at the risk of her own life. She sent them out another way—not through her door, but her window, and not back to their camp where they would be pursued, but to the mountains instead (Joshua 2:15-16). Her works were entirely different from those of Abraham, but both proved that a living faith is a working faith.

Remember our first lesson, we mentioned that the testing of our faith would be varied (James 1:3)? We learned that our various trials would bear different colors. Both Rahab and Abraham were tested, yet they were different people in character and different in their tests of faith. In their trials and by their works, both proved to be genuine in their faith. Both were willing to sacrifice what mattered most to them. For Abraham, it was Isaac; for Rahab, it was her own life. Both are mentioned in the great hall of faith in Hebrews 11!

If God asks, are you and I willing to sacrifice what matters most? True faith sacrifices everything, even our own lives. We are all given various tests to see if our faith is real, to see if we really have the faith to trust God even in the most difficult and puzzling situations. Did not Jesus say, "For whoever desires to save his life will lose it, but whoever loses his life for My sake and the gospel's will save it. For what will it profit a man if he gains the whole world, and loses his own soul?" (Mark 8:35-36). And now James uses a simple analogy to close this second chapter of his epistle.

James 2:26. For as the body without the spirit is dead, so faith without works is dead also.

The spirit (the immaterial part of man) imparts life to our material body, and without it, we are dead. Without the spirit, our body is a useless corpse. A dead body isn't any good, so that's why we bury it. A lifeless body without a spirit is comparable to faith without works. Faith without works is dead. As breath gives life to a physical body, likewise a living faith produces works! This is the third time that James has said that faith without works is dead (James 2:17, 20, 26). Spiritually dead is exactly what we are if we have only a profession of faith without a life of works. The faith that does not save is called "dead." Unless our faith produces holy living and holy works, it has no more of the characteristics of true religion than a dead body has of being a man. You might as well bury your faith and quit wasting your time with all your religiosity.

A good practice is to ask those whom you live with if your Christianity fleshes out at home. Ask your husband, your children or those closest to you, "Does my faith work?" "Is my faith working?" Mr. Talkative, John Bunyan's character in *Pilgrims Progress*, was a saint at church but a devil at home. The home is the testing ground to see if we are genuine Christians. No one can fool people at home for long. A faith that does not do loving deeds at home is questionable. If necessary, ask God to grant you saving faith, repent of your sin, and start living in obedience to Him. Christian faith must manifest its existence in active obedience to God's Word!

Summary

Those poor ducks in Kierkegaard's parable waddled in and out of church and never flew as God created them to do, because their "faith" was nothing more than mental assent. Few things are as unattractive as a waddling duck, and yet when they fly, they are so beautiful. Few things are as unattractive as a person who has all the religious trappings but doesn't live a life of obedience to God. And yet when they do obey, they are so beautiful, so attractive, and so desirable to be around. If we believe, then let us behave!

Questions to Consider
"Abraham and Rahab:
Examples of Living Faith"
James 2:21-26

1. Read James chapter 2 and share one truth God has impressed upon you from this chapter.

2. Memorize James 2:26.

3. Read James 2:21-26, especially noting the account of Abraham. Now read Romans 4, especially noting what Paul says about Abraham. A contradiction *seems* to exist between what Paul says about Abraham and what James says about Abraham. How do you reconcile this?

4. (a) What did Rahab believe about God? See Joshua 2:1-15. (b) How did she show it?

5. What qualities of faith did Abraham, the friend of God, have in common with Rahab, the harlot?

6. Choose one example from Hebrews 11 (besides Abraham or Rahab) and read the Old Testament account of his or her example of faith. What truths did you learn about genuine faith?

7. (a) In what way(s) have you exercised your faith lately to prove that it is genuine? (b) Is there something God is asking you to do that you are saying "no" to? Why? (c) Does what you confess at church match what you say and live at home?

8. Ask God to increase and strengthen your faith throughout the day. Look for specific opportunities to trust Him more fully. Record those opportunities as a reminder of the faithfulness of God.

9. We have now completed two chapters in James. What has God impressed upon you to change to prove that your faith is real? Put your answer in the form of a prayer request.

13

The Danger of the Tongue!

James 3:1-6

I read an amusing story about a lady who told her pastor that she wanted to put her tongue on the altar, to which he replied, "Madam, there isn't an altar big enough for your tongue!" I am sorry to say that women have the greater temptation, as well as the greater difficulty, in this area of uncontrolled speech. John Calvin commented, "Talkativeness is a disease of women and old age usually makes it worse."[42] He also said "There is nothing more slippery or loose than the tongue" (commenting on Psalm 38). For women, the power of self-control is most often tested in the use of our tongues. When you think about it, the words that we speak show what is truly in our hearts. As Jesus told the Pharisees, "Out of the abundance of the heart the mouth speaks" (Matthew 12:34).

We all have struggled with this at one time or another, and I am indeed thankful to God for a husband who keeps me on track in this area. Jesus taught that you and I are going to give an account before God on the Day of Judgment for every idle word we speak, and by our words we will either be justified or condemned.

---

[42] John Calvin, *Commentaries on the Epistles of Paul: Titus* (Baker Books, 1981), translated from Latin by William Pringle, p. 311. The Pastor of Geneva was commenting on Titus 2:3, "The aged women likewise [teach], that they be in behavior as becometh holiness, not false accusers ..." That slander and gossip is unfortunately a common sin among women, Calvin boldly points out, making James chapter 3 very key to a woman's sanctification, as it deals with the dangers of the tongue.

> A good man out of the good treasure of his heart brings forth good things, and an evil man out of the evil treasure brings forth evil things. But I say to you that for every idle word men may speak, they will give account of it in the day of judgment. For by your words you will be justified, and by your words you will be condemned. (Matthew 12:35-37)[43]

This truth impels us to see how great our responsibility is to keep our tongue under control. We are going to see the seriousness and gravity of an untamed tongue in the first twelve verses of James chapter 3. In fact, there is so much material to cover here that it will take two chapters to deal with this important topic. In this chapter, we will study the following topics: The inability to control our tongue (vv 1-4) and the iniquities of our tongue (vv 5-8). In the next chapter we will focus on the inconsistencies of our tongue (v 9-12).

> My brethren, let not many of you become teachers, knowing that we shall receive a stricter judgment. ²For we all stumble in many things. If anyone does not stumble in word, he is a perfect man, able also to bridle the whole body. ³Indeed, we put bits in horses' mouths that they may obey us, and we turn their whole body. ⁴Look also at ships; although they are so large and are driven by fierce winds, they are turned by a very small rudder wherever the pilot desires. ⁵Even so the tongue is a little member and boasts great things. See how great a forest a little fire kindles! ⁶And the tongue is a fire, a world of iniquity. The tongue is so set among our members that it defiles the whole body, and it is set on fire by hell. (James 3:1-6)

---

[43] Notice there will be some kind of accounting for both those who speak "good things" and those who speak "evil things," as the Lord used the generic term "man." Both lost and saved will give account for their idle words.

The Inability to Control Our Tongue

James 3:1. My brethren, let not many of you become teachers

Again, the introductory words are "My brethren." Take notice: the warning here is not to heretical teachers who need to be removed, but to *the brethren*. And the warning is that "not many of them should become teachers." The teaching ministry was highly esteemed in the early church. In fact the word *rabbi* means great one. To fear the rabbi or the teacher was equated with the fear of God. The duty to help a rabbi even exceeded the duty to help one's parents, so to be a rabbi, a teacher, meant to have power, prestige, and position. Due to these circumstances, many were selfishly seizing the opportunity to teach even though they were not qualified. According to the Apostle Paul, many were standing in the church service, which was much more informal than ours today, and spontaneously spouting off things they should not have been (1 Corinthians 14). As it is written in Ecclesiastes 1:9, "there is nothing new under the sun"—not even today. In our contemporary churches, we will put almost anyone in the position of teacher—just give us a warm body. But do we ever ask if they are spiritually qualified? Can they teach? Is that one of the gifts that God has given them? Are their lives consistent with what they teach? Since the teacher's work is administered primarily through the use of the tongue, to be in control of it is crucial. James is seeking to restrain teachers who were unqualified and yet were rushing into the office of teacher. This is why he warned, "Let not many of you become teachers." Why not, we ask?

James 3:1. Knowing that we shall receive a stricter judgment

Because, James says, we know that teachers shall receive "a

stricter judgment."[44] By using the word *we*, James includes himself among those whom he is warning. I hope that all of us who are teachers will pay special attention to this verse. It should put the fear of God in us and be the key in motivating each of us to bridle our tongue. Some who are teachers become unworthy, unwanted, because of pride or not practicing what they teach.

The future tense *shall receive* indicates when we as teachers will stand before the judgment seat of Christ and be judged according to the impact of our lives. Remember what James' half-brother warned?

> Not everyone who says to Me, 'Lord, Lord,' shall enter the kingdom of heaven, but he who does the will of My Father in heaven. Many will say to Me in that day, 'Lord, Lord, have we not prophesied in Your name, cast out demons in Your name, and done many wonders in Your name?' And then I will declare to them, 'I never knew you; depart from Me, you who practice lawlessness!' (Matthew 7:21-23)

Now when James says that teachers shall receive the stricter judgment, what does he mean by that? *Stricter judgment* implies degrees of treatment at the judgment seat, due to unfaithfully fulfilling the duties of the work that they rashly assumed. Those who undertake the office of teacher will be held strictly accountable for the way they use their position. I imagine this will include how they live, what they teach, and if they have taught the truth and not error. Why? Because we deliver our words with the intention of directing the lives of those who hear them. We must be attentive to the significance of the Christian teacher's task. It is a disgrace to Christ and a sacrilege to His name to be a teacher who is unprepared or does not live a godly life. I know many teachers who haphazardly prepare a message on Saturday night while watching television and many who do not practice what they teach! Jesus expressed it this way: "For everyone to whom much is given, from him much will be required; and to whom much has been committed, of him they will ask the more" (Luke 12:48).

---

[44] James has already used the word *judgment* in James 2:12-13: "So speak and so do as those who will be judged by the law of liberty. For *judgment* is without mercy to the one who has shown no mercy. Mercy triumphs over *judgment*" (emphasis mine).

It is reported that when the Scottish reformer John Knox was called to preach, he shed many tears and withdrew to the privacy of his room. He was grieved and greatly troubled at the prospect of such an awesome responsibility. He knew that God holds teachers of the Word accountable for what they say. John Calvin once stated that it would have been better for him to fall and break his neck while climbing to the pulpit than to preach the truth without first applying it to his own life. If anyone is ever offended by my teaching, I pray it will be because of the convicting power of God's Word and not because of something I have said in an unguarded moment, or because my life doesn't reflect what I teach. But just in case you think you're off the hook because you are not a "teacher," well hold on, because now James says:

James 3:2. For we all stumble in many things

At one time or another we have all said things that did not bring glory to our Lord. That we all stumble is a universal fact; all humans stumble. *Stumble* here is a moral lapse. It portrays the picture of a foot striking against some obstacle so as to cause the individual to trip or stumble. It is some failure that arrests the forward progress of our daily walk; but after recovering, we continue walking. The present tense indicates that such experiences of stumbling occur repeatedly in life. Indeed they do. In fact, as you read this and review your day, you probably recall saying something that you should not have said, for we all stumble in many things! James uses the pronoun *we* again, being certain to include himself with this admonition. He elaborates further.

James 3:2. If anyone does not stumble in word

If anyone does not stumble "in word" is not referring to teaching but to our speech in general. At this point, James moves from the specific to the general. Why does James begin his discourse with the tongue, and not the hands, the eyes, or the feet? Because it is with our words that we express what occupies our hearts and minds. Worth repeating are Jesus' words: "Out of the abundance of the heart the mouth speaks" (Matthew 12:34). When you think about it, our tongues are apt to go places that our feet, hands, and eyes would never take us. What are some ways in which we offend and stumble with our mouth?

Gossip, flattery, lying, hurtful joking, sexual overtones, profanity, harsh or angry words, negative speech, criticism, self-boasting, and demeaning others all come to mind. Saying too much can be our downfall, for as it is written: "In the multitude of words sin is not lacking, but he who restrains his lips is wise" (Proverbs 10:19). Perhaps some of us would benefit by remembering that if we can't improve on the silence, then don't break it!

Other ways we stumble with our mouths are by vocalizing praises to God that are not from our heart. Exaggerations such as "I never watch TV," when you do, or "I always go to bed at 9:00," when you don't, cause us to stumble. Slang that is not Christ-like is another form of unwholesome speech; words like *screwed up*, *gee whiz*, *golly*, *gosh*, which are mixed oaths. If you look up those words in the dictionary, you may be convicted to eliminate them from your vocabulary. For example, the etymology for the interjection *gee* is an abbreviated euphemism for *Jesus* and is defined as "an introductory expletive for emphasis and sometimes to express surprise or enthusiasm."[45] Did you know that every time you utter the word *gee* that you are disrespectfully invoking the name of our Lord and Savior Jesus Christ? When I was growing up my parents washed my mouth out with soap for saying those types of words. That left such an impression on me that I washed out my children's mouths, too, which they still remember! Some of us need to not only wash out our mouths, but our hearts, too, for out of the abundance of the heart the mouth speaks!

---

[45] *Webster's Third New World Dictionary* (Springfield, Mass.: Merriam-Webster, 2002), p. 943.

James 3:2. He is a perfect man, able also to bridle the whole body

Now if you are perfect and don't offend in any of these areas, then James says, "you are a perfect man, able also to bridle the whole body." *Perfect* in the Greek was used for animals that were full grown, and so it describes a Christian who has reached a maturity of character. This person is mature and has a ripeness and richness of knowledge and character. This person has reached the goal, not his own but God's. Not only is this person mature, but is able also "to bridle the whole body." This means that a Christian controls her whole body as a man controls a horse by the bridle. *To bridle* here in the Greek means to lead as with a bridle; it doesn't refer to the actual bridling of the horse, but the leading of the horse to the desired destination with the help of the bridle. Thus James is saying that if you can control your tongue, then you are able to bridle your whole body. If you can control your speech, then you can control any passion of your body! (Now there's a diet plan that's better than Weight Watchers® or Jenny Craig®. Maybe we could package and sell the James 3 diet!)

"Able" here means strong, powerful, an inner divine enabling. It is the divine nature that tells us to stop. It is the presence of mind in the person who stops and thinks: "Would Christ say that?" And if Christ wouldn't say that, then the *perfect* woman, the mature woman, does not say it either! James now gives us two powerful illustrations: The horse without a bit and a ship without a rudder.

James 3:3. Indeed, we put bits in horses' mouths that they may obey us, and we turn their whole body.

Although the horse was a well-known animal to James' readers, it was not an animal owned by the average man. In New Testament times, horses were primarily used for military purposes, so James' reader would most likely have thought of a prancing warhorse and not the humble plow horse. And it was actually the prancing warhorse that needed bridling the most! So James says, "Indeed, we put bits in horses' mouths." Average horses weigh between one to two thousand pounds, and yet they can be controlled with a bit that weighs only two pounds. The point is that when we put bits in horses' mouths we can make them go to the right or the left, and we can move their whole body and take them where we want to go.

Notice that the horse does not bridle itself, but he has to be bridled by a man. When it comes to humankind, it is God who fits us with a bridle and leads us in the right path. We must have the power from someone greater to bridle us, to lead us. It is that inner ability that James mentioned in verse 2. We cannot control our tongues on our own, even though we must do our part. When God does bridle us, He does not expect us to act like a horse that is only obedient because it is being coerced, but rather, He wants us to see the bridle as there for our benefit and to be obedient because we love God. No wonder David says, "Set a guard, O Lord, over my mouth; Keep watch over the door of my lips" (Psalm 141:3).

James then tells us why we put bits in horses' mouths, "so that they will obey us." This indicates that the aim in bridling the horse is to secure the obedience of the whole horse, not just the mouth!

When bits are securely inserted into the horses' mouths, then we are able to "turn their whole body." *Turn* means we can change the whole direction of. If we bridle our tongue, we can change the direction of our life. So then, two goals in controlling our tongue should be obedience to God and a change of direction for our whole life. An uncontrolled tongue leads to sin, guilt, and shame. A controlled tongue leads to peace, power and victory.

James 3:4. Look also at ships: although they are so large and are driven by fierce winds

Now James compares the tongue to a great ship, some of which were large in those days. We know how large they were from Acts 27:37 where it states that the ship in which Paul was shipwrecked carried 276 passengers, in addition to the cargo. James writes, "Look also at ships, although they are so large and driven by fierce winds ..." These large ships were subject to the fierce winds of the sea that could cause them to sail out of control and so it is with our tongues. The fierce winds of circumstance can batter us about and cause us to lose control of our speech. Once that process gets started, many times it can snowball and get out of control. No matter how bridled we think our tongue is, it can be moved by the fierce circumstances of life.

James 3:4. They are turned by a very small rudder wherever the pilot desires.

Even though these ships are so large, they are "turned by a very small rudder, wherever the pilot desires." The ancient rudder or helm was made in the shape of an oar and was connected to the ship's stern. It was very small when compared to the size of the ship—about as small as the tongue is compared to the body. But James says the pilot can turn the ship around with the helm, the little rudder. The ship is under the pilot's control. The word here for pilot is a noun, which means to guide straight. In other words, we can commit our tongues to the One who can guide us straight. As humans, we are like ships carrying heavy loads and burdens while encountering fierce circumstances. But if we have a good rudder, a good tongue, we can go through each difficultly blameless, without losing control. Our tongues will not help us, however, unless they are committed entirely to Jesus Christ. That James said both the horse and the ship are "turned" is significant. He uses the word *turn* in verse 3 and repeats it in verse 4. With both objects, there is a change of direction. In other words, there is repentance—first you are going one way, and then you turn around and go another. Just as the bit and the rudder are small objects relative to the size of the horse and the ship, so is our tongue small relative to the size of our body.

The Iniquities of Our Tongue

James 3:5. Even so the tongue is a little member and boasts great things.

Did you know the average tongue is only 3 inches long and one and a half inches wide, even though my husband claims I have the biggest tongue he has ever seen! How little that is compared to our bodies, which are five to six feet tall and weight one hundred to two hundred pounds. The tongue is petite, but powerful. It is one of the smallest members of our body, but it is the largest troublemaker by far. James says, it "boasts great things"! The tongue seems to be conscious of its power and influence and boasts largely of what it can do. David says, "My soul shall make its boast in the Lord" (Psalm 34:2). We need to let our tongues talk about the greatness of our God and not the greatness of ourselves.

James 3:5. See how great a forest a little fire kindles

James' readers would recognize this terminology, since during the long dry weather the terrain of Palestine was known to produce forest fires. Most of us know about the great Chicago fire in 1871. Tradition holds that it was started by a cow that kicked over a lantern in a barn. The destruction was placed at two million dollars. Many have seen the damage caused from a careless cigarette thrown from a car, or from a campfire that has been left to smolder, or from a forest fire that was intentionally set. And so there is potential for just as much destruction from a word spoken by the tongue. Our uncontrolled tongues can set our neighborhood on fire, our church on fire, our marriage on fire, and send our home up in flames. You can ruin someone's entire life by the power of your tongue. Did you know that ten minutes of unbridled temper can waste enough strength to do wholesome work for half a day? I think some of us need to keep our mouths shut and instead use that energy to clean our homes. Our physical energy is a gift from God—what a sin to waste it on idle words.

The Danger of the Tongue!

It is said that a physician can tell a lot about your physical health by looking at your tongue. So it is with our spiritual Physician. He can tell a lot about our spiritual well being by listening to what our tongues are saying. Just as our earthly physician tells us to stick out our tongue and say "ah" so that he can see what is wrong or right with our physical body, so our Heavenly Physician tells us to stick out our spiritual tongue and say "ah" so that He can tell what is right or wrong about our Spiritual body. I am afraid that sometimes what our Lord sees is an "open grave, deceptive, poisonous like a snake and full of cursing and bitterness," as Paul wrote in Romans 3:13-14. Jesus says our mouth speaks what is in our heart (Matthew 12:34), which are evil thoughts, murders, adulteries, fornication, thefts, slanders, blasphemies, covetousness, wickedness, lewdnesses, pride, and foolishness—all of these things come from within and defile a man. All three of the examples that James gives—the horse, the ship, and the tongue—are destroyed when left to themselves without someone to control them. The ship needs a pilot, the horse needs a rider, and the tongue needs a Savior. Just in case we haven't gotten the message, James goes on to say:

James 3:6. And the tongue is a fire, a world of iniquity.

To speak of the tongue as *a fire* was to use an Old Testament concept: "An ungodly man digs up evil, and it is on his lips like a burning fire" (Proverbs 16:27). James uses fire as a metaphor to describe the tongue's destructive nature. If left uncontrolled, the tongue is deadly like fire. It is not only a fire, but James says it is a "world of iniquity." *World* here is viewed as this present world system. The tongue is a system of iniquity, a system of evil. This present world system is in opposition to God and responsive to Satan. James is saying that the tongue is unjust and unrighteous in character. Fallen man shows himself to be a part of this evil world system by using his tongue to express the evils that are in his mind. The good and sanctified tongue will condemn unrighteousness, but the evil tongue will compliment it, flatter it, and make it appear righteous.

James 3:6. The tongue is so set among our members that it defiles the whole body

James says: "The tongue is so set among our members"; no other member of our body has comparable power and range of influence for evil. It can give utterance to every evil thought and motive and put every evil deed into words. James also says that our tongue "defiles the whole body." This means it stains or pollutes the whole body like a moral cancer. And like physical cancer, the tongue can influence all the members of the body and defile all its actions. It is interesting that James says a bridled tongue controls the whole body, and yet an unbridled tongue defiles the whole body. An unbridled tongue will disable us from controlling our passions, and a filthy tongue makes for a filthy person. Jesus said that it is not what goes into a man that defiles him, but that which comes out of the man defiles him.

> So He said to them, "Are you thus without understanding also? Do you not perceive that whatever enters a man from outside cannot defile him, because it does not enter his heart but his stomach, and is eliminated, thus purifying all foods?" And He said, "What comes out of a man, that defiles a man. For from within, out of the heart of men, proceed evil thoughts, adulteries, fornications, murders, thefts, covetousness, wickedness, deceit, lewdness, an evil eye, blasphemy, pride, foolishness. All these evil things come from within and defile a man." (Mark 7:18-23)

James 3:6. And sets on fire the course of nature; and it is set on fire by hell.

Not only that, but the tongue can set on fire the "course of nature." What does that mean? The Greek here, *wheel of nature*, is life being represented as a wheel that is set in motion at birth and continues rolling until death. Life is presented as a turning thing, a wheel. For a person to go along, constantly making evil use of her tongue, thinking that no one will stop her, that nothing will ever bother her, she is a fool. She does not stop to think that her tongue

The Danger of the Tongue!

affects everything she touches. She does not realize that her wheel of life may catch fire, and then she will have to stop and consider the consequences of her evil tongue. The more it burns, the faster it spins, until the whole wheel erupts in a blaze, spitting fire in all directions. But the tongue is only a fuse; the source of the deadly fire is hell.

"It is set on fire by hell." The term for hell here is *gehenna*, which was known by the Jews as a literal place where the Jews offered their children to Molech. It served as a receptacle of all sorts of putrefying matter and defiled the holy city, and so became symbolic for the place of everlasting punishment. It burned perpetually. Burning flesh and other rubbish, the fire never went out. *Gehenna*, hell, is represented as a place where the fires continually burn. The idea here is that which causes the tongue to do so much evil derives its origin from hell. Nothing could better characterize much of what the tongue does than to say that it has its origin in hell and possesses the spirit which reigns there. The word became almost synonymous with Satan Himself. As Jesus says in John 8:44 "You are of your father the devil ... when he speaks a lie, he speaks from his own, for he is a liar, and the father of it." We also know from Genesis 3:1 that Satan is behind all evil speech. All evil talk has its beginning in hell and will cause the whole body to burn in hell. The fire that we start with our tongues has been borrowed from hell, and it could lead us there if left uncontrolled. In Matthew 5:29-30, Jesus says that it would be better that one of your members be cut off than for your whole body to be cast into hell. Perhaps some of us would be wise to cut out our tongue.

Summary

Strong words come from this little book, and it should cause us all to think twice before using our tongues for evil purposes. (And we aren't finished yet. We have one more chapter on this important subject.) The tongue is dangerous when left uncontrolled. The test of how we control our tongue is another test to see if we are in the faith. That is why James says in verse three that a controlled tongue is a mark of a mature man, one whose faith is genuine. If your speech is no better today than it was a year ago, something is amiss. James has already told us in James 1:26 that if anyone among us seems to be religious, yet does not bridle his tongue, then his religion is useless. It is dead. A sign of Christian maturity is not simply how much of the Bible you know, or how many sermons you have heard, or how many theology books you have read, or even how many years you have been saved. A sign of Christian maturity is controlling the tongue and keeping it from complaining, faultfinding, backbiting, slandering, gossiping, lying, exaggerating and cursing.

It is said that in an old English churchyard is the epitaph of a woman who died on May 24th proclaiming: Beneath this stone, a lump of clay, lies Arabella Young, Who, on the Twenty-fourth of May, began to hold her tongue! Is that what would be inscribed on your tombstone if you should die today? It is said that we speak eighteen to twenty thousand words a day and spend twenty percent of our life talking. In one year's time that is sixty-six 800-page books that could have been written by your words! Have you stopped lately to examine what you are saying with your eighteen- to twenty-thousand words each day? But perhaps a more important question is: Will you be justified by those eighteen- to twenty-thousand words on that day, or will you be condemned?

Questions to Consider
"The Danger of the Tongue!"
James 3:1-6

1. Read James 3:1-6. (a) According to James, where does ungodly speech come from? (b) What words does James use to describe our speech?

2. Memorize James 3:6.

3. Read Proverbs 10:11, 19; 13:3; 15:1; 16:24, 27; 17:28; 29:20; and 31:26 making note of what each verse teaches about good speech and/or evil speech.

4. Read Acts 5:1-11. (a) How do you know that Ananias and Sapphira did not bridle their tongues? (b) What was the bigger issue here? (c) What principle(s) can we as wives glean?

5. Cite some biblical examples where misuse of the tongue resulted in defilement of the whole body (besides Ananias and Sapphira).

6. Proverbs 31:26 says this about the virtuous woman: "She opens her mouth with wisdom, and on her tongue is the law of kindness." (a) In what ways does this characterize the tone you set in your home? (b) Can you recall some examples where misuse of your tongue resulted in defilement of the whole body?

7. Do any of these forms of speech need to be "bridled" in your life? Gossip? Flattery? Lying? Hurtful joking? Sexual overtones? Profanity? Harsh, angry words? Negative speech? Criticism? Boasting of self? Putting others down? Saying too much? Praises to God (verbal or sung) that are not sincere? Extremes? Exaggerations? Un-Christ-like slang (gee-whiz, golly, gosh, darn, screwed-up, etc.)? Any others?

8. If you could replay the conversation around your dinner table last night, what would your talk reveal about you?

9. Ask the Lord to teach you to guard your tongue and to speak only what is edifying to others. (Perhaps use Psalm 19:14, Psalm 141:3, or Psalm 120:2 as your prayer request.)

14

Gaining Victory Over the Tongue!

James 3:7-12

Picture with me the following scenario: A large family was sitting around the table for breakfast one morning. As was customary, the father returned thanks, blessing God for the food. Immediately afterward, however, as was his bad habit, he begins to grumble about hard times, the poor quality of the food, the way it was cooked, and much more. His little daughter interrupted him and said, "Father, do you suppose God heard what you said a little while ago?"

"Certainly," replied the father with the confident air of an instructor.

"And did He hear what you said about the bacon and the coffee?"

"Of course," the father replied but not as confidently as before. And then his little girl asked him again, "Then, Father, which did God believe?"

Perhaps the above scenario describes what goes on in some Christian homes. We speak well of God in prayer and bless His name, only to lift our heads and complain about what we don't have. Or we begin to criticize or maybe even curse others. We will see a terrible inconsistency in this chapter. In the last chapter, we put one foot in the door of this important passage about our tongues. We learned of the inability to control our tongues in verses 1-4 and the iniquities of our tongue in verses 5-6. James wrote:

For every kind of beast and bird, of reptile and creature of the sea, is tamed and has been tamed by mankind. ⁸But no man can tame the tongue. It is an unruly evil, full of deadly poison. ⁹With it we bless our God and Father, and with it we curse men, who have been made in the similitude of God. ¹⁰Out of the same mouth proceed blessing and cursing. My brethren, these things ought not to be so. ¹¹Does a spring send forth fresh water and bitter from the same opening? ¹²Can a fig tree, my brethren, bear olives, or a grapevine bear figs? Thus no spring can yield both salt water and fresh. (James 3:7-12)

Now let's put the other foot in the door and complete the passages about the iniquities of the tongue in verses 7-8 before going on to the inconsistencies of our tongue in verses 9-12.

Iniquities of Our Tongue

James 3:7. For every kind of beast and bird, of reptile and creature of the sea, is tamed and has been tamed by mankind.

One danger of the tongue is its inability to be brought under control by men, in contrast to men who are able to control animals. "For" is the Greek word *gar* that introduces a fresh fact as a further proof or explanation of what James previously said in verses 1-6 regarding our tongue. James writes "For every kind of beast and bird, of reptile and creature of the sea," in order to declare that all animals are included under one of these categories. James then says that every animal in each one of these categories is "tamed and has been tamed by mankind." James is saying that it is possible for man to tame any animal. Now the word *tame* does not mean to domesticate, but rather to subdue or control. We know from Genesis 1:26 that man was given dominion over the fish of the sea, over the fowl of the air, and over every living thing that moved upon the earth. God gave us that power to subdue and control these animals. We have not been able to make pets out of all animals—and believe me there are some I wouldn't want for pets, even though my husband still thinks a snake would make a good pet—but we are able to capture and otherwise control any animal we wish. Even the wildest animals can be brought under man's control in the zoo. To my knowledge I have never seen an animal capture a man and put him in the zoo. Man's power in taming some of these wild beasts has been remarkable, as we often witness at the zoo and the circus. James goes on to say in verse 8, even though man has a remarkable ability to subdue animals, he cannot tame the tongue.

James 3:8. But no man can tame the tongue. It is an unruly evil, full of deadly poison.

No man can tame the tongue—only God can. This does not mean that we are always out of control with our tongues, but it does mean that without God's help we cannot permanently master our tongue. Not even the disciples had their tongues perfectly tamed. Think about the time Peter said to Jesus: "Even if I have to die with You, I will not deny You" (Matthew 26:35). And then used the very same tongue to deny Jesus with curses and swearing, saying "I do not know the Man!" (Matthew 26:74). Think of the Apostle John who said, "Beloved, let us love one another" (1 John 4:7), and with that same tongue he wanted to call down fire from heaven to blast a Samaritan village out of existence (Luke 9:54). No man can tame the tongue. The supernatural power of God is required to subdue it, the divine inner enabling that James mentioned in verse 2. James goes on to give us another description of our tongue.

In the first place, he says it is "an unruly evil." This means it is an evil without restraint. *Unruly* means restless and characterizes the tongue as being fickle and inconsistent. It cannot be trusted to stay submissively in its proper place. Always liable to break out in evil, the tongue is never at rest. *Evil* means the tongue is degraded in character and prone to be injurious. In the context here it forms the picture of a caged animal pacing back and forth seeking the opportunity to escape. We all have probably seen that very thing when visiting the zoo or going to the circus. That is the picture being conveyed of our tongue. It is possible to secure the animal so he cannot get out, but not so with the tongue. (Perhaps some of us need to use duct tape to secure our mouths!)

James gives a second description of our tongue. He says it is "full of deadly poison." One of the pictures conveyed here is that of a venomous snake as it prepares to strike.[46] The word *poison* is translated as an arrow indicating the human tongue has the ability to shoot arrows at others. Observe that James does not say our tongues are *half* full of poison, but full of poison. When I think of something that is full, I think of something that doesn't have room for anything else to go in it. What a sad commentary on our tongues! If we have committed our hearts to Christ, then that sack of poison contained in the tongue should be transformed into a blessing, not only for ourselves, but also for the benefit of others.

Most of us would never think of intentionally putting poison in our own mouth, and yet we will let poisonous, thoughtless words, emanate from it! We would never serve poisonous food at a meal, and yet we would contaminate our meals with gossip about neighbors, family, and church members. Jesus says, *"All things, whatsoever ye would that men should do to you, do ye even so to them"* (Matthew 7:12 KJV, emphasis mine). This would certainly include the things we say. Are you saying things about others that you would like them to say about you, at home, at church, to your children, your husband, and even your best friend? Do we stop and realize that God is present right beside us listening to every word we say? From Psalm 139, we know that the Psalmist says, "Lord, you know everything about me. You know when I sit or stand, and even when far away you know my every thought. Every moment you know where I am. *You know what I am going to say before I*

---

[46] Other passages in the OT previously used the metaphor of a venomous snake, from which James as a Jew would be well familiar: e.g., Psalm 58:3-5, "The wicked are estranged from the womb; they go astray as soon as they are born, speaking lies. Their poison is like the poison of a serpent; they are like the deaf cobra that stops its ear, which will not heed the voice of charmers, charming ever so skillfully." Psalm 140:1-3, "Deliver me, O LORD, from evil men; preserve me from violent men, who plan evil things in their hearts; they continually gather together for war. They sharpen their tongues like a serpent; the poison of asps is under their lips." Romans 3:13-14, "Their throat is an open tomb; with their tongues they have practiced deceit; the poison of asps is under their lips; whose mouth is full of cursing and bitterness."

even say it" (Emphasis mine). Do we think about that? The Lord is right there with us! I think we would be wise to ask ourselves this question before speaking: "Would I say this if Jesus Christ were standing right here in His earthly form?" Well, I must tell you, He *is* there with you!

In the last chapter, we mentioned some of the ungodly ways in which we use our tongue. At this point, I want to give you four definitions of inappropriate speech of which women are especially prone, even though sometimes we may be unaware that our speech falls in that category. The first one is gossip. What is gossip? Gossip is idle talk, and it is not always the truth about other people. "Did you know that Sally's father abused her?" "Did you hear about Bill and his tenth car accident?"

The second category of speech that I think women are guilty of is flattery. Flattery is praising too much or beyond the truth; it is to praise insincerely. "I just love being with you," when you don't, or "I sure missed you!" when you didn't. The connection between gossip and flattery is this: gossip is saying behind a person's back what you never say to her face; flattery is saying to a person's face what you would never say behind her back.

The third form of ungodly speech to which women fall prey is criticism. Criticism is unfavorable remarks or judgments; it is finding fault. A good example of this is when Moses sent forth the spies to observe the land that God gave to the nation of Israel, and they brought back an unfavorable report causing the whole community to grumble (Numbers 13:32). Another example is when Miriam and Aaron criticized Moses for marrying an Ethiopian woman (Numbers 12:1). A critical person rarely says anything good about anyone or anything.

The fourth and last area of sinful speech—and this list is not exhaustive—is slander. Slander is a false report meant to do harm to the good name and reputation of another. Perhaps a good question to ask yourself before saying anything about anyone is this: "Would I say this if the person were standing here?" If you wouldn't, then what you have to say should probably not be said. James continues in verses 9-12 to describe the inconsistencies, the fickle nature, of our tongues.

The Inconsistencies of Our Tongue

James 3:9. With it we bless our God and Father, and with it we curse men

James uses the pronoun *we* here to include himself. James himself was not perfect in this area, as he has already stated in verse two—for *we* all stumble in many things. James says we "bless our God and Father" and "curse men" out of the same mouth. *Bless* means to speak well of. Whenever the Jew spoke God's name, it was customary to add, "Blessed is He." In fact, it is said that devout Jews would not even step on a piece of scrap paper that had fallen in the street, because it might have God's name written on it. Evidently James had observed this contradiction in the Jewish Christians who would use this term, "Blessed is He," and then would actually curse someone who had angered them! James knew that this was a shameful sin! As modern-day Christians, we also speak well of God, don't we? We praise and celebrate his name and rarely speak evil of Him. We sing about Him, we talk about Him, and we bless Him. And yet out of the same mouth that we use to bless God comes forth cursing on our fellow man.

Curse here means to call down curses upon someone—not profane them—but call down a curse in order that one might experience vengeance. In order to call down curses, a person must think himself above those whom he curses. God abhors this double standard. Paraphrasing Paul, he said, "Don't think of yourself more highly than you should, but think soberly" (Romans 12:3). Paul also said, "In lowliness of mind let each esteem others better than himself. Let each of you look out not only for his own interests, but also for the interests of others" (Philippians 2:3-4). Are we looking out for the interest of others when we call down curses upon them? I think not!

James 3:9. Who have been made in the similitude of God

James says we curse those who "have been made in the similitude of God." Man is made in the similitude or likeness of God. We are all patterned after His likeness. Genesis 1:27 speaks of this: "So God created man in His own image; in the image of God He created him; male and female He created them." This means we possess the attributes of reason, will, and conscience, the ability to know and serve God, and the capacity to be conformed to God's moral and spiritual likeness. To curse a man is to insult the God whose likeness he bears. The idea here is when looking up to God, we recognize His superiority and bless Him, but, when we look down upon our fellow men and women, we have no respect for them, we do not bless them, and we even curse them. And when we curse them, we curse God's creation. James continues characterizing the mouth of men and women.

James 3:10. Out of the same mouth proceed blessing and cursing

"Out of the same mouth" is the setup for this fatal inconsistency. The praise to God loses its noble character and becomes tainted with the bitterness of the cursing towards others. No man can acceptably praise and bless God while feeling bitter hatred toward his fellow man who bears God's image. The Apostle John says, "If someone says, 'I love God,' and hates his brother, he is a liar; for he who does not love his brother whom he has seen, how can he love God whom he has not seen?" (1 John 4:20). You can't—it is impossible.

James 3:10. My brethren, these things ought not to be so.

By using the word *brethren,* James delivers this rebuke, like the others, with gentleness and affection. James is grieved with their inconsistencies. In other words, he is saying, "It's not right!" Of what advantage is cursing someone? It will not affect God in his judgment towards that person, it will not profit the man being cursed, and it will do the one cursing no good, except to bring judgment on him. The tongue that blesses God and the Father and curses men made in God's image is in trouble. On Sunday mornings how easy it is to sing, "O, for a thousand tongues to sing, my great Redeemer's praise," and then get in the car and fight all the way home or play "roast the preacher." How easy it is to spend time with Christian friends talking about things of the Lord, but when driving home curse the driver in the other car. Or come to a Ladies' Bible Study, and then gossip to your friend or family member. Or spend time in the morning with God in prayer and in His word, and then come out of your prayer closet and get angry with your husband or kids, or get on the phone and say things to others you shouldn't be saying! My sisters, these things ought not to be so.

A very sobering passage to consider is Psalm 50:16-23. The Psalmist here is rebuking the nation's hypocritical lifestyle. They recited God's laws and spoke of His covenant as their profession of faith (v 16). While appearing to be so righteous, they tolerated and participated in theft, adultery, and slander. They thought that by God's silence everything was okay. But the Psalmist says something different:

> Now consider this, you who forget God, lest I tear you in pieces, and there be none to deliver: Whoever offers praise glorifies Me; and to him who orders his conduct aright I will show the salvation of God. (Psalm 50:22-23)

The point here is that an uncontrolled tongue is a very serious matter in the sight of God. You might be reading this right now and thinking to yourself, "I just can't control myself." Oh? I remember an illustration Jay Adams once gave at a seminar I attended, and I will probably never forget it. Picture this: You and your husband are having a heated argument, and the phone rings. It is your pastor. "Hello? Yes, just fine, thanks." You can control your tongue, because you just did. The fact is, we choose not to. We choose to find pleasure in our sin.

To say, "I can't" should never be in the Christian's vocabulary. We can, we just won't! Maybe you like getting angry, maybe you like putting others down to make yourself feel good. I have seen—and I know you have too—those who have ruined people's good reputations with the power of the tongue. Friendships have been broken and destroyed because of the tongue; couples have divorced because of the tongue. Tragedies have altered peoples lives that otherwise could have been prevented if someone had only bridled her speech. Proverbs 18:21 puts it well: "Death and life are in the power of the tongue." As he so often does in this epistle, James again turns to the realm of nature to further illustrate this intolerable inconsistency.

James 3:11. Does a spring send forth fresh water and bitter from the same opening?

The question asked here calls for a negative answer. James uses the image of a fountain or spring as an analogy to the human heart. These fountains that James observed were not man made, but rather natural gushes of water from the mountain slopes. The people in James' day did not have the convenience of air-conditioned homes or cars as do we, and so these fountains of cool water were a great comfort to the traveler in the heat. A traveler would surely be surprised, if after taking a few sips of the sweet mountain water, it would suddenly turn bitter and be found undrinkable. James does not deny that there may be fountains of bitter water, but not out of the same opening in the mountain. Both kinds of springs exist, but never do both kinds of water flow from the same opening. Such things do not occur in nature and should not occur in man. If God meant it to be, He would have made two mouths, one for blessing God and one for cursing men. Bitter speech coming from our mouths, which should be sweet, is a tragedy indeed. James now asks a second question in verse 12, which also calls for a negative answer.

James 3:12. Can a fig tree, my brethren, bear

olives, or a grapevine bear figs?

Again, James uses that tender term "my brethren" to show affectionate concern while driving home this point to them. By using this term, he also wishes to remain on good terms with them. From the plant kingdom, James mentions three of the most common agricultural products native to his part of the world: The fig tree, the olive tree, and the grapevine. All three were used at one time or another to describe the Jewish nation. The fig tree was a common plant in Bible times and is first mentioned in Genesis 3:7 where Adam and Eve used fig leaves to make clothes for themselves. It was often used to represent the Jewish nation (Deuteronomy 8:8; Numbers 13:23; Hosea 9:10; and Joel 1:7).

The olive is an ancient tree, used in ancient times for medicinal therapy, religious ceremony, and as fuel for lamps. The wood from this tree was also used to carve cherubim for the temple doors and posts. Its first mention in the Bible is Genesis 8:11, and we see it used in Romans 11 to describe the blessings given to the Jewish people.

The grapevine was also used for a symbol of the nation and is used in Isaiah 5:1-7 to represent God's care for His people. Each of these well-known plants reproduced according to its own nature. Fig trees did not bear olives, nor did grapevines produce figs. Although today scientists and farmers are crossbreeding many plants and flowers and even food, that technology was not available in James' day! By now many of us have seen brociflower. But readers, broccoli is still broccoli, and cauliflower is still cauliflower!

James 3:12. Thus no spring yields both salt water and fresh.

James ends this passage by saying "no spring yields both salt water and fresh." Likewise, a fresh heart cannot produce bitter speech. Your speech reveals who you truly are, and true believers are identified by their speech! Out of our heart, our mouth speaks (Matthew 12:34, Luke 6:45). It is striking that James does not explicitly draw conclusions from these illustrations, but the examples so obviously condemn man's inconsistency that none is needed. These illustrations—the two fountains and the three plants—brilliantly

Gaining Victory Over the Tongue!

manifest the double-mindedness of blessing and cursing proceeding from the same mouth. No inconsistencies are found in these illustrations, and none should exist with our tongue.

If you had two bank accounts and in one you deposited ten dollars for every kind word you said and in the other one you deposited only five dollars for every unkind word, which account would have the most money, the kind account or the unkind account? That is something to think about. How easily we slip with our tongues. In fact, the very day I was studying this passage, a friend of mine shared with me how she had injured a family member with words that had been carelessly and unintentionally spoken, and we discussed how often we do that. I know many of us have great difficulty in this area, and James has already stated in the second verse of chapter 3 that to never stumble or offend in word is to be perfect. I know it is the desire of many of us to gain control in this area.

So as we complete these two lessons on controlling our speech, I want to give you three simple steps to help you gain victory over your tongue.

1. Admit your difficulty to God. Admission of any sin is always the first step in gaining victory. Proverbs 28:13 says, "He who covers his sins will not prosper, but whoever confesses and forsakes them will have mercy." Confess the sin of your speech. When we see our speech in light of God's omnipresence, then it should bring us to our knees in confession of our sins and dependence upon Him.

2. Pray! There must be an ongoing prayerfulness regarding our tongues—regular, daily, detailed prayer. "Keep my tongue from evil O God! Set a guard over my mouth!" One woman in our church has this verse by her telephone, which might be good for all of us to use: "You shall not go about as a talebearer among your people" (Leviticus 19:16).

3. Resolve to discipline yourself regarding the use of your tongue. You might say, "How do I do that?" Determine not to criticize, not to receive or give gossip, not to belittle or demean or falsely flatter, not to lie, and not to boast. Find an accountability partner who will hold you accountable and pray for you, and give them the go ahead to confront you when they see your speech out of line! As I have mentioned, I have a husband who holds me accountable for my speech, as well as other friends that pray for me and help me.

Summary

Our tongues are the smallest members of our bodies, but the largest troublemakers. The tongue is contained in our mouth and surrounded by our lips and teeth, and yet it escapes. If we are to bear evidence of a genuine saving faith, it must be controlled. Hypocrisy in our hearts is exposed by our speech. The unsaved world in which we live should listen to our speech and know that we are different. We should not be the ones they hear yelling at our kids in the grocery store. We should not be the ones they hear criticizing our husbands. We should not be the ones they hear telling off-color, much less dirty, jokes. Let us allow God to use our tongues to steer the world into eternal life and to delight other believers during the trials of life. Let us speak words that are gracious, words that are edifying, and words that build up. Will you say with the songwriter, "Take my lips and let them be filled with messages for thee?" Will you "let the mind of Christ our Savior live in you from day to day, by His love and power controlling all you do and say?"

Questions to Consider
"Gaining Victory Over the Tongue" (Part 2)
James 3:7-12

1. Read James 3, especially noting verses 7-12. What are some reasons given here why God might not accept your praise?

2. Memorize James 3:10.

3. Compare and contrast the ungodly man's speech with that of our Lord in Psalm 12.

4. Read Exodus 15:20-21 and Numbers 12:1-16. (a) Who is using her mouth to bless God and to curse men? (b) Who was she speaking evil of and why? (c) What happened to her? (d) What principles can you learn for your life in avoiding this awful sin of murmuring?

5. (a) Read the following verses to see what terms are used to describe the tongue. (b) Do any of them describe your speech lately? Psalms 5:9; 10:7; 12:3; 15:2-3; 50:19; 52:2-4; 109:2; 120:2-3; Proverbs 6:17; 10:31; 12:19; 17:4; 17:20; 25:23; 28:23.

6. (a) Read Colossians 3:1-17 and Ephesians 4:22-32, noting what our speech was like before our conversion and then after our conversion. (b) Does your speech reflect the old man or the new man according to these passages?

7. (a) What are some ways you think we can use our tongues for good? (b) For evil?

8. Is there anyone that you need to seek forgiveness from for the

way you have used your tongue? Perhaps from gossip, hurtful words, slander, or lying? Confess it and determine to put off all evil speaking!

9. We have now studied two lessons regarding our speech. What has the Lord revealed to you in this area, and what change(s) do you need to make? Put your answer in the form of a prayer request.

15

Wisdom – From Above or From Below?

James 3:13-18

One of the things that grieves me more and more as I rub shoulders with Christians is the lack of wisdom. What is wisdom, and what does the Bible say about it? The book of Proverbs is full of words about wisdom. "The fear of the LORD is the beginning of knowledge: but fools despise wisdom and instruction" (Proverbs 1:7). "Wisdom is the principle thing, therefore get wisdom" (Proverbs 4:7). "For wisdom is better than rubies; and all the things one may desire cannot be compared with her" (Proverbs 8:11). "Happy is the man who finds wisdom, and the man who gains understanding" (Proverbs 3:13). In talking about the virtuous woman, Proverbs 31:26 states, "She opens her mouth with wisdom; and on her tongue is the law of kindness."

Proverbs is not the only book in the Bible that speaks of wisdom. As we mentioned in our introductory lesson in this Bible study, the Epistle of James is also considered to be wisdom literature. As we now arrive at the second passage in the Epistle of James regarding wisdom (James 1:5-6 was the first), James asks and answers a vital question for us all: How can we know if the wisdom we possess comes from God or comes from the world? Initially the verses in this chapter may appear to be disconnected from the previous verses that we just studied on the tongue, but that is a wrong assumption. We saw that even though the tongue is contained in our mouth and surrounded by our lips and teeth, it escapes. What is the cause of that? Is it lack of intelligence? No! It is a lack of wisdom and a lack of discernment. James has been expounding on the importance of responsible speech, and now he is going to elaborate that wisdom enables us to speak responsibly. James is not changing the subject here, because when you think about it, a man or woman who possesses heavenly wisdom will have godly speech. That is why he asks in verse 13, "Who is wise and understanding among you?"

> Who is wise and understanding among you? Let him show by good conduct that his works are done in the meekness of wisdom. ¹⁴But if you have bitter envy and self-seeking in your hearts, do not boast and lie against the truth. ¹⁵This wisdom does not descend from above, but is earthly, sensual, demonic. ¹⁶For where envy and self-seeking exist, confusion and every evil thing are there. ¹⁷But the wisdom that is from above is first pure, then peaceable, gentle, willing to yield, full of mercy and good fruits, without partiality and without hypocrisy. ¹⁸Now the fruit of righteousness is sown in peace by those who make peace. (James 3:13-18)

From these six verses, we will see the characteristics of *the wise* (v 13), the characteristics of *demonic wisdom* (vv 14-16), and the characteristics of *divine wisdom* (vv 17-18).

The Characteristics of the Wise

James 3:13. Who is wise and understanding among you?

This question is posed in reference to public speaking and means that if there are wise and understanding persons among them, then they are the ones that should be selected for the office of teaching. The third chapter in the Epistle of James begins with an encouragement not to rush into the office of teacher because of the stricter judgment that teachers will receive. Then James expounds on speech and the dangers of having an unbridled tongue; and while doing that, he warns that just because someone is not a public speaker does not mean they are off the hook. Why not? Because we all use our tongues to speak; and because we influence those around us for better or worse with our speech. We all are teachers in one way or another. Therefore, we need wisdom before we speak; we need wisdom that is from above.

What is wisdom anyway? The Greek word is *sophos,* the characteristic that describes an individual who possesses moral insight and skill in deciding practical issues of conduct. This *sophos* wisdom is from God.[47] The phrase *wise man* describes the person who possesses "wisdom" and who can be a resource for instructing others. The wise man has a deep discernment of the underlying principles of life. Not only should teachers possess wisdom, but James also says that they should have "understanding." This is the only time this term occurs in the New Testament, and it refers to a specialist who is able to apply his fuller knowledge to practical situations. In other words, he or she can put wisdom into practice. This would be the person who sees the big picture and knows how to get things done. The combination of these two attributes produces a person who is able to be a reliable guide to others, and the person who possesses this kind of wisdom and knowledge must also lead a good and upright life.

James 3:13. Let him show by good conduct that his works are done in the meekness of wisdom.

In other words, from a good life, from an upright life, let him show his works with meekness of wisdom. James used the verb *show,* while today we might say "show and tell." Wisdom is not measured by degrees but by deeds, which is why James says that the wise should show her *works,* her acts of righteousness. This should typify a woman who has a holy life, a changed life; and the product of her new life should be her works. Her life will show good works

---

[47] The Jewish concept of *sophia* from the Old Testament, added the element of Godly living. An early church father, Clement, defines wisdom as: "An understanding of things human and divine, and their causes, and implies thoughtfulness, penetration, grasp of relations of things, and the right use of one's knowledge for the highest ends." Robert L. Thomas, *Editor, Exegetical Digest of the Epistle of James* (1976), p. 30.

not just once in a while, but her whole life will be characterized by good works and will display what has happened to her heart. I have seen many men and women who are teachers or preachers possessing wisdom and knowledge, but not an upright life. This greatly concerns me, as we seem to have lost our zeal for personal holiness, for sanctification—being set apart from this world. To be a teacher who possesses knowledge and wisdom yet lacks an upright life is only bringing about a stricter judgment from God. Now let me also say that these good works should not be merely outward displays of religiosity, because that is the hypocrites' sin that Jesus condemns in Matthew 6 and Matthew 23. He tells the hypocritical leaders that they outwardly appear righteous unto men, but within they are full of hypocrisy and iniquity. So that is a warning to us all!

Notice how these works should be performed. With harshness? No! They should be done in "the meekness of wisdom." This means with gentleness of wisdom. Gentleness or meekness is that wonderful quality that characterizes our Lord. Isaiah foretold this quality of Jesus: "He will feed His flock like a shepherd; He will gather the lambs with His arm, and carry them in His bosom, and gently lead those who are with young" (Isaiah 40:11). Jesus says of Himself, "Come to Me, all you who labor and are heavy laden, and I will give you rest. Take My yoke upon you and learn from Me, for I am *gentle* and lowly in heart, and you will find rest for your souls" (Matthew 11:28-29, emphasis mine). Gentleness or meekness is not passivity, or weakness, but strength under control. We know that meekness is also a fruit of the spirit. It is the opposite of arrogance; the meek person does not feel a need to fight for his rights or acceptance of his personal views, but his life will be characterized by modesty. The Apostle Paul said, "[We are] to speak evil of no one, to be peaceable, *gentle*, showing all *humility* to all men" (Titus 3:2, emphasis mine). Paul also said that "a servant of the Lord must not quarrel but be *gentle* to all, able to teach, patient, in *humility* correcting those who are in opposition" (2 Timothy 2:24-25, emphasis mine). When confronting a brother, Paul instructed the Galatians to do so in a spirit of *meekness* (KJV) or *gentleness* (Galatians 6:1-2). A Christian who is not meek is a contradiction of terms. This should give us all food for thought, especially those of us who are teachers.

What happens if that wisdom is not expressed in meekness?

The Characteristics of Demonic Wisdom

James 3:14. But if you have bitter envy and self-seeking in your hearts

Apparently some in James' day were misusing their knowledge, letting it become the basis for self-glorification. They had "bitter envy," which means they possessed harsh zeal and selfish ambition; they promoted themselves. It is this envious attitude of the heart and mind that causes us to feel sorrow when someone excels us in some manner. It is an evil jealousy. From these words it appears that the bitter zeal they possessed manifested itself by wanting to get ahead of others, which led them to boastful claims of superiority. *I am better than you!* They also had *self-seeking* in their hearts. This term *self-seeking* derives from a word that depicts the day laborer that regards monetary compensation as the only reward for work. It is a selfish and self-willed attitude coupled with a feuding and contentious spirit. For example, if Betsy gets a job at church to head up a committee, don't envy her, rather support her, help her, pray for her, and assist her in any way you can.

James 3:14. Do not boast and lie against the truth.

If the motive in your heart is generated from bitter envy and self-seeking, James says, "do not boast and lie against the truth." Stop boasting. Glory not. This word means to boast of one's self to the detriment of another. This means you are standing up and looking down with smug satisfaction upon others and declare you have arrived. Paul saw the dangers of boasting and prayed, "God forbid that I should boast except in the cross of our Lord Jesus Christ" (Galatians 6:14). In effect James is saying, "Do not boast and be arrogant, and thus prove false to the Truth!" Bitter envying, strife, and self-seeking is contrary to the true wisdom of God, and boasting is usually a companion of lying. Any person, and especially a teacher, who is acting in such an evil way and yet claims to be wise is lying against the truth, against the wisdom of Jesus Christ. If a teacher is dominated by jealousy and selfish ambition, she is instructed to stop boasting and to stop lying against the truth. Regardless of the wisdom she possesses, she contradicts the truth of the gospel with ungodly attitudes such as boasting and lying. "Don't kid yourself," James says, "attitudes, speech, and works that are accompanied by bitterness and jealousy are not indicative of the kind of wisdom that comes from above."

James 3:15. This wisdom does not descend from above, but is earthly, sensual, demonic.

James tells us that "this wisdom does not descend from above." If you think that sort of wisdom comes from God, then you are wrong, for the true wisdom that is from above is very different. The wisdom that *is not* from God has three characteristics: it is *earthly*; it is *sensual*; it is *demonic*. It is interesting that the believers' three enemies, the world, the flesh, and the devil, all derive from ungodly wisdom.

The first characteristic of ungodly wisdom is that it is *earthly*, which means it has its origin in the world and is exhibited by men who are governed by worldly principles. Earthly wisdom is temporal and mundane. It is concerned with the physical world, not the spiritual world. In 1 Corinthians 1:20 the Apostle Paul refers to a wisdom that is of the world. To the Philippian believers, Paul would later speak of the enemies of the cross who set their minds on *earthly* things.

> Brethren, join in following my example, and note those who so walk, as you have us for a pattern. For many walk, of whom I have told you often, and now tell you even weeping, that they are the enemies of the cross of Christ: whose end is destruction, whose god is their belly, and whose glory is in their shame—who set their mind on earthly things. (Philippians 3:17-19)

The second characteristic of this worldly wisdom is that it is *sensual*, which means it is from the flesh. This wisdom is natural and unspiritual, springing from mental and emotional impulses. We get our English word *psychology* from it—its origin is from the sensual as opposed to the intellectual and moral nature. The people that I know who have been grounded in psychology are like that—they are emotional, unstable. Sensual wisdom is not godly wisdom.

The third characteristic of this ungodly wisdom is that it is *demonic* or *devilish*. Evil spirits rather than the Holy Spirit promote this wisdom. Satan tempted Eve in the Garden of Eden leading her to believe that his advice would make her wise—"You will be like God, knowing good and evil" (Genesis 3:5)—and yet it was demonical wisdom. In 1 Timothy 4:1 we see a warning about deceitful doctrines that are influenced by demons. The Apostle John writes that other spirits besides the Holy Spirit can energize and inspire preachers and teachers (1 John 4:1-6). Satan, the spirit of the Antichrist, is behind this ungodly wisdom, and he is always trying to convince us that his ways are right. Beware of his tactics! Now that James has shown us the origin and given us a description of ungodly wisdom, he then warns:

James 3:16. For where envy and self-seeking exist, confusion and every evil thing are there.

How can we know when we are following the world's wisdom? There will be confusion and every evil thing. First let's discuss "confusion," which means disorder and turmoil. This word is related to the adjective *unstable* that we encountered in James 1:8, which referred to the double-minded man. Instead of promoting harmony, this wisdom causes disruption and unruliness. All sorts of confusions, from arguments in churches to personal tensions and frustrations, are sure to result when Christians seek earthly wisdom. "For God is not the author of *confusion* but of peace, as in all churches of the saints" (1 Corinthians 14:33, emphasis mine). The same Greek word for *confusion* in 1 Corinthians 14:33, (*akatastasia*), is used in James 3:15, so it is clear that the wisdom conveyed here is not from Him.

Where envy and self-seeking exist, there is also every "evil work," which means every evil practice. In the Greek this actually means "good for nothing." Every evil action you can think of exists alongside of false wisdom. Such wisdom is worthless in the sight of God, James says, although in man's sight it may seem great and worthy. It should be very clear from these verses that human wisdom unaided by the Holy Spirit is not a safe guide to spiritual truth.

If left to itself, human wisdom quickly becomes tainted with sinful jealousy and personal ambition, and it will eventually lead to evil deeds. The fact that it can and is happening in the church makes this truth especially alarming. Dear readers, I strongly encourage you to measure everything you hear and everything you read by God's Word. When you seek counsel from others, make sure they use God's Word to back up the advice they give. If you read a lot, be careful. I have seen a lot of garbage labeled "Christian literature" that is no more Christian than *Sports Illustrated Magazine*. Here is something else that concerns me. Even when counselors do use the Holy Scriptures for backup, what appears to be sound counsel in the beginning may not have any connection with the original principle inherent in the Scripture. What I am saying is please be careful and please seek God's wisdom. So how can we tell when a person is using divine wisdom? James tells us how to discern that in verses 17-18.

The Characteristics of Divine Wisdom

James 3:17. But the wisdom that is from above is first pure, then peaceable, gentle, willing to yield, full of mercy and good fruits, without partiality, and without hypocrisy.

These are the fruits of wisdom. James contrasts the wisdom from above with the false wisdom of verse 15. This divine wisdom has a heavenly origin and is from God. It gives emphasis to spiritual and eternal issues. By the way, you don't need a formal education to obtain this wisdom. Seven characteristics given of this wisdom are:

1. "It is Pure." *Pure* is number one on the list, because it is the heading to the rest. Out of purity fall the other six characteristics. The first effect that godly wisdom has on the mind is to make it pure. Purity reflects the heart of the wise person who has been regenerated—it is a pure heart! The Greek word for pure means to be innocent or free from blame, and wisdom from above purifies the heart and the life. We know Christ Himself is pure, so obviously wisdom that is from Him would reflect His purity. If someone gives you advice that is not pure or free from blame, it is not from God. For example, a fellow Christian might convince you to go see a movie by telling you how good it is. When you get there and view it, you realize it is unwholesome. This fellow Christian's recommendation would call into question his or her purity.

2. "It is Peaceable," means it will cause a man to live in peace with others. It does not cause strife. Being peaceable will tend to settle disputes rather than provoke them; but it does not pursue peace at the expense of purity. It will not compromise with sin to maintain peace with God. John MacArthur says,

> Godly wisdom, purity, and peace go hand in hand. Peace is wisdom in action and is never established at the expense of righteousness ... Some people equate peace with evading issues, but true peace can be very confrontational.[48]

Even Jesus says, "Do not think that I came to bring peace on the earth; I did not come to bring peace but a sword" (Matthew 10:34). Jesus knew that sinful people have to be confronted with the truth before they can experience the peace that surpasses all understanding (Philippians 4:7). But the person who has wisdom from above will not go around stirring up discord. We know from Proverbs 6:19 that sowing discord among the brethren is one of the seven things that God considers an abomination!

3. "It is Gentle." This means it is mild, inoffensive, fair, and reasonable. The Greek word here means moderation without compro-

---

[48]John MacArthur, Jr. *Drawing Near: Daily Readings for a Deeper Faith* (Crossway Books, 1997), April 22 devotional.

mise. This means one is considerate of others and makes allowances for their feelings, weaknesses, and needs. It is interesting that we get our English word *gentlemen* from the Greek word *gentle*.

4. "It is Willing to Yield." This phrase does not occur anywhere else in the New Testament. It means to be easily persuaded, submissive, and obedient—not stubborn. *Willing to yield* does not mean being easily persuaded to do the wrong things. Instead the person that has wisdom from above is not stiff and unyielding. This is the person that will listen to the ideas of others and be willing to change if necessary.

5. "It is Full of Mercy and Good Fruits." Mercy is a characteristic of someone who shows compassion to others. A good example of this would be the Good Samaritan mentioned in Luke 10. He showed godly wisdom in helping the traveler who was beaten and robbed and left for dead. He gained nothing from that act of mercy, except the blessings that come from doing the will of God. The victim could not pay him back. That is mercy. *Good fruits* here means just and kind actions, which are a result of our works of mercy.

6. "It is Without Partiality." This characterizes a person who is unwavering, undivided. There is no indecision about one's commitment to God. Such a person has clear discernment of God's will and can be confident regarding the wisdom of his or her actions. She can walk a straight path without wavering from the truth and is not double-minded but stable in all of her ways. This is the antithesis of the man mentioned in James 1:7.

7. "It is Without Hypocrisy." This means there is no mask or disguise, no lying, deceit, or pretense. In ancient Greece, a hypocrite was one who played the part of an actor. The term has come to describe one who in public acts different from his true character. Therefore, the person *without hypocrisy* is the person who is at home what she is at church. She is in private what she is in public. She does not attempt to pretend or make a good impression.

These seven characteristics of wisdom—purity, peace, gentleness, willing to yield, full of mercy and good fruits, without partiality, and without hypocrisy—are from God. They are from God because they are consistent with His character. In verse 18, James then closes his discourse on wisdom with the result of exercising heavenly wisdom.

James 3:18. Now the fruit of righteousness is sown in peace by those who make peace.

The "fruit of righteousness" characterizes the godly life. It is the fruit of that which is sown in a godly life. Isaiah said, "The work of righteousness will be peace, and the effect of righteousness, quietness and assurance forever" (Isaiah 32:17). It is "sown in peace." James here pictured a farmer who understands in the broader sense that he is actually sowing a crop when he plants a seed. A farmer sows his seed in peace, not in the middle of a tumultuous climate. Righteousness cannot effectively be sown where there is strife and turbulence. In other words, these men, these women, are engaged everywhere in scattering these blessed seeds of peace, and the result shall be a glorious harvest. These people are peaceful, and they promote peace. They are not concerned with self-promotion. Their motive is love, not envy or jealousy. They are motivated by heavenly wisdom, and they bring men and women into peaceful relationships. Righteousness is the crop that is reaped.

Summary

Godly wisdom is another test to determine if we are genuinely in the faith. We all reap what we sow. Some of us are reaping havoc by the ungodly wisdom we have sown. Others of us are reaping a righteous harvest by the godly wisdom we have sown. What about you? Think about the following questions: Do the words you communicate come from above? Do they show godly wisdom? When you give advice to others, can it be backed up with God's Word? Is your advice backed up by a holy, upright life?

The wisdom you pass on to others, is it pure? For example one might say: "Live together before you get married to see if it works!" But God says to "flee fornication" or "sexual immorality (NKJV)" (1 Corinthians 6:18). Is the wisdom you pass on peaceable? Does your advice bring peace? If you know someone who is in sin, do you avoid confronting him or her because you don't want to rock the boat? True peace confronts sin. Is the wisdom you give gentle? Do you come on like a bull in a china shop with others? Or are you gentle when you give advice? Is the wisdom you give willing to yield? Will you listen to someone else's ideas for change, especially if they have a better biblical idea? Is the wisdom you pass on full of mercy and good fruits? When you give advice, do you back it up with acts of compassion? Do you seek to meet the needs of those you advise? Is your wisdom without partiality? Do you vacillate on decisions for yourself and others, or are you firm in your convictions? Is your wisdom without hypocrisy? Do you follow your own advice, or are you hypocritical saying "Do what I say, not what I do!" In thinking about earthly wisdom, would you say when you give advice to others that it causes envy, strife, confusion and every evil thing? Do you leave paths of confusion and strife everywhere you go and with each life you touch? Or do you leave paths of peace and wisdom everywhere you go and with each life you touch? May God help us to be women who are wise!

Questions to Consider
"Wisdom – From Above or From Below?"
James 3:13-18

1. Read over James chapter 3 and share at least one truth that God has convicted you of in this chapter.

2. Memorize James 3:17.

3. Read James 3:13-18. Answer the following questions. (a) What indicators does James list that prove a man's wisdom is not from God? (b) How does "do not boast and lie against the truth" relate to envy and strife? (c) Why do you think the word *pure* is the first characteristic of godly wisdom mentioned?

4. Choose one chapter from Proverbs and compare and contrast the world's wisdom with God's wisdom. (a) What did you learn about depending on your own wisdom? (b) Why should you depend on God for wisdom?

5. (a) Read the book of Jonah and note the various ways that the wisdom of Jonah did not descend from above. (b) What does this teach you about pursing godly wisdom?

6. Will wisdom from above always produce peace? Prove your answer biblically.

7. Notice your responses this week in tense situations. (a) Did you display wisdom that is worldly or wisdom that is divine? (b) Did you demonstrate peace making, or did you foster more divisions?

8. How are the truths that you know (wisdom) being made manifest by a godly life? "For everyone to whom much is given, from him much will be required" (Luke 12:48b).

9. As you reflect on this passage regarding wisdom, what do you need help in? What is your prayer request?

16

Wars and Worldliness

James 4:1-4

The story is told of a young father who, upon hearing a commotion in his backyard, looked outside to see what was going on. He saw his daughter and several of her playmates in a heated quarrel. He went outside to intervene and to see what in the world was going on that would have caused her and her playmates to be in such turmoil. His daughter said, "Daddy, we're just playing church!" This is a very sad, but unfortunately true indictment on many of our churches today. But "there is nothing new under the sun" (Ecclesiastes 1:9), right?

James has already dealt with a few of the issues going on in the church at Jerusalem. Chapter 2 addressed the sin of showing partiality precipitated by conflicts between the rich and the poor, and chapter 3 addressed the conflict among leaders who were competing for the prestigious office of teacher. Many were using their tongues to curse each other as we also saw in chapter 3.

James is not the only New Testament writer who deals with conflicts among the brethren. In 2 Corinthians 12:20, the Apostle Paul also addressed the church at Corinth regarding their conflicts: contentions, jealousies, outbursts of wrath, selfish ambitions, backbitings, whisperings, conceits, and tumults. In fact, he is so concerned about their conflicts that he finally tells them to examine themselves as to whether they are even in the faith (2 Corinthians 13:5).

The church at Philippi was having a problem with conflicts as well, as Paul commands one of the brethren to help the women,

Euodia and Syntyche, to be of the same mind in the Lord (Philippians 4:3). These two women could not get along! Problems in churches are not a new thing. I have heard of churches that fight over something as minor as the color of carpet in the auditorium. Where does this discord come from? What is the real reason behind these hostilities? People often blame environment and circumstances for conflict; it is not external conditions, but rather internal selfish desires that ignite conflicts. The Epistle of James gives us the answer why some have conflicts, but I will give you a hint: the answer lies within ourselves, within our hearts, not from the outside, not from the world. About wars and fights, James writes:

> Where do wars and fights come from among you? Do they not come from your desires for pleasure that war in your members? ²You lust and do not have. You murder and covet and cannot obtain. You fight and war. Yet you do not have because you do not ask. ³You ask and do not receive, because you ask amiss, that you may spend it on your pleasures. ⁴Adulterers and adulteresses! Do you not know that friendship with the world is enmity with God? Whoever therefore wants to be a friend of the world makes himself an enemy of God. (James 4:1-4)

In these first four verses of Chapter 4, James gives us the *reason* for their worldliness (vv 1-3), and then his *rebuke* for their worldliness (v 4).

The Reason for Their Worldliness

James 4:1. Where do wars and fights come from among you?

James' sudden transition from the beautiful picture of being a peacemaker in the last verse of chapter 3 to the appalling picture of starting a war in chapter 4 startles the reader. He is obviously aware that not all the brethren are peacemakers. Believe me, I have been in ministry long enough to agree with Pastor James. Too often we see fights and wars among the Christian brethren, and it is a reality that

Satan uses some of the brethren to sow discord. James asks rhetorically, "Where do wars and fights come from among you?" *Wars* here refers to a prolonged state of hostility, not to international wars, such as World Wars I and II or the Vietnam War, the Persian Gulf War or the war against terrorism and Iraq. When James says these wars are among you, he is indicating that they are *in* you, referring to the inner feeling of frustration and agitation, which is not of God.[49] James identifies not only wars, but also *fights*, or as we might say, contentions. He doesn't tell us what they were fighting about, but one can assume that it may be from what James has covered thus far in his epistle. James asks, where do these contentions come from? Did your upbringing make you act this way? James says, "No!"

James 4:1. Do they not come from your desires for pleasure that war in your members?

James says that they come from "your desires for pleasure that war in your members." The Greek word for *desires for pleasure* is *hedonon,* from which we get our English word *hedonism*. It refers to sinful pleasures, self-gratification, and ministering to oneself. It is that sinful desire for satisfaction, which is self-seeking and causes us to fight with one another so that we might get our own way. This is done at the expense of the interests of others. Isn't that why we argue? We want our own way.

For example, we may not like the way our husband wants to do something, so we argue for our own way; and might I add, many times we argue, sad to say, until we get our own way. Drip, drip, drip! Or maybe we don't like the way some in our church handle the ministry that God has given them, and so we manipulate until it is done our way—as if our way is right!

The desire for pleasure, the desires to have our own way, James says, creates "war in our members." This describes the passions of the flesh constantly fighting to have their own way and to

---

[49] That these two terms refer to factional bickerings in the local church is agreed upon by Clement, who was an early church father. *The Epistle of Clement of Rome* (xlvi).

be victorious over the spirit. These two words, *that war,* depict the desires for pleasure as soldiers carrying on a military campaign aimed at securing the satisfaction of their cravings. The *members* here are not members of your family or members of your church; they are members of your human body. These are drives, lusts, and compulsions. Paul speaks of this warring in his members in Romans 7:23. For example, this might be sexual pleasures you are fighting for, or material pleasures that you are warring for. You may want to exalt yourself; you may think you and only you have the right idea, saying "But we have always done it this way." This describes a person who is unwilling to yield. Maybe you war over your personal schedule. Do you stop and think that your time is all God's time? Elisabeth Elliot insightfully quips, "Interruptions are divine appointments."

Before my own redemption, my husband used to say that he was going to inscribe "She did it her way" on my tombstone. What an awful indictment on my life before Christ! These corrupt passions, James says, are the cause of wars and fights. James expands this thought of evil warring in our members in verse 2.

James 4:2. You lust and do not have

Lust (Greek, *epithemeite*) here means to long for, strongly desire, or to crave for. What things they were lusting after is not mentioned, but obviously it was for self-gratification. James writes, "You lust and do not have." You lust, you desire, you are longing for something, but you are not receiving it. Their lust did not bring about the desired result. Isn't that so true? Sometimes we lust over something as simple as dining at a particular restaurant, and then when we get our way, we can hardly enjoy the food knowing we sinned to get there! It reminds me of what the Psalmist says about the Israelites in Psalm 106:14-15: "[They] lusted exceedingly in the wilderness, and tested God in the desert. And He gave them their request, but sent leanness into their soul."

Amnon is another example of lusting for something, and yet it did not bring about the desired satisfaction. Remember, he raped his half-sister, Tamar, in 2 Samuel 13? The Scriptures tell us that afterwards he hated her so exceedingly that the hatred that he hated her with was greater than the love he had. So if you can't get your way by lusting, James says the next step is that you kill. You kill and desire to have. This means you are bent on murder, which indicates a murderous spirit. James is describing here the attitude of murder, or he could actually be speaking of murders, which were taking place. Remember James was writing to Christian Jews, of which some were former Zealots, that would have accepted murder as a religious way to solve disagreements (Acts 9:1). Perhaps they thought that this might secure their religious freedom. You might say, well I would never stoop that low to get my way. Murder someone so I can get my way? Never! Oh? In Matthew 5:22, Jesus tells us something different. "But I say to you that whoever is angry with his brother without a cause shall be in danger of the judgment. And whoever says to his brother, 'Raca!' shall be in danger of the council. But whoever says, 'You fool!' shall be in danger of hell fire." Here Jesus is equating anger with murder. The Apostle John tells us that if we hate our brother we are a murderer and that no murderer has eternal life abiding in him (1 John 3:15). Like Jesus before, James is forcing his readers to realize the depth of their evil in their bitter hatred toward each other.

James 4:2. You murder and covet and cannot obtain.

All wars, all fights, could be avoided if we would just be content with the things that we have and not desire what is not ours. Maybe you have set your heart on a new car or a new home, a new dress or a new piece of jewelry, or a position of prestige; but in order to get what you want, you must argue and fight and sometimes use unethical means. Many times such desires make us miserable and at the same time create an awareness of the struggle within the members of our bodies. Paul describes this internal conflict to the Christian church in Rome:

> My own behavior baffles me. For I find myself doing what I really loathe but not doing what I really want to do ... I often find that I

have the will to do good, but not the power. That is, I don't accomplish the good I set out to do, and the evil I don't really want to do I find I am always doing. Yet if I do things that I don't really want to do then it is not, I repeat "I" who do them, but the sin, which has made its home within me. My experience of the Law is that when I want to do good, only evil is within my reach. For I am in hearty agreement with God's Law so far as my inner self is concerned. But then I find another law in my bodily members, which is in continual conflict with the Law, which my mind approves, and makes me a prisoner to the law of sin, which is inherent in my mortal body. For left to myself, I serve the Law of God with my mind, but in my unspiritual nature, I serve the law of sin. It is an agonizing situation, and who can set me free from the prison of this mortal body? I thank God there is a way out through Jesus Christ our Lord. (Romans 7:15-25, Phillips translation)

Paul tells us the "way out" in 1 Corinthians 10:13: "No temptation has overtaken you except such as is common to man; but God is faithful, who will not allow you to be tempted beyond what you are able, but with the temptation will also make the way of escape, that you may be able to bear it." Most of us just don't want to use the escape hatch that God has provided, because sin does have its pleasure for a season. So what happens when we give into that desire of our heart? There is war within our souls, and there is not satisfaction in our heart.

James 4:2. You fight and war. Yet you do not have because you do not ask.

James summarizes, "you fight and war." We have bitter quarrels and disputes. "Yet we do not have because we do not ask." We fail to ask God for things that our hearts are set on, perhaps because we know our desires are selfish and it would be inappropriate to ask God for such things. The way to obtain anything that we really need is to seek God in prayer. If what we request is withheld, it will be because that is what is best for us. Many of us have lost the vision of what prayer is really all about (we are going to learn more about prayer in James 5), so at this point we need to ask ourselves why we pray. Do the things we are asking of God bring pleasure and relief, or do we really want God to be glorified through our prayers? Do we say "Thy will be done" or "my will be done?" I like what Elisabeth Elliot says:

> I had been praying for something I wanted very badly. It seemed a good thing to have, a thing that would make life even more pleasant than it is, and would not in any way hinder my work. God did not give it to me. Why? I do not know all of his reasons, of course. The God who orchestrates the universe has a good many things to consider that have not occurred to me, and it is well that I leave them to Him. But one thing I do understand: He offers me holiness at the price of relinquishing my own will. 'Do you honestly want to know Me?' He asks. I answer yes. 'Then do what I say,' He replies. 'Do it when you understand it; do it when you don't understand it. Take what I give you; be willing not to have what I do not give you. The very relinquishment of this thing that you so urgently desire is a true demonstration of the sincerity of your long life prayer: Thy will be done. So instead of hammering on heaven's door for something which is now quite clear God does not want me to have, I make my desire an offering. The longed-for thing is material for sacrifice. Here, Lord it's yours. He will, I believe, accept the offering. He will transform it into something redemptive. He may perhaps give it back as He did Isaac to Abraham, but He will know that I fully intend to obey Him."[50]

This is the bigger issue, isn't it? We need to ask ourselves, what does God want, will this glorify Him? Sometimes we do not have because we do not ask for the right things. God is not a genie in heaven who bows to our every wish and desire. He is God Almighty. The Apostle Paul wrote, "Indeed, O man, who are you to reply against God? … Does not the potter have power over the clay?" (Romans 9:20-21). God is the potter; we are the clay! In his letter to the Romans, Paul quoted the Old Testament Scriptures: "For who has known the mind of the Lord? Or who has become his counselor?" (Romans 11:34).

Sometimes we are ignorant in our requests because we do not know God's Word. Sometimes we need to go to the Word to see

---

[50] Elisabeth Elliot. *A Lamp for My Feet* (Ann Arbor, Mich.: Vine Books, 1985), 53-54.

what He has already revealed as many times the answer is there. I will never forget when someone told me that they were praying that God would stop them from divorcing their mate if it wasn't His will. God's will was already clearly revealed in the Bible, as this individual did not have Scriptural grounds for divorce. Sometimes we lack sensitivity to the Spirit to know what God's answer is. Next James tells the brethren that even though they asked, they didn't receive because they asked incorrectly.

James 4:3. You ask and do not receive, because you ask amiss, that you may spend it on your pleasures.

James now tells them that even though they asked, their requests were inappropriate. The first statement is not meant to imply that they did not ask at all, but they were not asking in a true sense. They had prayed but not according to God's will. Some prayers we pray God will not answer—did you know that? First John 5:14 says, "Now this is the confidence that we have in Him, that if we ask anything according *to His will* [for His purposes], He hears us" (Emphasis mine). Earlier in 1 John 3:22, it is also written: "Whatever we ask we receive from Him, because we keep His commandments and do those things that are pleasing in His sight." The key is that in order to receive anything from God we must be keeping His commandments and doing things that are pleasing in His sight. Jesus tells us that we must be abiding in Him before He is obligated to answer our petitions (John 15:7). The Psalmist says that if I regard iniquity in my heart the Lord will not hear me (Psalm 66:18). Many hindrances impede our prayers, so a careful student of the Word will study those to make sure that her praying is not being hindered.

Obviously these readers were not asking according to God's will and were praying with selfish intentions. They were asking "amiss." *Amiss* is a strong adverb, which means in a base way or a mean way. This is a strong indictment of selfishness in prayer. That type of prayer says, "Give me this and give me that." James says you are praying that way in order that you may "spend it on your pleasures." *Spend* means to waste, to squander, and to consume. This could be anything that seeks to please the flesh. The prodigal son is a good illustration of this as he wasted his substance on riotous living (Luke 15:13). For example, we may ask for wealth, not for the purpose of feeding the hungry, or giving to the destitute, but for the purpose of a new car, a new house, or a new dress. That is a wrong motive. We might ask God to stop the mouth and evil deeds of our enemies, but our motive should not be vengeance but the glory of God. The brethren's worldly, self-centered desires had invaded their prayer life and perverted their relationship to God. Anything that tends to put self before Christ and before others can be considered asking amiss.

We should evaluate our prayer life and ask ourselves the question: What am I asking God for and what are my real reasons behind my request? I would encourage you to listen to yourself pray and see what you are asking from God. The exposure of their true worldliness, their fighting and warring with each other is now followed by a sharp rebuke to the worldly minded in verse 4. The thoughts are not disconnected, as one who is worldly finds pleasure and satisfaction in the world and not in God. Arguing, fighting, and lusting for our own pleasures are characteristics of worldliness. James addresses what is wrong and identifies the root cause, and so in verse four he rebukes them.

The Rebuke for Their Worldliness

James 4:4. Adulterers and adulteresses

At this point, James identifies them as "adulterers and adulteresses." (NKJV, KJV) The word *adulterer* is not in the original text—only *adulteresses*. (NASV, NIV, RSV) The word *adulteress* is to be understood in the same ethical sense as *you murder* in verse 4:2. *Murder* is a reference to the fifth commandment and specifies what the readers do to mankind. *Adultery* is a reference to the sixth commandment and specifies what the readers do to God. Why does

James use this term? James is not a male chauvinist, but he uses this term because the unfaithfulness of the nation Israel to the Lord was always compared to a female's unfaithfulness to her mate. The Jew reading this epistle would understand this terminology.[51] Even as we come to the New Testament, we see that believers are referred to as the Bride of Christ (Ephesians 5:22-33 and Revelation 21:2). The church is married to Christ, we are his bride, and to love the world is to be unfaithful to Him. After James calls them adulteresses he then posed a question.

James 4:4. Do you not know that friendship with the world is enmity with God?

James expresses surprise and shock! By this statement, we infer that they must have known that to be friendly with the world meant to be enemies of God, but they are letting the knowledge lie dormant. This is strong language and speaks of committing spiritual adultery. James is rebuking them and calling them to repent! "Friendship with the world" means to have love or have affection for the world. Their apparent friendship of the world just further pointed to their pleasure-seeking activity that he has been talking about in verses 1-3. James is not talking about casually rubbing shoulders with the world, but falling in love with the world. James has already told us in 1:27 that pure religion is to visit orphans and widows in their trouble and to keep oneself unspotted from the world. If we walk with the Lord and abide in His presence throughout the day, even though we live in this sinful world, we must remain without blemish and unspotted by the world. We remain unspotted when our wills and our affections are not attached to this world. James says if you have friendship with the world, it is enmity with God.

---

[51] For example: Deuteronomy 31:16, "And the LORD said to Moses: 'Behold, you will rest with your fathers; and this people will rise and play the harlot with the gods of the foreigners of the land, where they go to be among them, and they will forsake Me and break My covenant which I have made with them.'" Psalm 73:27, "For indeed, those who are far from You shall perish; you have destroyed all those who desert You for harlotry." Jeremiah 3:20, "'Surely, as a wife treacherously departs from her husband, so have you dealt treacherously with Me, O house of Israel,' says the LORD."

James 4:4. Whoever therefore wants to be a friend of the world makes himself an enemy of God.

The word "whoever" in the Greek is emphatic. It indicates a deliberate choice to give allegiance to the world rather than to God. It is the opposite of Abraham, who was called the friend of God, as James wrote in 2:23. Demas is a good illustration of one who deserted the cause of Christ because of his love of the world (2 Timothy 4:10). This friendship with the world is diametrically opposed to friendship with God. It is an attitude of personal hostility—of war against God. You cannot embrace both God and the world. When it comes to one's allegiance to Christ, there can be no gray area in a believer's life. Either you belong to God or you belong to the world. One of the worst crimes imaginable is to be a traitor to one's country. Worse than that is for a believer to betray God by rendering allegiance to the world which opposes Him. If you love the world, then you hate God, and therefore cannot belong to Him. I did not say that—God did. Inspired by God, the Apostle John wrote, "Do not love the world or the things in the world. If anyone loves the world, the love of the Father is not in him" (1 John 2:15.)

Summary

Now some of us may have an erroneous idea of worldliness. Some of us might say worldliness is going to movies, watching television, having a tattoo, wearing too much jewelry or flashy clothes, mixed swimming, and so on. James, however, approaches the matter of worldliness differently. Questionable practices are really just the symptoms; James focuses on the disease. James does not view worldliness as just a list of taboos, but as an attitude of unfaithfulness to God. It is the condition in one who is lured away from loyalty to God by the attractions of the non-spiritual world system. Worldliness is a matter of our orientation. Either we are oriented towards God or the world. We cannot have it both ways. The spirit of worldliness can be a problem for our churches as well as a problem for our personal lives. The worldly person is a self-centered person.

James seems to be pleading here: What has happened to your spirit of discernment? What has happened to your godly wisdom? Do you no longer know the difference between good and evil, between righteousness and sin? Have you completely lost your sense of values? That is exactly what happened in James' day, and that is exactly what is happening to Christians today. If you are a friend of the world, then you are God's enemy. We will see in the next chapter that James calls these friends of the world to repent—it is a call to salvation. Worldliness is again another test to determine if your faith is genuine or not. If you love the world, your faith in God is suspect. Who are you fighting with this day, and what are you fighting about? Is it so that you might obtain your own selfish desires? Are you committing spiritual adultery by being a friend of the world? These are serious issues for us to consider. A favorite quote of my husband's by C.S. Lewis is: "If we insist on keeping Hell, or even earth, we shall not see Heaven. If we accept Heaven, we shall not be able to retain even the smallest and most intimate souvenirs of Hell."

Questions to Consider
"Wars and Worldliness"
James 4:1-4

1. Read James chapter 4. (a) According to James 4:1-4, what is the source of fighting? (b) How does this attitude manifest a desire to be a friend of the world? (c) Why do you think James calls these people adulterers and adulteresses?

2. Memorize James 4:4.

3. (a) What are the ways in which Oholah (Samaria) and Oholibah (Jerusalem) were committing spiritual adultery in Ezekiel 23? (b) How does God say that He will judge them?

4. (a) In Mark 10:35-45, what was the problem with what James and John were asking of Jesus? (b) Does Jesus grant their request? (c) How does this relate to what James says in 4:1-3? (d) What principle(s) can you glean for your prayer life?

5. Read Matthew 7:7-11. (a) Does this passage mean that God will give me anything that I ask of Him? (b) Why or why not? Prove your answer from Scripture.

6. Evaluate your prayer life. (a) Are you asking for things amiss so that you may spend them on your pleasures? In what ways? (b) Or do your prayers include "Thy will be done?" How does this manifest itself? (c) Do you want God to be glorified or do you just want relief from your difficulty? Give examples.

7. (a) How do you demonstrate self-will (wanting things your way) in your own life? (b) What can you do to put that off and demonstrate God's will instead?

8. What are some ways in which you think you may be committing "spiritual adultery" (being a friend of the world)?

9. After meditating on question 6, what changes need to be made in your prayer life? What is your prayer to God?

17

The Remedy for Worldliness

James 4:5-10

The story is told of two boys who were playing. One was unkind to the other, really hurting his friend. Feeling bad, he said, "I am sorry, Georgie." His friend said, "What kind of sorry, the kind-so-you-won't-do-it-again sorry?" I also know of a true story which happened to "yours truly" several years ago. It seemed like I was going to my husband Doug way too often to ask forgiveness for a particular area of transgression. Finally one day he said, "I am not going to forgive you until you repent." Now let me tell you, at first his response blew me away, but it was just the jolt I needed to realize I was coming time and time again confessing my sin to him, but not with the mindset of repenting or turning from that sin. It was a turning point for me in this area, and it was what God used to get to me to sincerely consider if I was serious about repenting or not. This experience was used by God to get me to turn from this sin. Most of us would agree that modern-day Christianity has lost sight of what sin and genuine sorrow over sin really is. We see people go forward in evangelical meetings sorry for their sin, but then they leave and do not make any changes in their lives. Some have an emotional feeling for the moment, but it does not last. Some are worse than that—instead of tears and mourning over sin, we see laughter and barking. We take sin lightly, and as evangelicals we are paying for it.

We have been looking at James 4 and the forms of worldliness. We saw in the last chapter that James rebuked them for their fights, wars, contentions, and lusts. He rebuked them for this form of worldliness and ended by calling them adulteresses. We ended on a very sobering note where James warned them that their affection for the world proved that they were enemies of God. They could not have it both ways; they could not be friends of the world and friends of God concurrently. We are going to see the remedy for worldliness, and it is not walking down the aisle in a revival meeting. James writes:

> Or do you think that the Scripture says in vain, "The Spirit who dwells in us yearns jealously"? ⁶But He gives more grace. Therefore He says: "God resists the proud, but gives grace to the humble." ⁷Therefore submit to God. Resist the devil and he will flee from you. ⁸Draw near to God and He will draw near to you. Cleanse your hands, you sinners; and purify your hearts, you double-minded. ⁹Lament and mourn and weep! Let your laughter be turned to mourning and your joy to gloom. ¹⁰Humble yourselves in the sight of the Lord, and He will lift you up. (James 4:5-10)

In this chapter we will see that the remedy for worldliness is a complete *devotion* to God (vv 5-7) and a complete *dejection* of self (vv 8-10).

A Complete Devotion to God

James 4:5. Or do you think that the Scripture says in vain, "The Spirit who dwells in us yearns jealously"?

Now you might have scratched your head after reading this sentence and remarked, "Say what? What does this mean?" Do not worry, since this is a difficult verse to interpret. But I believe the best interpretation is this: the Spirit (i.e., the Holy Spirit), which He has made to dwell in us, jealously desires us. The sense is that God wants our full allegiance, and the Holy Spirit, the one who indwells each Christian, yearns for the believer's complete devotion. This really goes along with verse 4:4, where James was explaining that Scripture was clear in its teaching that God's people are espoused (married) to Him and that He won't tolerate love to Him *and* the world. The incoming Holy Spirit, who sealed our redemption, wants our undivided love. This is similar to the physical realm: you want your husband to love you and you only. You do not want to share your husband with another woman, nor should you. By the same token, our Lord is jealous over us, and He does not want our love shared with the world. That is spiritual adultery. God is jealous over us; He wants our complete devotion.

Now what particular passage of Scripture is James referring to here? James is referring to the teaching of the Scriptures as a whole and not a specific scripture. There is no passage in the Bible that says, "The spirit that dwells in us yearns jealously." Doesn't the whole of scripture teach us this? Doesn't it teach us that we either show allegiance to the world or to God? Something would be wrong if God could watch His children be seduced by the world and not be divinely jealous.[52] *Yearns* here means to have a strong lust for, as in a longing affection for a lover. The great encouragement is that God does not cast us off when we stumble, when we are tempted to the lusts of the world. Instead, He gives us more grace. God gives us the grace to withstand the temptations of the world. That is why James then says that He gives more grace.

---

[52] For example: Exodus 20:4-6, "You shall not make for yourself a carved image, or any likeness of anything that is in heaven above, or that is in the earth beneath, or that is in the water under the earth; you shall not bow down to them nor serve them. For I, the LORD your God, am a jealous God, visiting the iniquity of the fathers on the children to the third and fourth generations of those who hate Me, but showing mercy to thousands, to those who love Me and keep My commandments." Exodus 34:12-17, "Take heed to yourself, lest you make a covenant with the inhabitants of the land where you are going, lest it be a snare in your midst. But you shall destroy their altars, break their sacred pillars, and cut down their wooden images (for you shall worship no other god, for the LORD, whose name is Jealous, is a jealous God), lest you make a covenant with the inhabitants of the land, and they play the harlot with their gods and make sacrifice to their gods, and one of them invites you and you eat of his sacrifice, and you take of his daughters for your sons, and his daughters play the harlot with their gods and make your sons play the harlot with their gods." Deuteronomy 6:13-15, "You shall fear the LORD your God and serve Him, and shall take oaths in His name. You shall not go after other gods, the gods of the peoples who are all around you (for the LORD your God is a jealous God among you), lest the anger of the LORD your God be aroused against you and destroy you from the face of the earth."

James 4:6. But He gives more grace.

More grace literally means greater grace. Greater grace means effective help given by God far beyond what man deserves. It is perpetual, like wave upon wave, day after day. *Grace* means unearned favor expecting nothing in return. You might say, "Greater than what?" Greater than the temptations of the world, the flesh and the devil; greater than anything the world has to offer. It is the idea that Paul speaks of in Romans 5:20 where he says, "Where sin abounded, grace abounded much more." God graciously works in our lives so that we actually experience a greater measure of His grace than we would have otherwise thought possible. When you look back on the temptations to sin in your life since you became a Christian, don't you sometimes wonder how you ever resisted them? What keeps *you* from drowning *your* kids, what keeps *you* from killing someone, from stealing, from lashing out in anger? I will tell you what keeps you from those heinous sins—it is the grace of God. Except for the grace of God, we would all be like Osama Bin Laden, Saddam Hussein and Adolph Hitler. He gives more grace, which is a wonderful promise for the believer, but James then says something interesting.

James 4:6. Therefore He says: "God resists the proud, but gives grace to the humble."

This statement comes from Proverbs 3:34: "Surely He scorns the scornful, But gives grace to the humble." That God resists the proud is a solemn warning. A proud person is haughty, arrogant, and places herself above others. God "resists the proud." *Resist* is a verb that vividly pictures God as placing Himself in battle array against such an individual. God is against the proud and the self-sufficient. There is no other sin mentioned in the Bible that arouses God in such a way as to transform His lovingkindness into fury. It was pride which turned angels into devils. They wanted to rise above God, and therefore, God cast them down. Pride is the sin the Lord hates, because it is a sin that sets itself most against Him. Pride is the root cause of every sin you commit. Pride will always get in the way of your spiritual progress. Notice some of the very serious warnings about pride:

> These six things the LORD hates, yes, seven are an abomination to Him: a proud look, a lying tongue, hands that shed innocent blood, a heart that devises wicked plans, feet that are swift in running to evil, a false witness who speaks lies, and one who sows discord among brethren. (Proverbs 6:16-19)

> The fear of the LORD is to hate evil; pride and arrogance and the evil way and the perverse mouth I hate. (Proverbs 8:13)

> Everyone proud in heart is an abomination to the LORD; though they join forces, none will go unpunished. (Proverbs 16:5)

The bad news is that God does resist the proud. But, praise God, James says the good news is that "He gives grace to the humble." This is a message of encouragement. God continually imparts His grace to those who take a lowly position and have a humble attitude. They are humble and have a deep awareness of their sinfulness and dependence on God. I think the closer one gets to God, the more one loses her sense of pride and sees her sinfulness. That's the heart of the believer. To those who are humble God gives His grace; but if you are proud, then don't expect it. If, however, you are humble, you can count on it! Because of God's amazing grace, we should abandon our pride. James now gives ten imperatives, *ten commands* to those who are arrogant. These are a call to repentance, a call to salvation to the lovers of the world at war with God.

James 4:7. Therefore submit to God.

The first command is to "submit to God." If you wish to be saved, if you wish to be the opposite of God's enemy, then be under His submission. Put yourself under God. This is a military term, which means to get yourself into your proper rank. If you desire His grace, then submit to Him. Submission is accepting God's will for our lives instead of imposing your will and accepting God's providence as the best provision for our lives. This means we will turn away from friendship with the world and focus on our friendship with God. This submission is a permanent thing, just like His grace. Once you do submit yourself to God, you will find it hard to be under the command of anyone else, including yourself. I see the same principle in action when learning of a wife's joy when submitting to her husband. Once you start submitting to the husband that God has placed over you as your authority, and once you begin to see your husband as a God-given authority, then you will experience such freedom that you can't imagine ever submitting to any other man. This command to submit is in the middle voice, which means it is a voluntary submission to God. God does not want forced obedience; He wants a willing heart.

James 4:7. Resist the devil and he will flee from you.

If you are wholeheartedly submitting to God, then you can "resist the Devil." This is the second imperative James gives. This military term means to stand against, as taking your position in battle. Chase him away! Resist him in whatever way he may tempt you: allurements, flattery, promises, and worldly temptations. Be like Joseph when Potiphar's wife attempted to seduce him—he fled the scene and got out (Genesis 39). If you are in a conversation you shouldn't be in—get out. If you are watching a movie you shouldn't be watching—walk out! If someone says something to arouse anger in you, don't get angry—resist him. Both Paul and Peter tell us how we are to resist the devil.

> Finally, my brethren, be strong in the Lord and in the power of His might. Put on the whole armor of God, that you may be able to stand against the wiles of the devil. For we do not wrestle against flesh and blood, but against principalities, against powers, against the rulers of the darkness of this age, against spiritual hosts of wickedness in the heavenly places. Therefore take up the whole armor of God, that you may be able to withstand in the evil day, and having done all, to stand. Stand therefore, having girded your waist with truth, having put on the breastplate of righteousness, and having shod your feet with the preparation of the gospel of

peace; above all, taking the shield of faith with which you will be able to quench all the fiery darts of the wicked one. And take the helmet of salvation, and the sword of the Spirit, which is the word of God; praying always with all prayer and supplication in the Spirit, being watchful to this end with all perseverance and supplication for all the saints. (Ephesians 6:10-18)

Be sober, be vigilant; because your adversary the devil walks about like a roaring lion, seeking whom he may devour. Resist him, steadfast in the faith, knowing that the same sufferings are experienced by your brotherhood in the world. (1 Peter 5:8-9)

Sometimes we hear people say and pray that we have some kind of authority to rebuke or bind Satan. That notion is not taught in the Word of God. I wish we did have that power; then we would not have so many temptations. But even Michael the archangel treated Satan with respect when contending with the devil. Michael did not dare to bring a reviling accusation against Satan, but instead said, "The *Lord* rebuke you" (Jude 9, emphasis mine). Also take note of what the Lord said to Satan when Joshua the high priest was standing before the angel of the Lord. "And the Lord said to Satan, 'The Lord rebuke you, Satan!'" (Zechariah 3:2). So, if you resist Satan, then what happens? This is wonderful news—"he will flee from you."

That is a promise from God! *He will flee from you* assures us that we can be successful in resisting the devil. If you have an attitude of indecision and doubt when facing the devil, this will only make him bold and aggressive in his attacks, but confronting him with a strong will and firm confidence in God's promises unmasks him as a coward. Satan cannot lead us into sin without our consent. As long as we are submissive to the control and guidance of the Holy Spirit, we can stand victorious against all of Satan's tricky devices. As the Apostle John says, "Greater is He that is in you, than he that is in the world" (1 John 4:4 KJV). We are to submit to God and resist the devil. In verses 8-10 we continue with the ten imperatives and see that we are to have a complete dejection of ourselves.

A Complete Dejection of Self

James 4:8. Draw near to God and He will draw near to you.

The third command is to "draw near to God." Isn't it interesting that resisting the devil will result in our drawing near to God? When you run from something or someone, then we usually run *to* something or someone, right? Run from the enemy, Satan, and run to your Friend, God. This term *drawing near* conveys the thought of entering into communion with God as acceptable worshippers. The Jewish audience to whom James was writing would understand this, as this was a common Old Testament concept describing the priests and their responsibilities in approaching the tabernacle and its sacred ceremonies (Leviticus 21:21-23). It is impossible for sinful man and woman to draw near to a Holy God without the energizing power of the Holy Spirit. It is the faith of God implanted in our hearts through the operation of the Holy Spirit that gives us the desire to draw near to God. It is the implanted word that we saw in James 1:21, which is able to save our souls.

How can you draw near to God? Some practical ways are: prayer, reading His Word, meditating on His Word, memorizing His Word, and sitting before Him. Do you ever do that—just sit before Him in quietness? Music is another way that we can draw near to God. Being with godly people is another. What are the results when you draw near to God? They are great results! He will draw near to you! What a deal!

James 4:8. Cleanse your hands, you sinners

We cannot draw near to God with dirty hands. That is why James then gives the fourth command, "cleanse your hands, you sinners." The Jewish reader would understand what James meant here as the Old Testament priests had to wash their hands in a bronze laver filled with water, "lest they die" (Exodus 30:19-21). As water removed physical filth from their hands, they became aware that spiritual filth also had to be removed. Our hands are symbols of our actions. Therefore to *cleanse our hands* means to recognize that they are dirty with sin and need to be washed. Cleansing our hands, or confessing our sins, is another way we draw near to God (1 John 1:9). It is impossible for you and me to think that we can draw near to a Holy God with dirty hands and hearts. We must confess and repent of our sins.

James 4:8. And purify your hearts, you double-minded.

Not only do we need to cleanse our hands, but also to "purify our hearts." This fifth command calls for an inner purification. The cleansing of our hands is a metaphor of our outward activity, and purifying our hearts is symbolic of our inward activity—our thoughts and attitudes. Outwardly, the hands may appear clean, but the heart may not be pure. The psalmist asks, "Who may ascend into the hill of the Lord? Or who may stand in His holy place? He who has clean hands *and* a pure heart" (Psalm 24:3-4, emphasis mine). Clean hands do not necessarily indicate a holy life. If you want a clean life, you must have a clean heart. "For out of the *heart* proceed evil thoughts, murders, adulteries, fornications, thefts, false witness, blasphemies. These are the things which defile a man, but to eat with unwashed hands does not defile a man" (Matthew 15:19-20, emphasis mine). The heart represents our inner life. How do you get a pure heart? By being separated unto God, by being devoted and obedient to Him. Purity carries the idea of separation unto God. This is another way in which we draw near to God.

Now James calls them "double-minded." Why? Because they are divided and inconsistent in their thoughts and deeds. In James 1, we explored this term *double-minded*, which described the man who doubts when asking for wisdom. He is unstable in all his ways—he is double-minded. Double-minded in the Greek means people with two souls. They want to have a heart for the world and a heart for God.[53] "Mr. Facing Both Ways" as John Bunyan said! We want the world to see our clean hands, but when it comes to the heart, which no one can see but God, we are double-minded. We know the world can't see our hearts, so we convince ourselves that God cannot see what's inside. This is a call to salvation. If we are two-souled, if we are facing both ways, then what is the remedy? How can I become united in hands and heart? How can I love God with all my soul? James gives us the answer in verses 9 and 10.

James 4:9. Lament and mourn and weep! Let your laughter be turned to mourning and your joy to gloom.

James rapidly gives the sixth, seventh and eighth commands: "lament," "mourn" and "weep." He means for us to do these things on account of our sins. We should not take sin lightly. These sins are the ones he has already spoken about—namely pride, which we said, was the root cause of all sin. *Lament*, in other words, be miserable. Feel miserable and wretched on account of your sins. Do you? You should. When a true realization of sin sets in, the feeling of wretchedness will follow. Paul said, "O wretched man that I am who will deliver me from this body of death" (Romans 7:24). Job said, "Therefore I abhor myself, and repent in dust and ashes" (Job 42:6). Isaiah wrote, "Woe is me, for I am undone, because I am a man of unclean lips, and I dwell in the midst of a people of unclean lips" (Isaiah 6:5).

Mourn indicates the grieving and sorrow a repentant sinner should experience with such intensity that it cannot be concealed. What did Jesus say in the Sermon on the Mount in Matthew 5:4? "Blessed are those who mourn, for they shall be comforted." In this sermon Jesus is talking about mourning over sin.

---

[53] As mentioned previously, the *double-minded* has one soul turned toward God and the other soul toward the world. One soul believes God, and the other soul disbelieves God. The Old Testament would have provided James with this concept of a united soul, as every day the Hebrews would repeat: "Hear, O Israel: The LORD our God, the LORD is one! You shall love the LORD your God with all your heart, with all your soul, and with all your strength" (Deuteronomy 6:4-5). James' Jewish audience would have understood this completely.

To *weep* adds the element of an outward display of sorrow. Do you weep over your sin? The ninth command is, "Let your laughter be turned to mourning and your joy to gloom." Now, dear ladies, there are times when laughter is appropriate, but laughter is inappropriate when you and I are mourning over sin. The laughter mentioned here is a reference to flippant laughter of careless unconcern. A person who has given his or her life to Christ cannot laugh at sin. The flippant laughter is to be turned to something different—*to mourning, to gloom*. The word *gloom* occurs only once in the New Testament, and it means dejection or sorrow. It is not melancholy, but it is sorrow on account of sin. God has made us so that we should feel sorrow when we are conscious that we have done wrong, and it is appropriate that we should do so. We should experience heaviness and gloom when living in unconfessed sin, as it is a miserable place to be. James is calling for genuine repentance, not some casual apology or mild expression of regret, but sorrow. Not "Oh sorry God, I goofed today. You know how I am. See ya." Remember the good old days in Nehemiah? The Israelites read the Word one-fourth of the day, and for another fourth of the day they also *confessed* their sins and worshipped the Lord (Nehemiah 9:3). Our consciences are so dulled to sin. Something is amiss today as our confession takes only a fourth of a minute of our day. We are neither to laugh nor rejoice in the presence of sin. In verse 10, James wraps up the whole of the ten imperatives, the ten commands to repentance.

James 4:10. Humble yourselves in the sight of the Lord, and He will lift you up.

Finally, James summarizes his thoughts with the tenth command, "Humble yourselves in the sight of the Lord." He is telling us that we should allow ourselves to be humbled in the eyes of the Lord or before Him. The sense of our unworthiness in His presence can only produce humility. What will happen if you allow yourself to be humbled? "He will lift you up," James says. He will exalt you. In James 1, we saw that the Lord exalts the man of humble circumstances or physical conditions. We now see that He exalts the humble of spirit—the one who is truly broken over her sin. What does this mean? He will exalt us from the condition of a brokenhearted child to that of a forgiven child. He will wipe away our tears; He will remove the sadness from our hearts; He will fill us with joy. We need not stay in a continual period of mourning. The prophet Isaiah declared that the Lord "anointed him to give us beauty for ashes, the oil of joy for mourning, and the garment of praise for the spirit of heaviness" (Isaiah 61:3). Why? So that we might be called "trees of righteousness, the planting of the Lord," and "that He may be glorified!"

Summary

James has clearly given us the remedy for worldliness. He has clearly shown us the steps to make sure our faith is genuine. Now some of you might be asking, "Well, how do I know if I really am repentant? How do I know if I have submitted my life to the Lordship of Christ? Is there any way to measure that?" Yes, there is. Paul wrote:

> Now I rejoice, not that you were made sorry, but that your sorrow led to repentance. For you were made sorry in a godly manner, that you might suffer loss from us in nothing. For godly sorrow produces repentance leading to salvation, not to be regretted; but the sorrow of the world produces death. For observe this very thing, that you sorrowed in a godly manner: What diligence it produced in you, what clearing of yourselves, what indignation, what fear, what vehement desire, what zeal, what vindication! In all things you proved yourselves to be clear in this matter. Therefore, although I wrote to you, I did not do it for the sake of him who had done the wrong, nor for the sake of him who suffered wrong, but that our care for you in the sight of God might appear to you. (2 Corinthians 7:9-12)

How would Paul know if they were repentant? Paul gives seven ways for us to be certain if our sorrow for sin is a godly sorrow leading to repentance or whether it is just worldly sorrow that leads to death:

(1) *Carefulness.* Genuine repentance produces a diligence to deal with the issues of sin in your life. A worldly sorrow will produce a carelessness and lack of concern over sin.

(2) *Cleansing of yourselves.* If you are truly repentant, then you will be seeking the forgiveness of God and others. Worldly sorrow will produce rationalizing your sin, excusing it, and defending yourself.

(3) *Indignation.* Genuine repentance will produce righteous anger that you have offended a holy God and anger that you have allowed sin in your members. Worldly sorrow will produce anger at yourself, others, and at the mess you are in.

(4) *Fear.* Genuine sorrow will produce a fear of God and fear of His displeasure. Worldly sorrow produces a fear of consequences and fear of others.

(5) *Vehement desire.* A longing for, an intense craving, to settle the issue and see relationships restored. Worldly sorrow will not produce a longing for true restoration.

(6) *Zeal.* Zeal to remove the sin and to see the work of reformation in great earnest. A worldly sorrow will be content to be lethargic about sin. There is no real battle against sin, no fighting against sin, no hatred of sin.

(7) *Full punishment.* This will produce an avenging of the wrong. This person no longer tries to protect himself, no matter what the cost. Worldly sorrow will produce no real effort to correct the real problem, which is the heart.

I would encourage you to get serious about your sin. Do not take a casual approach to it. Weep and mourn over your sin. Be zealous about fighting sin in your life and be diligent to take care of offenses that you have committed. If and only if your life is manifesting these things can you be assured that you are not among the many "Christians" who are double-minded, thus proving their faith dead!

Questions to Consider
"The Remedy for Worldliness"
James 4:5-10

1. Read James chapter 4. (a) How does the person in verses 1-4 differ from the person in verses 7-10? List as many contrasts as you see.

2. Memorize James 4:6-7.

3. Read Hebrews 10:19-25. (a) What steps do we need to take to draw near to God according to this passage? (b) What do you think these mean? (c) What steps do you take when you draw near to God?

4. Find an example in the Word of someone who resisted God, and note the results. Share principles you can glean for your own life.

5. Find an example of someone who humbled herself or himself before God, and note the results. Share principles you can glean for your life.

6. According to this passage in James, how can one know if she is genuinely repentant?

7. Recall a time when you knew God was resisting you because of your pride. What did you learn about God? About yourself?

8. Notice this week the ways in which you draw near to God and the ways in which you resist Satan.

9. How might you better draw near to God? Write your answer in a form of a prayer request to God.

18

The Danger of Slander!

James 4:11-12

One Sunday morning I was visiting with a man in our congregation, and we were talking about gossip and how destructive it is. He said that he had recently asked his grown daughter if she could recall the most hurtful time in her life. Her answer was "when I was slandered by a group of kids from church." Thankfully, our church was not the one they were attending when this slander occurred, but I am not foolish enough to believe that gossip isn't practiced in our church as well. Slander! It is so destructive—so hurtful! At one time or another, slander has probably injured each of us. As someone once said, "Into the space of one little hour sins enough may be conjured up by evil tongues to blast the fame of a whole life of virtue."

Perhaps many of you breathed a sigh of relief after we finished studying the tongue in James 3, but guess what? We are not finished. We not only have these verses in chapter four on the tongue, but James is going to address the topic briefly again in James 5. Evidently, because of James' repetitious warnings regarding the tongue in his epistle, it posed a serious problem for these readers. And I fear it is a serious problem for some of us too, which is why we need these repetitious warnings. In addition to speaking evil of one another, we are also going to address the awful sin of judging one another. We could all use some admonishment in this area.

So far in chapter 4, James has been writing of *worldliness*, which he defines as warring, fighting, lusting, asking amiss in prayers, being spiritually unfaithful, and lacking humility. In verses 5-10, James then called his readers to repent of this worldliness, to stop being an enemy of God and submit to His Lordship. His words are a call to salvation. As we have seen in verses 7-10, true repentance manifests itself in how we respond to the Lord, but true repentance will also manifest itself in how we respond to others as well. As we humble ourselves before God, we will also humble ourselves before others, and that humility will manifest itself in edifying speech regarding others, not in slandering and judging. The opposite is true as well, as a haughty spirit towards God will manifest itself in a haughty spirit towards others. James addresses this haughty attitude in verses 11 and 12.

> Do not speak evil of one another, brethren. He who speaks evil of a brother and judges his brother, speaks evil of the law and judges the law. But if you judge the law, you are not a doer of the law but a judge. [12]There is one Lawgiver, who is able to save and to destroy. Who are you to judge another? (James 4:11-12)

Two predominate themes emerge from this passage: the *character* of a judgmental spirit (v 11) and the *condemnation* from a just Savior (v 12).

The Character of a Judgmental Spirit

James 4:11. Do not speak evil of one another, brethren.

After telling the brethren to humble themselves before God, James then admonishes them saying, "Do not speak evil of one another, brethren." It is uncertain whom the *brethren* were, but it was probably a fellow brother or sister in the Lord. It is by the goodness of God that specific names aren't mentioned, because I always wonder about Euodia and Syntyche, whom Paul beseeched to be of the same mind in the Lord. He asks someone in the church to help those women, because, we assume, they were not getting along and were depreciating one another (Philippians 4:2-3). How would you like your name forever recorded in the Word of God as an example of disagreeable behavior? Yikes!

This *speak evil of* in the original language means to talk another down or talk against another. It involves slandering and speaking harshly. In this verse, it is likely that James is referring back to those fights and wars that he recorded in James 4:1. Usually this verb means to slander someone when she is not there to defend herself. In later Greek usage the word *katalaleo*[54] seems to have had the additional significance of speaking about others behind their backs in a derogatory manner. The evil here is probably speaking against others—against their actions, their motives, their manner of living, etc. It reflects backbiting, faultfinding, and harsh criticism. As we saw in the last chapter, where humility is lacking, the door is wide open for evil, slanderous, disparaging, and depreciating speech. What is the opposite of humility? Pride. Pride is why we speak evil of our brother and judge our brother.

If you are in the habit of criticizing others, it is because you feel you are much better than they—this is pride. Backbiting is really a variation of self-exaltation. As believers in Christ, we are bound to each other. We are brothers and sisters with ties that bind us together as a family. We sing the song "They'll Know We Are Christians By Our Love," and I pray that this is how the world will truly know us. Speaking evil of our brother and slandering our brother is serious business. In fact, read Psalm 50 where true religion and false religion are contrasted, especially noting verses 16-23. Slander is a serious sin, serious enough that God says, "Lest I tear you in pieces!" (Psalm 50:22). Psalm 101:5 says, "Whoever secretly slanders his neighbor, Him I will destroy." The Apostle Paul says, "Let all bitterness, wrath, anger, clamor, and evil speaking be put away from you, with all malice" (Ephesians 4:31). However, speaking evil is not the only way we judge others, is it? James adds another element that is just as bad when judging others.

---

[54] *Biblesoft s New Exhaustive Strong s Numbers and Concordance with Expanded Greek-Hebrew Dictionary*. 1994, Biblesoft and International Bible Translators, Inc. The verb *katalaleo* is made up of two words, *laleo* meaning "to speak" and *kata* meaning "against." Hence, it suggests a speaking against someone.

James 4:11. He who speaks evil of a brother and judges his brother

In addition to speaking evil of a brother, James exposes another unacceptable behavior in this passage, i.e., "judging a brother." To judge someone entails what goes on in our heart and mind. This judging would be harsh and would include judging one's motives and conducts. Although we don't verbalize it, much of the time we are speaking evil in our minds. Wouldn't it be awful if others could read our minds and know what we are thinking of them? Of course, God knows what we are thinking before we even think it. James has given us several admonitions about the poor. Let me give you some illustrations of how we might judge someone based only on outward appearance.

When you see a poor person, do you immediately think he is lazy and a poor money manager? Wouldn't it be better to ask him how he got that way and seek a biblical solution to relieve him? When you see a rich person, do you automatically think she is snobby or dishonest? Instead of judging her character by her wealth, why not thank God that He has chosen to bless her and then encourage her to generously give back to the Lord? When you see someone with a sour look on her face, do you presume she is an unbeliever? Instead, why not go talk to her, discover what is troubling her, then pray for her. When politicians come to mind, do you automatically equate them with dishonesty? Instead, why not give honor to them as Paul says in Romans 13:4, realizing they are "God's minister to you for good." Pray for our leaders as we are commanded in the Scriptures. When someone forgets you at Christmas or your birthday when they normally remembered in the past, do you automatically think they don't care for you anymore? If someone forgets you, maybe they just really forgot. Maybe they are just getting older, or getting Alzheimer's disease. We need to overlook these things. We need to get our focus off ourselves. Take your hurt to the Lord in prayer.

Just think how terrible it would be if God specialized in speaking evil of us and condemning our faults as we do of others.

None of us would be able to bear it. So now you might say, why is it so bad to speak evil of others? James says that if you speak evil of your brother and judge your brother, you speak evil of the law and judge the law.

James 4:11. Speaks evil of the law and judges the law.

By judging you are setting yourself up to judge not only your brother, but *the law*. The word for *law* (Greek, *nomos*) means the law governing the Christian life, the perfect law of liberty (James 1:25) and the royal law of loving our neighbor as our self (James 2:8), which we studied in chapter 10. James says that you cannot claim to love your neighbor as yourself while speaking maliciously behind her back. Re-read this principle that the Lord gave Moses. The Lord clearly states that we are not to slander our brother or hate our brother in our heart.

> You shall not go about as a talebearer among your people; nor shall you take a stand against the life of your neighbor: I am the LORD. You shall not hate your brother in your heart. You shall surely rebuke your neighbor, and not bear sin because of him. You shall not take vengeance, nor bear any grudge against the children of your people, but you shall love your neighbor as yourself: I am the LORD. (Leviticus 19:16-18)

If a brother or sister has sinned, the loving approach is to go to them directly and try to help with the hope of pointing out the blind spot. I fear that too many Christians would rather deal with another's sins by gossiping and slandering the individual, instead of going to them directly. About this issue Jesus said, "Moreover if your brother sins against you, go and tell him his fault between you and him alone. If he hears you, you have gained your brother" (Matthew 18:15). Clearly it is easier to whisper your displeasure in someone else's ear rather than directly confront someone about her sin.

So James is saying that when you violate this royal law of loving your brother, this law of moral obligation that God has written in the heart of man, you are in effect criticizing the law, implying that it is not good and should be abolished. By criticizing the law, you are breaking the whole law again. Remember James has already said that whoever keeps the whole law yet stumbles in one point is guilty of all (James 2:10). By speaking evil of the law and judging the law, you think that you are above the law. You have become a judge of the law. We think our opinions are better than God's! James says:

James 4:11. But if you judge the law, you are not a doer of the law but a judge.

You are no longer acting as one who is obligated to obey the law, but you are usurping the office of the judge whose function is to determine a man's actions. We have already seen the term *doer* in James 1:22-23, where we are told to be *doers* of the Word. In that passage, James says that if you are not a *doer* of the Word, you have deceived your own self. Now he says that if you are speaking evil of others, you are not a *doer* of the law, but you are a judge. Once again, James is clearly making distinctions between the spurious and the genuine believer. If slandering and judging others mark your life, then James says your faith is suspect.

I want to stress that this does not mean that, as Christians, we cannot exercise discernment, wisdom, or form opinions. Instead it means that the child of God must not become a gossip or have a critical spirit. James is not saying that we cannot make moral judgments regarding each other based on our conduct, because we know Scripture commands us to evaluate the conduct of others and to take appropriate action. For instance, some people will tell you that it is not right to judge anyone, and they will quote the verse from Matthew 7:1 that says "Judge not, that you be not judged." The people who use this verse use it for their own means but don't complete Jesus' thought. They will interpret it to mean that you had better not make a judgment about someone else or you will be in big trouble with God. They don't account for the verse's context, which is directed to people who are ignoring the log in their own eyes while fixating on the speck in someone else's. Jesus does not forbid judgment. Rather, He forbids us from judging when we haven't dealt with the sin in our own lives. It is our duty to exercise judgment. For example, Matthew 7:15 says we are to beware of false prophets. How can we beware if we do not judge them against the standard of God's Word? Jesus said, "You will know them by their fruits" (Matthew 7:16). Paul commanded the Corinthian Christians to judge sinfulness in their midst and excommunicate offenders (1 Corinthians 5:1-5). The Apostle John instructs his readers to put teachers to the test and make the appropriate decisions about them (1 John 4:1-4). We are to judge adultery, murder, lying, and stealing as sins. And if anyone is engaging in this kind of behavior, we must judge them as being sinful (1 Corinthians 5:9-13). John 7:24 says, "Do not judge according to appearances, but judge with righteous judgement." What James is forbidding is a critical spirit, judging motives of other people, and the attitude that seeks to run others down. James is prohibiting a judgmental spirit that usurps the authority that belongs to God, causing us to act as gods. The right of judgment belongs to God and God alone. Judging belongs to God and God alone because it is God and God alone who is able to save and destroy, as James says in verse 12.

The Condemnation From a Just Savior

James 4:12. There is one Lawgiver, who is able to save and destroy.

"There is one Lawgiver" and it is not you or me; it is God. What are you trying to be? God? When you set yourself up as a judge of others and of God's law, you are trying to dethrone God and to establish your own law of judgment. It's as if you are saying, "God, I think I can judge better than You. Move over and let me take the reign on Your throne." There are two characteristics that James gives of this Lawgiver. He is able to save and to destroy.

"There is one Lawgiver, God, and He is able to save and destroy." The *save* here involves a complete act at a certain time, to rescue from danger and destruction, to save a suffering one from perishing. We know that man can never come to God in his own strength. If he is left to himself, he will perish. As the Apostle Peter says, the Lord is "not willing that any should perish but that all should come to repentance" (2 Peter 3:9). God is the only one who can save man. You and I simply do not have that power. Paul says that Christ Jesus came into the world to do what? To save sinners! (1 Timothy 1:15). Yes, He saves, but He also destroys! This means to destroy utterly and completely. This denotes an act once and for all with finality to it. If man rejects the offers of grace, it brings final execution of the sentence of his sin, which is death. This death is an eternal separation from God. It will be final and it will be irrevocable. Jesus says, "Do not fear those who kill the body but cannot kill the soul. But rather fear Him who is able to *destroy* both soul and body in hell" (Matthew 10:28, emphasis mine).

James 4:12. Who are you to judge another?

James wraps up his thoughts on judging others by saying: "Who are you to judge another?" The emphasis is on the *you*. "And *you*, who do you think you are to place yourself above God?" Who are *you* anyway? Are *you* able to destroy both body and soul in hell? Do *you* think *you* are without flaw? Are *you* the holy standard? Can *you* save a soul from hell? Romans 2:1 says "You are inexcusable, O man, whoever you are who judge, for in whatever you judge another you condemn yourself; for you who judge practice the same things." Barnes writes, "Who art thou, a weak and frail and erring mortal, yourself accountable to that Judge, that you should interfere, and pronounce judgment on another, especially when he is doing only what that Judge permits him to do?"[55]

Unfortunately, too many Christians try to help God in His capacity of lawgiver. They are like the man who said he was afraid

---

[55] Albert Barnes, *Barnes Notes on the New Testament: James* (Baker Book House, n.d.), p. 77.

The Danger of Slander!

he was going to be of no use in the world because he only had one talent. His pastor said, "That shouldn't discourage you. What is your talent?" asked the pastor. The man replied that it was the talent of judging others, of criticizing. The pastor said, "Well, I advise you to do with it what the man of one talent did with his—BURY IT!" Can't you just imagine that by now James is a little disgusted with them? And how much more is God disgusted with us? Someone may look perfect from a distance, but as we get closer, the flaws show. If you and I want intimate friendships who will feel our heartbeats and whose heartthrobs we can feel, we must take them with their faults and love them. Because there are sin issues, any corrections we make must be in love, not because it is our job to judge them. Part of loving someone is rebuking sin, and we should not shy from that, but we are forbidden to judge motives.

Summary

Perhaps you are convicted of this terrible sin of slander and judging others. You might say, "What do I need to do?" Repent of course, but perhaps we need get to the root of the problem by examining our motives. Why do we speak evil of each other, and judge one another?

(1) *Revenge*. We get hurt over something that someone else did to us or said about us or to us, so we want to retaliate. And yet what does the Bible say in Matthew 5:44? "Love your enemies, bless those who curse you, do good to those who hate you, and pray for those who spitefully use you and persecute you." Paul tells us that vengeance is the Lord's and that He will repay (Romans 12:19).

(2) *Pride or self-righteousness*. We think we are more spiritual, and so we want to let others know how spiritual we really are and how unrighteous someone else is. Let us not forget James 4:6: "But He gives more grace. Therefore He says: 'God resists the proud, but gives grace to the humble.'"

(3) *Too much idle talk*. Sometimes I think we speak evil of others just because we talk too much. There is too much empty talk. Proverbs 10:19 says, "In the multitude of words sin is not lacking." Just think what would happen if we used that empty talk to build each other up or pray together. When you are with other people, do you try to raise the level of conversation from the mundane—the weather, sports, clothes, houses—to the eternal—heaven, the Lord, answers to prayer? Remember that wonderful verse in Malachi 3:16 that says "Then those who feared the LORD spoke to one another, and the Lord listened and heard them; So a book of remembrance was written before Him for those who fear the LORD and who meditate on His name."

We need to be iron sharpening iron— not busybodies wandering from house to house speaking things we ought not to speak. I want to encourage you to always be thinking of ways you can elevate the conversation to speak of eternal things, to sharpen the thinking of those you are with, to challenge one another in the areas of holy living. Now I am not saying that discussing other things is not necessary, because it is. But when we spend all of our time talking about the mundane and earthly, we open ourselves up to idle talk and evil chatter. I am sure that each of you would agree with me that speaking against our brothers and sisters in Christ is a serious sin. But according to these two verses that we have looked at in this chapter, it is one of the worst of all sins for two reasons: (1) We exalt ourselves above the law, and (2) we exalt ourselves above God. May God help us to be women who judge with righteous judgment, but who do not judge the motives and intents of one another's hearts!

Questions to Consider
"The Danger of Slander!"
James 4:11-12

1. (a) What does James say in 4:11-12? (b) Now, review the book of James and note where else the topic of the tongue is spoken about. (c) Why do you think James mentions this so often? (d) What would "speaking evil" include?

2. Memorize James 4:11-12.

3. Read Matthew 7:1-5 and John 7:24. (a) Is Jesus contradicting Himself? (b) How do you know?

4. Read Numbers 12. (a) What was the sin of Miriam and Aaron? (b) What was the result of their judging Moses? (c) What principles can you glean regarding judging others—especially those in leadership?

5. (a) What is Paul saying in 1 Corinthians 5:9-13? (b) Do you think the churches today are practicing this? (c) What can we do to change that?

6. Observe your speech and thoughts regarding other people this week. Do the things you say and think about others show a righteous judgment or a judgmental spirit?

7. Try as much as you are able to elevate your conversations this week from the mundane to the eternal. What have you learned about your speech?

8. We have now had several instructions regarding the tongue. Is your speech any better, and is it God-honoring? What is your prayer to God?

19

To Plan or Not to Plan?

James 4:13-17

The day I had planned to study this lesson, I had not planned to study this lesson. Are you confused? Let me start over. The day I had planned to study this lesson, I woke up and went through my usual morning routine; I spent time with the Lord, went on a walk, and did various household duties. Then I showered and got dressed. Only this particular morning I dressed up, because I was taking a friend to lunch for her birthday, or so I thought. I finished the last minute things I needed to do; and as I was just about to head out the door, my friend called and said, "I am going to need to cancel today." For a moment I stood there and said to myself, "OK, self, now what are you going to do with this time you have?" And quite a chunk of time it was. So I decided to execute Plan B (by the way our Plan B is often God's Plan A); I began my study of this lesson in James.

These types of unexpected events happen to all of us, and often they occur multiple times a day. We plan, only to have our plans thwarted. In fact, the second time I had the opportunity to work on this lesson, my day went like this: I unexpectedly woke up at 2:30 a.m., so my day started unusually early. Next I heard about the plane crash in New York City—this happened on the November 12 that followed September 11, 2001. My husband had just left for Colorado by car; but an hour after his departure, I noticed his garment bag was still at our house. I called him, and guess what I did then? I met him halfway to deliver his clothes. And so the day went, not as I planned, but as God planned. So we ask ourselves the question: "Should Christians plan or not?" And what should be our attitude when our plans change? Should we pout and cry and get mad at God? No, we should not.

The fourth chapter of the Epistle of James begins with quarrels and ends with planning in relation to the will of God. "How is this related?" you might be asking. Planning without a proper sense of the uncertainty of life and without consulting the Lord is another form of worldliness. In the last number of chapters we have been considering worldliness: the worldliness of fighting and warring, the worldliness of asking amiss in our prayers, the worldliness of spiritual unfaithfulness, the worldliness of pride, and as we noted in the last chapter, the worldliness of speaking evil and judging our brothers and sisters. James is simply transitioning from one form of worldliness to another. Worldliness can manifest itself in an arrogant attitude of self-sufficiency, in planning one's life without acknowledging God. Therefore, James has some very practical concepts for us to ponder as we complete chapter 4 in the Epistle of James.

> Come now, you who say, "Today or tomorrow we will go to such and such a city, spend a year there, buy and sell, and make a profit"; [14]whereas you do not know what will happen tomorrow. For what is your life? It is even a vapor that appears for a little time and then vanishes away. [15]Instead you ought to say, "If the Lord wills, we shall live and do this or that." [16]But now you boast in your arrogance. All such boasting is evil. [17]Therefore, to him who knows to do good and does not do it, to him it is sin. (James 4:13-17)

The last five verses in James chapter 4 present us with three major themes: planning without God is *self-reliance* (vv 13-14); planning with God is *sovereign reliance* (v 15); and planning without God is *sin* (vv 16-17).

Planning Without God Is Self-Reliance

James 4:13. Come now, you who say, "Today or tomorrow we will go to such and such a city, spend a year there, buy and sell, and make a profit."

So what is Pastor James talking about in verse 13 when he says: "Come now." He is saying, "Listen, you who say, or attend to this, you who say." The picture of traveling Jewish businessmen was not unusual in the first century. These energetic Jewish traders would have precisely planned their agenda, "today or tomorrow," and the exact location of their enterprise, "such and such a city." You can almost visualize a finger pointing it out on the map! We do the same thing today, don't we, when we are getting ready to go on a vacation? The strategy is well formulated: the duration of their intended business venture, "spend a year there"; the precise nature of their activity, "buy and sell"; and the anticipated outcome, i.e., "make a profit." The Greek word here for *make a profit* (kerdesomen) means the desire of gain, the love of gain. Selfish gain was their passion, and that was why they were traveling and trading. Selfish gain should not be the motivating power behind the Christian businessperson.

God wants businesspeople whose primary goal is not the accumulation of money, but the glory of God and creating a maximum impact for the kingdom. This notion is so contrary to our way of thinking, but not to God's way of thinking and not according to His Word. When you think about your job or your spouse's job, do you desire to make money so that you can accumulate material possessions, or do you desire to make money to give back to God and help those in need? James is rebuking the Christian's thinking, which had become worldly by focusing on profit as the primary reason for making money as opposed to using it to be a blessing to others. By the way, parents must be alert not to brainwash their children with the idea that making money is everything. Some parents lay guilt trips on their children, pushing them to select a profession that will enable them to be better off financially than their parents. Other parents may dissuade their children from undertaking Christian work because it doesn't pay well. Instead we should train our children to pursue the Lord and His will for their life. We must encourage them to use the gifts and abilities that God has given them according to His will, not our own. From this verse, we must not conclude that James is arguing against planning wisely, for we should be wise planners indeed.

Jesus Himself taught His followers the importance of calculating resources before beginning an enterprise. He agrees that it is normal for us to plan, for He said, "For which of you, intending to build a tower, does not sit down first and count the cost, whether he has enough to finish it" (Luke 14:28). What is condemned here is planning that eliminates God, planning that thinks human intelligence and ingenuity will suffice. Remember James' half-brother's memorable parable?

> Then He spoke a parable to them, saying: "The ground of a certain rich man yielded plentifully. And he thought within himself, saying, 'What shall I do, since I have no room to store my crops?' So he said, 'I will do this: I will pull down my barns and build greater, and there I will store all my crops and my goods. And I will say to my soul, "Soul, you have many goods laid up for many years; take your ease; eat, drink, and be merry."' But God said to him, 'Fool! This night your soul will be required of you; then whose will those things be which you have provided?' So is he who lays up treasure for himself, and is not rich toward God. (Luke 12:16-21)

The scenario depicted here in James clearly reflects their self-confidence. They assume that their plans are in their control, and no consideration is given to their dependence upon God and the uncertainty of life. The whole picture rings true today, doesn't it? Do we pray and seek God's counsel before making plans for our future, for our day? We might say, "Tomorrow I will have lunch with so and so, take the kids to school, clean the house, etc." Many times we plan our schedules without first consulting Him, and, readers, the results of that can be disastrous. How much less heartache and even headache we might have if we would consult the Lord for the decisions we make day to day. In verse 14, James reminds his readers that their knowledge of what will happen tomorrow is too uncertain to give them the confidence in making such firm plans.

James 4:14. Whereas you do not know what will happen tomorrow. For what is your life? It is even a vapor that appears for a little time and then vanishes away.

According to the previous verse, they were making plans for a *whole year* when they could not even see *one day* into the future. "Whereas you do not know what will happen tomorrow." None of us knows with certainty whether we will live to see the dawning of tomorrow, yet we plan as if we did. Proverbs 27:1 says, "Do not boast about tomorrow, for you do not know what a day may bring forth." Since September 11, 2001, I have often pondered the probability that none in the World Trade Center or those in the hijacked airplanes, when they woke up that morning or went to bed the night before, thought that it would be their last day on earth. We count our years by our birthdays, and yet God says in Psalms that we are to number our *days*, so that we may gain a heart of wisdom! (Psalm 90:12).

After James reminds us of tomorrow's uncertainty, he asks a broader question: "What is your life?" What sort of life do you have? "It is even a vapor that appears for a little time, and then vanishes away." My friends, your life is a puff of smoke or vapor, like breath appearing momentarily on a cold morning and disappearing, not even leaving a trace behind. Or a teakettle that gives off steam only to disappear against the ceiling. Blow out a match and watch how fast the smoke fades away—that is your life! We have already looked at this same concept in James 1:10, where James said that the rich man was like a flower of the field that passes away. Job says, "Oh, remember that my life is a breath" (Job 7:7)! The Psalmist says that our life is "a breath that passes away and does not come again"

(Psalm 78:39). How can we think that we can build any solid plans or hopes on a mist? It is rather silly, isn't it? How foolish we are to ignore God and then proudly plan for our lives that are as fleeting as a vapor. Every birthday that rolls around seems to shout at me, "You are dying, Susan Joy Heck!" As believers in Jesus Christ, should we not take death into consideration when planning? In verse 15, James continues to tell them that the error was not in what they said, but in what they did not say.

Planning With God Is Sovereign-Reliance

James 4:15. Instead you ought to say, "If the Lord wills, we shall live and do this or that."

Instead of relying on our own plans, James says, "Instead you ought to say, 'If the Lord wills, we shall live and do this or that.'" *If the Lord wills* is an acknowledgement that we want God's direction and approval and will do nothing without His consent. Now you might say, "Isn't James going a little too far here?" Well, let's look at some of the numerous examples in the Scriptures. Paul says, "I will return again to you, God willing" (Acts 18:21); "I will come to you shortly, if the Lord wills" (1 Corinthians 4:19); "I hope to stay a while with you, if the Lord permits" (1 Corinthians 16:7); "I trust in the Lord Jesus to send Timothy to you shortly ... I trust in the Lord that I myself shall also come shortly" (Philippians 2:19, 24).

James is not suggesting that we must always say, "If the Lord wills"—"If the Lord wills, we will go get a hamburger for lunch," or "God willing, I will see you next week"—because it could become a meaningless repetition, but we must have that outlook on life when making any plans. Nor is he condemning those who do say that. I often say to others when planning something, "If the Lord wills" or "God willing." I personally think that Christians might be wise to use the phrase more than they do, but only if they mean it from a sincere heart. The Puritans often used *Lord willing* in their speech and correspondence. It was a habit with them.

There is nothing wrong with planning, but there is something wrong with planning and leaving God out of the picture. Some of you may be list makers, like I am. Elisabeth Elliot says she has a list for everything: an everyday list, a grocery list, a Christmas list, a packing list for her suitcase, a prayer list, and several other lists. But when unexpected circumstances happen—at least unexpected to her—she says God is her Sovereign Lord, and she will not worry. She says, "He manages perfectly, day and night, year in and year out, the movement of the stars, the wheeling of the planets, the staggering coordination of events in order to hold things together. There is no doubt that He can manage the timing of my days and weeks. So I can pray in confidence, Thy list, not mine, be done."[56] This is an area where the Lord has matured me, and I thank Him for it. I know my husband thanks God, too! I used to become irritated when my schedule was interrupted or changed, but now I halfway expect it, and it does not trouble me as it once did. James is not saying, again I repeat, James is not saying that planning is sinful, but planning without committing your plans to the Lord and seeking His face is wrong. What does Psalm 37:5 say? "Commit your way to the Lord, trust also in Him and He shall bring it to pass."

We would be wise to take the time each morning to think about the day ahead and consider our agenda before God. I don't think we would be wise stewards of our God-given time if we were to wake up and just let the day happen. In fact, I usually plan my day the night before. It is a good idea to think about the next week, to look ahead that far, but always keeping God and His will in the forefront of your mind. When making promises to your children, it is also a good idea to convey, "If the Lord wills." Now that James has instructed us in the importance of including God in our plans, he then gives us God's opinion of excluding Him.

---

[56] Elisabeth Elliot, *Lamp for My Feet*, p. 77-78.

Planning Without God Is Sin

James 4:16. But now you boast in your arrogance. All such boasting is evil.

James says, "But now you boast in your arrogance. All such boasting is evil." *Boast* means to speak loudly about something you have a right to be proud of. *Arrogance* here is self-glorification in a negative sense. It is braggart talk.[57] Remember in James chapter 1 we saw that the brother of humble circumstances was to rejoice—to speak loudly about something he had a right to be proud of? This brother of humble circumstances was to rejoice. What a contrast here! We boast about our successes, our plans, our trips, our retirement, our houses, and ourselves. The word *boasting* also suggests these people were wandering in an unreal world and boasting to others about what they thought they had found! The only proper boasting for a believer is to boast in the Lord. Why, you might ask? Because self-boasting gives credit to self and not the glory to God, who is the Giver of the life you have.

Do you recall why the Lord struck Herod? The Lord struck him down because he did not give God the glory. Worms ate him, and he died (Acts 12:23). James says all such boasting is "evil." This means it is bad, useless, and good for nothing. How true is this! Boasting does no one any good, especially to the one who is boasting. What about the person who has to listen to it—BORING! Boasting is evil because it does not glorify our Lord. The man or woman who brags about their activities independent of God shows how empty they really are. As humans in the sight of God, James says you are declared good for nothing! And now that James has illuminated your thinking on this, he ends on a sober note!

---

[57] The Greek term translated *arrogance* is *alazoneias*, denoting pretensions of worldly thinking, as if they could control the future which is only within the control of the providence of God. It is the presumption of the self-sufficient who know nothing of the providence of God.

James 4:17. Therefore, to him who knows to do good and does not do it, to him it is sin.

James concludes by saying, "Therefore, to him who knows to do good and does not do it, to him it is sin." In effect he is saying that whoever *now* knows to plan their activities with a dependence on God but does not do so, is guilty of sin. These businessmen failed to plan with God in mind, and therefore acted arrogantly. This is sin. This law is universal—if someone knows the right thing to do and does not do it, he or she is guilty of sin. What should sober us here is that this is not just an unfortunate omission, but it is a sin. These words should make us tremble and repent. As Luke says, "For everyone to whom much is given, from him much will be required" (Luke 12:48). Once God has given us light, we are to walk in that light. In fact, many things have been illuminated for us since we began to study the Epistle of James—things that are good, things that are right for us to do, such as rejoicing in trials, asking God for wisdom during trials, enduring trials, not becoming angry with God or His Word, but receiving it with meekness, putting away all wickedness, being a doer of the Word and not a hearer only, taking care of widows and orphans, keeping ourselves unspotted from the world, not showing partiality, showing genuine faith by our works, bridling our tongue, not fighting, resisting the devil, and mourning over our sin, just to name a few. And so James says to us all, now that you have been enlightened to do the right thing and now that you know what good you should be doing, do it—if you choose not to, then to you it is sin!

In no way do I want to distract you from the main point of this chapter, which is the danger of planning without the Lord, but many times I am asked the question: "How can I be certain if something is a sin issue when it is not clearly pointed out in the Word?" These gray areas create uncertainty, so I want to give you ten questions to ask yourself when facing them.

(1) *Does it build me up spiritually?* Some things in which we choose to participate are just time robbers and hold little value. I often think of Paul's prayer for the church at Philippi: "that [they] may approve the things that are excellent" (Philippians 1:10). Ask yourself, "Is this the best thing I can do with my time?"

(2) *Does it bring me under its power or will it enslave me?* The Apostle Paul says, "All things are lawful for me, but all things are not helpful. All things are lawful for me, but I will not be brought under the power of any" (1 Corinthians 6:12). For instance, it is not a bad thing if you like to shop, but if you spend money that you do not have, then shopping has brought you under its power.

(3) *Is this an activity that will create an appetite for more?* A good example would be watching television. In and of itself, watching television is not a sin, unless the content is sinful. But if watching television creates an appetite for more to the point that you cannot turn the thing off, then perhaps God would be pleased to have you turn it off!

(4) *Will this destroy my ability to think logically?* The Scriptures are replete with the command to be sober minded, to have our wits about us! (Titus 2:6; 1 Peter 5:8). We are a generation that dulls our mind with illegal as well as legal drugs. In fact, I recently heard about a dog on Prozac®! These drugs can be very dangerous and produce long-term side effects.

(5) *Is this something that will weaken my intimacy with God?* The first commandment is "You shall have no other gods before Me" (Exodus 20:3). So if something takes precedent over your relationship with God and commandeers your love and passion for Him, it is in serious question. One of our Sunday school teachers said, "Whatever disrupts your communion with God, or weakens your appetite for the Bible, or dulls your concern for others, must be set aside."

(6) *Will it cause me to neglect my Bible Study and prayer time?* Many women get involved in all kinds of activities that may not be harmful or evil, but they rob them of the time they should be spending with God. They are encumbered with many things, but not sitting at the feet of Jesus!

(7) *Will it cause my body to rule over my spirit and soul?* A good example of this would be one's obsession with weight to the point of bulimia or anorexia. Some women will go to any means to maintain a certain weight. This is sinful and wrong. God does not care about your dress size—He cares about your heart!

(8) *Will this cause someone else to stumble?* Paul said, "But when you thus sin against the brethren, and wound their weak conscience, you sin against Christ. Therefore, if food makes my brother stumble, I will never again eat meat, lest I make my brother stumble" (1 Corinthians 8:12-13). Will this make your sister stumble?

(9) *Do I have an uneasy conscience about it?* It is written in Hebrews 13:18: "For we are confident that we have a good conscience, in all things desiring to live honorably." If you have the red flag of uneasiness, then don't do it. If in doubt, don't!

(10) *Can I ask God to bless this?* That question alone would probably veto many of those gray areas that we wonder about.

So, from now on when you wonder whether something is a sin, ask yourself these questions to try and determine what is God's best for you in this situation. One thing we do know: that thing that you know to be good or right, and you don't do, that is a sin.

Summary

So now we return to the object of our lesson, which is planning without the Lord. Think about your tomorrows. They may bring sickness, sorrow, or tragedy. They may bring a long awaited answer to prayer, like the salvation of someone you love. They may bring prosperity, a new friendship, or an opportunity to share Christ. Maybe your tomorrow will not come, as it did not come for those killed on September 11, 2001. They never saw September 12—all their plans were like vapor! Each of us in this room has an expiration date, just like items at the grocery store. The only thing different about our expiration date is that only the Lord knows when it is. He is the only One who knows the appointed time of our departure from this world. God may choose this very day to take you or me to our eternal home—either by death or maybe by the Rapture!

In Charles Swindoll's book, *Seasons of Life*, he relates a time that he was taking a leisurely drive on a Sunday afternoon.

> I was driving up to Forest Home with easy listening music coming through the speaker. A quiet drive on a mellow Sunday afternoon. Then I saw something up ahead. Before I realized what it was, it flashed in my mind as something terribly wrong—out of place—distorted. An overturned car—I could see it now. An ambulance screamed somewhere back. I felt like someone had pushed a fist into my stomach. Someone was directing traffic ... I got too close of a look at the vehicle resting on its crumpled top. The scene hangs in my mind ... the bystanders staring in open-mouthed disbelief ... two men dragging limp bodies out of the wreckage onto the pavement. All of the passengers were either dead or terribly mutilated. Such a warm, peaceful Sunday. The day was bright and filled with leisure hours. But for three people, that moment the world flipped—violently, crazily, fatally—upside down.... Naturally, I wondered if those victims knew our Lord—if they could smile at eternity. My pulse shot up so that I had to grip the wheel with both hands. Under my breath I mumbled Proverbs 27:1—Do not boast about tomorrow, for you do not know what a day may bring forth. James 4:13-14 was certainly written with that

particular proverb in mind. I said it out loud—several times—as the traffic resumed speed ... "Come now, you who say, "Today or tomorrow we will go to such and such a city, spend a year there, buy and sell, and make a profit, whereas you do not know what will happen tomorrow. For what is your life? It is even a vapor that appears for a little time and then vanishes away." [58]

---

[58] Charles Swindoll. *Seasons of Life* (Multnomah Press, 1983), p. 157)

Questions to Consider
"To Plan or Not to Plan"
James 4:13-17

1. Read over James 4 while asking yourself which form of "worldliness" needs to be removed most from my life?

2. Memorize James 4:13-15.

3. Read Proverbs 16:1-9. What do these verses teach you about wise planning?

4. Read Joshua 9. (a) Did the men seek the Lord's counsel about the Gibeonites? (b) What is the irony in what Joshua says in verse 22? (c) What does this teach you about planning without the Lord, especially when dealing with unbelievers?

5. (a) Give an example of someone in the Word who knew to do right and did not do it. (b) What was their sin? (c) What were the consequences? (d) What does this teach you about walking in the light that you have, being obedient to what you know?

6. Write down your plans for tomorrow. Wait until the next day, and then write down what actually took place. (a) What does this teach you about your plans versus God's "divine appointments"? (b) Also, how did you react when things did not go as you had planned?

7. Recall a time when you did not consult the Lord for some plan(s) you were making and the result(s).

8. What are you planning this week? Write a prayer request that would include "if the Lord wills" in your planning.

20

Warnings to the Rich

James 5:1-6

Flip Wilson, a popular comedian in the seventies, once said, "If money talks, all it ever says to me is goodbye!" However, money was not saying goodbye to the readers addressed in the first six verses of James, chapter 5. They were rich, and their riches were sinful. They were using their wealth for selfish purposes and were also persecuting the poor in the process. We need to understand a fact that will help us to unlock chapter five. A middle class society did not exist in biblical times, so the gulf between the rich and the poor was very wide. But nothing is new, as the tension between the rich and the poor is still evident today.

If you are a careful reader of the Scriptures, you understand that wealth is nothing but a gift from God, and that He has entrusted it to mankind to use wisely. However, the God who has made us and supplied us with money with which to live also holds us accountable for how we carry out that stewardship. These warnings are sobering for the rich in James' day, and I trust they will be for us as well. James warns:

> Come now, you rich, weep and howl for your miseries that are coming upon you! ²Your riches are corrupted, and your garments are moth-eaten. ³Your gold and silver are corroded, and their corrosion will be a witness against you and will eat your flesh like fire. You have heaped up treasure in the last days. ⁴Indeed the wages of the laborers who mowed your fields, which you kept back by fraud, cry out; and the cries of the reapers have reached the ears of the Lord of Sabaoth. ⁵You have lived on the earth in

pleasure and luxury; you have fattened your hearts as in a day of slaughter. ⁶You have condemned, you have murdered the just; he does not resist you. (James 5:1-6)

Two major themes emerge from this text: a *warning* to the rich (v 1) and the *reason* for the warning (vv 2-6).

A Warning to the Rich

James 5:1. Come now, you rich

With the initial words in this verse, "come now," Pastor James is summoning his readers to give careful attention to what he will say next. Notice that James does not call them brethren as we have seen frequently throughout this letter. (See James 1:2, 16, 19; 2:1, 5, 14; 3:1, 4:11; 5:7, 9, 10, 12, 19.) Instead he calls them "you rich." So who were these rich?

Evidently, they were non-Christian Jewish owners of large estates in the communities where these readers lived. These rich had no time for God. They rejected Him, and there seemed to be little hope for their salvation. You might say, "Hey, didn't you tell us that James wrote this epistle to Christians, or at least to those who thought they were Christians, to call them to test or examine their faith? Did James suddenly forget who his readers were?" The answer is no.

Warnings, which were directed to Israel's oppressors, were very common in the Old Testament. For example, one warning to Babylon says, "Wail, for the day of the LORD is at hand! It will come as destruction from the Almighty" (Isaiah 13:6). There were warnings to Moab (Isaiah 15:2), to Damascus (Isaiah 17:1), and to many other nations as well, although these prophecies were primarily directed to God's covenant people. It is highly unlikely that these nations would have ever heard or read those prophecies, but knowing that God would ultimately deal with their oppressors would encourage James' readers.

As we have mentioned, the Epistle of James is steeped in Old Testament terminology, and so James was informing his readers that there would be a day of judgment for the ungodly rich and that believers must not become disillusioned or envy the rich. He was probably also aware that his words would reach some of the rich and perhaps even alert them to the danger they were in. Therefore James commands them to "weep and howl," which is a term that refers to the howling of wolves and means that they were to have tears accompanied by loud lamentation. It is the emotional outburst of those who have disregarded God's claims and will be overwhelmed with the realization of their loss when He appears in judgment. They will realize that all their money did not buy them a passport to heaven and the privilege of being in God's presence for eternity.

James 5:1. Weep and howl for your miseries that are coming upon you!

Notice that James does not call them to repentance, nor does he tell them to "lament and mourn and weep" for their sins as he did in chapter 4:9, but he tells them to "weep and howl for [their] miseries that are coming upon [them]." *Howl* is a term used twenty-one times in the Old Testament to describe the violent grief of those who stand face-to-face with divine judgment. The vivid use of the present tense *coming* suggests that the judgments could be seen on the horizon. Like tidal waves, nothing could stop them, and these miseries were already approaching and on the verge of striking.

One probable misery was this: Remember earlier we learned that James wrote this epistle approximately A.D. 50 and that Jerusalem fell in A.D. 70? It is interesting that sixty years after Jerusalem fell, she had no history because the destruction was so devastating. Could these rich have imagined such a catastrophe? Hardly! And yet think of all the warnings that Scripture gives mankind, all the prophecies that were written, many which have already been fulfilled. Yet have these warnings changed the way some of us live? Unfortunately not!

But the greatest misery for the unsaved rich and for all who are unsaved is not the destruction of Jerusalem, but life without Jesus Christ and an eternity in hell. In Luke 16:19-31, Jesus Himself gives us a sobering reminder of the dangers of being rich and proud.[59] The rich man in the story is still burning in hell today, while the beggar Lazarus was carried by the angels to the bosom of Abraham. When we think of the miseries of hell, we should ask ourselves, "Is it really worthwhile to make money our god down here and to be separated from God for all of eternity?" Harrison Ford, an actor who has made millions with his movies, once quipped, "You only want what you don't have."

"What don't you have?" the interviewer asked.

"Peace," Harrison replied, "and I hope to find it when I die." This is a very sad commentary of the rich without Christ. Many like Harrison Ford will enter eternity looking for peace only to find torment, if they don't repent and trust Christ. In verse 2, James continues with some descriptive words regarding the futility of the rich.

---

[59] Jesus taught: "There was a certain rich man who was clothed in purple and fine linen and fared sumptuously every day. But there was a certain beggar named Lazarus, full of sores, who was laid at his gate, desiring to be fed with the crumbs which fell from the rich man's table. Moreover the dogs came and licked his sores. So it was that the beggar died, and was carried by the angels to Abraham's bosom. The rich man also died and was buried. And being in torments in Hades, he lifted up his eyes and saw Abraham afar off, and Lazarus in his bosom. Then he cried and said, 'Father Abraham, have mercy on me, and send Lazarus that he may dip the tip of his finger in water and cool my tongue; for I am tormented in this flame.' But Abraham said, 'Son, remember that in your lifetime you received your good things, and likewise Lazarus evil things; but now he is comforted and you are tormented. And besides all this, between us and you there is a great gulf fixed, so that those who want to pass from here to you cannot, nor can those from there pass to us.' Then he said, 'I beg you therefore, father, that you would send him to my father's house, for I have five brothers, that he may testify to them, lest they also come to this place of torment.' Abraham said to him, 'They have Moses and the prophets; let them hear them.' And he said, 'No, father Abraham; but if one goes to them from the dead, they will repent.' But he said to him, 'If they do not hear Moses and the prophets, neither will they be persuaded though one rise from the dead'" (Luke 16:19-31).

The Reason for The Warning

James 5:2. Your riches are corrupted, and your garments are moth-eaten.

Wealth in biblical times was commonly held in grain, clothing, and precious metals, as well as in flocks and herds. Today we might say that our stocks and bonds are useless. Corrupted or rotted may refer to hoarded grain stored in great barns, which Jesus warned against in Luke 12:15-21. Their moth-eaten garments are likewise worthless. These rich had large wardrobes in storage in addition to the clothes that they wore, and James called them moth-eaten. If you have ever seen a moth, you know they look harmless. They aren't like annoying flies, or stinging bees, or noisy crickets. In fact, they are rather cute, but in spite of their harmless appearance, we all dread the moth for the destruction they inflict upon our clothes. That is exactly what the rich are facing here, destruction. It is silent, unnoticed, and seemingly benign, but once the garment is moth-eaten, it is almost impossible to repair it. How true that is in the case of the rich. Once they begin to suffer the consequences of their money, the cure is difficult. Just as the hole in the garment is hard to repair, so the hole in a life is also hard to repair. Jesus gives us a similar warning in His Sermon on the Mount:

> Do not lay up for yourselves treasures on earth, where moth and rust destroy and where thieves break in and steal; but lay up for yourselves treasures in heaven, where neither moth nor rust destroys and where thieves do not break in and steal. For where your treasure is, there your heart will be also (Matthew 6:19-21).

In James 1:10, we learned that the godly response of a rich man is to be humble about his circumstances, not to accumulate wealth for personal gain. James goes on to describe what will happen to the personal assets of the rich.

James 5:3. Your gold and silver are corroded, and their corrosion will be a witness against you and will eat your flesh like fire.

James adds, "Your gold and silver are corroded." Now we know that gold and silver do not rust, so what is James saying here? He is using a metaphor: what you think is so important will be about as worthless as rusted-out iron in the day of judgment. It has no spiritual value. In fact, he says, "their corrosion will be a witness against you." In the judgment their corrupted wealth will stand as a witness to their misuse of God's provision. No excuses will diminish the evidence of their hoarded wealth used for selfish purposes. Just like us, they will not impress God on judgment day with all their possessions. Cars, houses, boats, clothes, jewelry, savings bonds, and anything else that have been hoarded will only be a witness against us. If Jesus asks, "Did you give to the poor?" The answer "no" will be a witness against us. If Jesus asks, "What did you do with that money I gave you?" and we reply that we heaped up treasures to live in pleasure, it will be a witness against us. And not only will it be a witness against us, but James says that it "will eat your flesh like fire."

These serious words should cause us to shudder for the souls of the rich. Remember in James 3:6 one of the descriptions of our tongue is that it is set on fire by hell? Here James uses the same term to describe their wealth as eating their flesh up as fire. The fires of judgment will be fueled by their corrupted wealth. James probably selected the words *your flesh* to remind the rich that their chief concern had been to provide for their own physical comforts, but in the day of judgment their rusted wealth will eat into their pampered flesh like a festering sore. Its effect will be like fire, torturing while it devours. The wicked are not all going to suffer with the same degree of punishment. The more wicked and oppressive a man or woman has been here on earth, the more God will punish him or her in hell. James has clearly taught that mercy will be withheld from those who have shown no mercy (James 2:13). God will individually deal with each person in hell even as He will deal with each believer individually in heaven (Mark 12:40; Luke 12:42-48; Matthew 11:24; and 1 Corinthians 3:8). There is no lumping all of us together. Christ saves us individually, works in each of our lives individually, rewards us individually, and punishes us individually. No one will be holding our hand on judgment day.

James 5:3. You have heaped up treasure in the last days.

James summarizes: "You have heaped up treasures in the last days." *The last days* in this sentence begin with Christ's first coming and will end with the return of the Lord Jesus. It is as though James is reminding them of the reality of eternity. You have thought of your last days, your retirement days, upon this earth, but what about when your last days are over? That would certainly fall under the category of making plans without consulting God, as we saw in James chapter 4. I wonder how differently you and I would spend our money if we would consult Him and realize that we will be accountable to Him for how we spent it? The rich not only misused their money by heaping and hoarding it, but they misused their money by oppressing the poor, by withholding their wages.

James 5:4. Indeed the wages of the laborers who mowed your fields, which you kept back by fraud, cry out; and the cries of the reapers have reached the ears of the Lord of Sabaoth.

The rich were even withholding wages from the laborers who had worked in their fields. This graphic scene is not drawn from their business dealings with other rich men, but with their treatment of the laborers. *Laborers* were agricultural employees who were dependent upon their daily earnings to meet their material needs. In those days no labor laws existed to protect the workers, so the rich often treated workers unfairly, and in this instance they were cheating them out of their wages. Remember in James 2:15 the brother or sister who was naked and destitute of daily food? They were dependent on the day's wages for their food. These laborers had reaped the rich man's fields—the reference here is to the wheat and barley harvests that were cut and shucked by hand. This work had been completed (reaped), and the pay had been earned, and yet the cruelty of the rich was evident in the words "kept back by fraud." This means the rich were depriving them of their pay at the end of the day.

Can you imagine what you would feel if your husband did not get that paycheck he so deserved each pay period? Or if you are a single mother who works outside the home, or a single woman who supports herself, can you imagine how you would feel if your hard-earned wages were withheld without cause? It would be a cruel and mean boss who would do such a thing, wouldn't it? You would probably do what James says these victims are doing—they "cry out." This is not a whimper, but a loud cry or scream, an appeal for justice. It is interesting that the laborers here are crying out because their wages have been withheld from them, yet in verse 1 we see that the rich will be howling because of the misery that will come upon them by hoarding that same money. How ironic! God doesn't hear the weeping and howling of the rich, but he hears the cries of the poor.

We know this because James writes: "the cries of the reapers have reached the ears of the Lord of Sabaoth." *Lord of Sabaoth* means the Lord of Hosts. This is one of the most majestic titles of the God of Israel, and it not only expresses His majesty and power as creator and ruler of the world, but also as commander of the hosts of heaven. *Lord of Sabaoth* stresses that the poor and the helpless have the Lord of hosts on their side, and when He hears their cry, something will be done. As David said, "This poor man cried out, and the Lord heard him, and saved him out of all his troubles" (Psalm 34:6). It is also written, "He shall regard the prayer of the destitute, and shall not despise their prayer" (Psalm 102:17). In verse 5, we shall see that a third example of the misuse of their money was their indulgent living.

James 5:5. You have lived on the earth in pleasure and luxury; you have fattened your hearts as in a day of slaughter.

"You have lived on the earth in pleasure and luxury," means that they lived in high style on this earth, a life of luxury and self-indulgence. It is the same picture that Jesus drew of the rich man "who was clothed in purple and fine linen and fared sumptuously every day" (Luke 16:19). *On the earth* seems to indicate that their delights were limited to the things of this world. What does Colossians 3:2-3 say about that? It says, "Set your mind on things above, not on things on the earth. [Why?] For you died, and your life is hidden with Christ in God." The rich lived in *pleasure and luxury*. The *King James Version* translated the phrase as "been wanton," which means they were sportive or joyous. The Greek word translated "been wanton" actually means to live in luxury or to be voluptuous. Since the central concern of the rich man is to indulge in the luxuries of earth, James elaborates: "You have fattened your hearts as in a day of slaughter." Just like ignorant cattle that are encouraged to eat well just before being led to the slaughterhouse, these rich men seem blissfully ignorant of impending judgment. *A day of slaughter* is used for "a day of judgment." They lived only to eat and drink and enjoy life. It is the same idea conveyed in the homily: Eat, drink and be merry, for tomorrow we all die! Others explain that these men are like beasts, which, on the very day of their slaughter, gorge themselves in unconscious security.[60]

We see this happening in our day as well, don't we? People in America indulge themselves in pleasure, giving no thought to the account they will someday have to give to God! By such a course, they are unwittingly preparing for their own destruction, just as cattle are fattened prior to being slaughtered. Both are ignorant of what is getting ready to happen to them. The rich were preparing themselves for the day of judgment like animals gorging themselves for the day of slaughter.

> There will be many fat and well to do people appearing before the great and just Judge to be condemned eternally, simply because they fattened their hearts so that they became senseless and deaf to the call of Christ to believe on Him and accept Him as Lord and Savior.[61]

---

[60] Vincent's *Word Studies of the New Testament,* Electronic Database. 1997, Biblesoft.

[61] Spiros Zodhiates, *The Patience of Hope* (AMG Publishers, 1981), p. 71.

A fourth and final example of how they misused their money and power was by persecuting the just.

James 5:6. You have condemned, you have murdered the just; he does not resist you.

You have condemned refers to the fact that these rich Jews controlled the Jewish courts of law. Recall from James 2:6 that the rich men were oppressing the poor, dragging them into the courts, and persecuting some unmercifully. In James 5:6, we see that they were being persecuted to the point of death. James said that not only did they *condemn*, but they "murdered the just." By this he was saying that they had exploited the laborers and taken advantage of their passivity and desire for peace. Before the rich would kill the poor, they would have them legally condemned, as we saw in James 2. The rich controlled the courts and could condemn whomever they wanted. Here in these United States, we know nothing of that kind of persecution.

How do the laborers respond? James says that, "he does not resist you." Amazing! This means that the laborer did not set himself against the rich. While the rich were taking advantage of the laborers' passive attitude, the just were not even holding a grudge against their oppressor and murderer. Most today would not consider responding that way, why—we would retaliate or sue. Yet the Christian's example is Jesus Christ, who was hated, but did not hate. He was crucified, but He prayed that His crucifiers might be forgiven. The Apostle Peter tells us that "when He was reviled, [He] did not revile in return; when He suffered, He did not threaten, but committed Himself to Him who judges righteously" (1 Peter 2:23). Jesus taught on this issue, saying ...

> You have heard that it was said, 'An eye for an eye and a tooth for a tooth.' But I tell you not to resist an evil person. But whoever slaps you on your right cheek, turn the other to him also. If anyone wants to sue you and take away your tunic, let him have your cloak also. And whoever compels you to go one mile, go with him

two. Give to him who asks you, and from him who wants to borrow from you do not turn away. (Matthew 5:38-42)

Summary

So we've reviewed Pastor James' warning to the rich, that they should howl because of the agony of a coming eternal hell if they don't repent and trust Christ (v 1); and the reason for the warning, because their coveting and hording wealth and not meeting their employer payroll (vv 2-6).

You might say, "Well, that was all fine and interesting, but how can I apply these verses to my life? I am not guilty of those awful things. I don't hoard money. I don't deprive others of their wages. I don't kill poor people, and I don't indulge myself." Even so, there are some lessons we can learn for ourselves, therefore, there are some questions that I would like to ask. (1) Do you hoard money? (2) Are you guilty of over-accumulating wealth? (3) Have you ever or are you now defrauding anyone? (4) Is there a financial deception in your life? (5) Are you self-indulgent in any area of your life? (6) How do you respond when you are treated unjustly? (7) Do you view a lost rich man as in need of a Savior? (8) When spending money, do you ask yourself, "Will this advance the kingdom of God?" (9) When you spend money, do you consider if it is a need or a want? (10) Do you buy what you can't use or don't need? (11) Do you spend more than you make? (12) Do you give sacrificially to the Lord with an enthusiastic heart to advance the kingdom?

Money is deceptive because it brings a false sense of security. As someone said, "Money can buy a bed, but it can never buy rest. It can buy food, but never satisfy the soul. It can buy luxury, but never buy contentment. It can buy you a house, but never buy you a home. It can buy a church, but it will never buy you a Savior." My admonition to you is: "For we brought nothing into this world, and it is certain we can carry nothing out. Loving money leads to all kinds of evil, and in their struggle to be rich, men and women alike have lost their faith and caused themselves untold agonies. But you, O [woman] of God, keep clear of such things. Set your heart on integrity, true piety, faithfulness, love, endurance and gentleness" (1 Timothy 6:7-11 paraphrased).

Questions to Consider
"Warnings to the Rich"
James 5:1-6

1. Read James Chapter 5:1-6. (a) What are the miseries for which the rich will weep and howl? (b) What is wrong with the way these rich viewed their possessions? (c) Does James condemn them for being rich or for being materialistic?

2. Memorize James 5:1.

3. (a) Review the previous chapters in James and note the other references to the rich and the poor. (b) Why do you think James repeats this so many times?

4. Read Amos 6. (a) What luxuries were the rich enjoying? (b) What warnings does Amos give to those living in pleasure? (c) What lessons are there for you in this passage?

5. (a) According to Leviticus 19:13 and Deuteronomy 24:14-15, what did the Mosaic Law say about wages for the laborers? (b) What did the prophets Jeremiah (Jeremiah 22:13) and Malachi (Malachi 3:5-6) say would happen to those who did not pay their laborers? (c) How do these passages compare to what James is saying in 5:1-6?

6. (a) Make note of how King Ahab lived out James 5:5-6 in 1 Kings 21. (b) What warnings are there for you if you find yourself living for pleasure and worldly things?

7. (a) Are there any material possessions that you are holding on to tightly? (b) Why? (c) What measures will you take so that these miseries will not come upon you in that day?

8. Is there an area in which God is speaking to you regarding finances and your handling of those? What is your prayer?

21

The Patience of Job

James 5:7-11

Put yourself in the following situation. You are at the grocery store. You have a specific amount of time and a very busy evening ahead of you. In fact you have company coming for dinner. You get a shopping cart with a wheel that drags. You choose your groceries, and, of course, they have moved things around since the last time you were there. The lines are long, and you get in the line where the cashier is in training. She is extremely slow. Finally it is your turn, but the cash register tape runs out, and, of course, she doesn't know how to change it, so she goes for help. Needless to say, you are delayed. What is your response?

Or picture this scenario. It's "family night," so your family is going out to eat. You have been looking forward to it the entire day. In fact, you have hardly eaten a thing all day so that you can really relish this meal. By now you think you are starving! When you arrive at the restaurant, it is *really* busy, but this is the place the family has chosen. The hostess tells you it will be a forty-five-minute wait. When you finally get a table, you are told they are short on help, so there's another delay in getting to eat. Then you order your favorite item on the menu only to find out they're out of it. What is your response? Do you respond with patience or with impatience? Do you see God in the picture, or do you forget that you're even related to Him?

In the last chapter, we saw the terrible persecution that New Testament Christians were suffering at the hand of their rich neighbors. Some of this persecution was even in the form of murder! This hardly compares to the above scenarios, does it? And yet, the admonition to them is the same admonition to us—be patient. James admonishes these poor readers, the ones being persecuted, to be patient! In his epistle, James gives his readers three examples to follow when in need of patience: The *patient farmer*, the *persistent prophets*, and the *patriarch, Job*. These would be especially helpful to them during their time of persecution. James says:

> Therefore be patient, brethren, until the coming of the Lord. See how the farmer waits for the precious fruit of the earth, waiting patiently for it until it receives the early and latter rain. ⁸You also be patient. Establish your hearts, for the coming of the Lord is at hand. ⁹Do not grumble against one another, brethren, lest you be condemned. Behold, the Judge is standing at the door! ¹⁰My brethren, take the prophets, who spoke in the name of the Lord, as an example of suffering and patience. ¹¹Indeed we count them blessed who endure. You have heard of the perseverance of Job and seen the end intended by the Lord--that the Lord is very compassionate and merciful. (James 5:7-11)

The three major ideas we will study are: the example of the *patient farmer* (vv 7-9); the example of the *persistent prophets* (v 10); and the example of the *patriarch, Job* (v 11).

The Example of the Patient Farmer

James 5:7. Therefore be patient, brethren, until the coming of the Lord.

After James completes his discourse on the eternal implications of worldly wealth, he reverts to addressing the Christian brethren again, saying, "Therefore be patient, brethren, until the coming of the Lord." *Therefore* points back to the sufferings that James had mentioned in verses 1-6. Because of these hardships, James says, "Be patient, brethren." This patient attitude is to be extended towards others. Be long tempered, James is saying. That does not mean that they are supposed to be passive, but to refrain from retaliation and have an attitude of self-restraint. Patience is one of the fruits of the Spirit that Paul mentions in Galatians 5:22. Patience should be a fruit that all believers bear. This is the same word that is used to describe God's attitude of forbearance toward our sins: "But You, O Lord, are a God full of compassion, and gracious, *longsuffering* and abundant in mercy and truth" (Psalm 86:15, emphasis mine). Can you imagine how hard that must have been for these brethren to be patient when they were undergoing such persecution? Their persecution was terribly unjust. They were receiving no pay for their labor and some were even being murdered! And look what James says. He says they must be patient how long? Until tomorrow? No! "Until the coming of the Lord."

Until Christ comes, we, as Christians, are obligated to leave vengeance with God and maintain a patient spirit. I know that is difficult for many of us. Maybe it is hard for you to be patient with a strong-willed child or a difficult marriage. Perhaps you struggle being patient with that neighbor who is always out to get you. Whatever difficult person or trying situation tests our patience, when compared to what James' readers were experiencing, our struggles seem insignificant, don't they? James is acutely aware of how hard it is for them to be patient, so he gives them the first example of patience by using a farmer who waits for the precious fruit of the earth.

James 5:7. See how the farmer waits for the precious fruit of the earth, waiting patiently for it until it receives the early and latter rain.

Of the farmer, James writes, "See how the farmer waits for the precious fruit of the earth, waiting patiently for it until it receives the early and latter rain." The farmer waits patiently for the grain to grow. Time is required to mature the crop, so he does not become impatient. He realizes that there is absolutely nothing he can do to speed up the process initiated by the rain, for rain will come when God decides it should. Jewish farmers in Palestine would plow and sow in what we know as the autumn months. The "early rain" would soften the soil; the "latter rain" would come in the early spring to help mature the harvest. Remember that modern irrigation techniques were unknown, so they must depend on the rain to water their crops. What good would it do the farmer if he became angry at the plants because they were late in producing a harvest? Would the growing process accelerate if he said, "I told you to hurry up and grow. What's the matter with you vegetables anyway?" This does not affect the plants, does it? So what good does it do for us to be angry with those who are persecuting us or, for that matter, to get impatient with anyone? Just as the farmer exercises patience and longsuffering while waiting for his crops to produce, so should we be patient and not vengeful to others in light of the Lord's return. James makes this point in verse 8.

James 5:8. You also be patient. Establish your hearts, for the coming of the Lord is at hand.

Just like the farmer, "you be patient." We must not lose our temper and be filled with hatred against those who oppress us. You might ask, "How do I get this patience?" James gives us two ways to develop it. The first way looks into our hearts, and the second way looks up to heaven. (1) *Establish your hearts*. This clause conveys the thought of strengthening and supporting something so that it will stand firm and immovable. It means to prop yourselves up. Let your faith be firm and unwavering. Do those sound like words we have studied before? In James 1:6, he told us that we are not to be double-minded, but instead steadfast. Don't become weary and fretful; take courage in your circumstances.

The second way to develop patience is to look up and realize (2) *the coming of Lord is at hand*. As the Apostle Paul said, "For I consider that the sufferings of this present time are not worthy to be compared with the glory which shall be revealed in us" (Romans 8:18). How do I take courage? Not by looking at circumstances or people, but by raising my eyes heavenward and realizing that the coming of the Lord draws near. We must look for the kingdom to come—we must not live for the kingdom here and now. These small irritations—what do they matter in light of eternity?

"The coming of the Lord is at hand," means His coming is imminent, at hand, near. This could happen at anytime.[62] The Lord's return should bring us hope and help give us the inner strength we need when facing difficult situations. Our hearts would be propped up and established if we lived in the constant expectation of His coming. Evidence that His coming is near are the biblical prophesies that have already been fulfilled and the pervasiveness of evil that we see in the world today. Even so, hostility from others is not easily endured, and James realized that our human nature wants to lash out or at least complain when going through trials. That's why in verse 9 he commanded his readers to withhold complaining during hardships.

James 5:9. Do not grumble against one another, brethren, lest you be condemned. Behold, the Judge is standing at the door!

The command, *Do not grumble* means do not groan, do not sigh, and do not murmur. A state of suffering from which one longs to be free prompts this expression of grumbling, sighing, and murmuring. Audible sounds may be expressed, but actual words are not usually spoken. This can be an inner sigh and not necessarily an open complaint. Notice that their grumbling was against each other instead of their rich oppressors. What is the warning here? James is warning us about our natural tendency to lash out to those near and dear to us (our husbands, our children) when we are suffering. My sisters, these things ought not to be so! For example, your well-planned day may not unfold as you had hoped because of spilled milk, a phone call with bad news, a broken washing machine, coffee spilled on your favorite shirt, a failure in your car's transmission, the flu, and so on. And what are we tempted to do? We are tempted

---

[62] When we say, "the coming of the Lord is at hand," it doesn't mean that it was immediately at hand. This would not be true, as Christ's coming hasn't happened almost 2,000 years after James wrote this. How would his immediate audience receive this? To speak of something "at hand" would suggest something could happen at any time. There is nothing essential that has to happen before an imminent event.

to take it out on our children or our husband, who by the way, have done nothing to us to deserve such unjust treatment.

The reason James commands us not to grumble or murmur against one another is because "the Judge is standing at the door." Do we realize that although our inward feelings of bitterness and criticism may not be overtly expressed, we are candidates for judgment by the One to whom we answer? In James chapter 4, we saw that when we judge our brother in our heart we are no longer a doer of the law, but a judge of the law. The very next verse asks, "Who are you to judge another?" (James 4:11-12). This admonition (here in James 5:9) not to murmur and grumble is because "the Judge is standing at the door." This caution of judgment may not be too distant in the future. *Standing at the door* means that He is right there ready to open it and return for His own. This phrase stresses His impending arrival. The Judge is actually facing the doors and ready to push them open as He enters the judgment hall. This should be both a comfort and a warning to us. It is a shallow Christian who sees only God's love and grace without seeing His inevitable return for us and the judgment to follow. The Apostle Peter reminds us that in the last days some will scoff and say, "Where is the promise of his coming?" They are ignorant, he says. The Lord is not slack concerning His promise. He will come as a thief in the night, the heavens and earth will pass away, and all will be burned up. Because of this, Peter says, we should be living holy and godly lives (2 Peter 3:3-14, paraphrase). James now returns to their difficult circumstances and encourages his readers to look not only at the patient farmer, but also to the persistent prophets.

The Example of the Persistent Prophets

James 5:10. My brethren, take the prophets, who spoke in the name of the Lord, as an example of suffering and patience.

My brethren, take, means to hold before your mind, my brethren. Who are they to take hold in their mind? "The prophets who spoke in the name of the Lord." The prophets encourage us to be mindful of a God who cares for us when we are suffering for his sake. Paul said, "For whatever things were written before were written for our learning, [Why?] that we through the patience and comfort of the Scriptures might have hope" (Romans 15:4). Some of the prophets who set an example for us are: (1) Elijah, who announced to wicked King Ahab that there would be drought in the land for three and a half years and who himself had to suffer in the drought (1 Kings 17); (2) Daniel, who suffered much affliction for God and was thrown in the lion's den (Daniel 6); (3) Jeremiah who was thrown into an abandoned well to die yet was fed and protected by God (Jeremiah 37 and 38); (4) Ezekiel, was told his wife would die (Ezekiel 24); and (5) Hosea, who was told to take an adulterous wife as an example of unfaithful Israel (Hosea 1).

These five men did not abandon their faith, but were willing to suffer for it. In fact, the phrase "who spoke in the name of the Lord" indicates why they suffered affliction. It was for God's "name" that they suffered. As Paul says in his letter to Timothy, "All who desire to live godly in Christ Jesus will suffer persecution" (2 Timothy 3:12). Their faithfulness to God amidst difficult times was a mark of their true character, a mark that they were truly in the faith. They persevered in the faith as all saints do! We call this the "perseverance of the saints." James then completes his sentence by saying the prophets were an example for us in two ways. They were "an example of suffering and an example of patience." The prophets have shown us how to endure hard times and how to endure them with a patient spirit. Are you familiar enough with the Old Testament prophets to know how they did endure? Could you follow their example? By the way, James was not a stranger to these difficulties. He could practice what he preached. Church history tells us, as we learned in the first chapter, that James was murdered because of his confession of his faith in Jesus Christ. The Jewish authorities tried to prevent James from standing on the wing of the Temple and talking about his faith in God. The Jews were so enraged to hear him give such powerful testimony for Jesus that they responded by throwing him down and stoning him. Tradition holds that a priest tried to stop the murder, but a fuller ran up to James and beat him to death with the club he used to beat his clothes. That happened in A.D. 62—twelve years after he wrote this epistle. I feel certain that at his death James clung to these words that he penned by the inspiration of the Holy Spirit. James ends this section on patience with something astonishing in verse 11.

The Example of The Patriarch Job

James 5:11. Indeed we count them blessed who endure. You have heard of the perseverance of Job

By using this word translated as *indeed,* James calls special attention to this matter of patient endurance by saying, "we count them blessed who endure." The Greek tense indicates that it was a common practice to admire such a brave display of perseverance by others and then to consider them blessed or happy. Jesus says, "Blessed are you when they revile and persecute you, and say all kinds of evil against you falsely for My sake. Rejoice and be exceedingly glad (Matthew 5:11-12)." Why does Jesus say this? He says this because (1) great is your reward in heaven. Remember what we are told in James 1:12? Blessed is the man who endures trials, for when he has been approved he will receive the crown of life.

The second reason Jesus says why we should rejoice and be glad is because (2) they persecuted the prophets who went before them in the same way (Matthew 5:11-12). The third and final example James gives us to follow when considering patience and perseverance is the patriarch Job.

James says, "You have heard of the perseverance of Job." By the way, here is a little bit of Bible trivia. This is the only place in the New Testament where Job's name is mentioned. But the fact that James says, "you have heard" indicates that the readers were very familiar with the story of Job in the Old Testament. As we have discussed, the Epistle of James is written to a Jewish audience and steeped in Old Testament terminology. So he gives them this example of Job. Why? He does this because Job endured incredible suffering. He lost his wealth, all of his children, and his physical health—he suffered from boils over his entire body. He suffered such insensitivity from his friends that Job called them *miserable comforters* (Job 16:2). His wife even told him to curse God and die, and yet he continued to trust God through his trials. In all this, Job did not sin (Job 2:10). What incredible perseverance! Using Job as an example, James is saying to look not at circumstances, but look at the end. See the big picture.

James 5:11. And seen the end intended by the Lord--that the Lord is very compassionate and merciful.

The big picture will show them "the end intended by the Lord, that the Lord is very compassionate and merciful." Even though Job's circumstances were difficult, his endurance and perseverance enabled him to see that God's blessings were abundant if he would be willing to let God choose the time to give them. *The end* refers to the termination, the close, or the last act. The second meaning of *end* is the purpose or aim. Whatever God permits has a purpose in the end. Many times we cannot understand the purpose of something until its end. It is not enough for us to note the sufferings of Job and the patience he exercises, but we must look at the end of the whole story. What was the outcome? Did God bless and reward Job for his patience? It is written that the Lord blessed the end of Job's days more than his beginning. He had fourteen thousand sheep, six thousand camels, one thousand oxen, and one thousand female donkeys. He had seven sons and three daughters, and in the land, no daughters were as fair as Job's. He lived 140 more years and saw his grandchildren and even his great grandchildren (Job 42:12-17).

We can never see the end from the beginning, but God knows it, and in that knowledge we must find comfort. Ecclesiastes 7:8 says, "The end of a thing is better than its beginning; the patient in spirit is better than the proud in spirit." I can recount many instances in my life, and I know you can too, where there has been persecution, suffering, grief, and disappointment. But the end has been so very good, and I wouldn't trade it for all that God has done. James says the Lord is "very compassionate and merciful." The Lord is big-hearted, which is what this word *compassionate* means. It literally means he is very, very compassionate, or full of tender compassion. James adds that He is also merciful. He cares about our miseries, and he is full of mercy. We must not think God is hard and cold. He does have a father's heart, even when he allows darkness to come. Isaiah says, "Can a woman forget her nursing child, and not have compassion on the son of her womb? Surely they may forget, yet I will not forget you. See, I have inscribed you on the palms of My hands" (Isaiah 49:15-16). Deuteronomy 33:27 is another comforting verse: "The eternal God is your refuge, and underneath are the everlasting arms." Jeremiah 31:3 tells us that "I have loved you with an everlasting love."

Summary

So what is causing you to be impatient today? Traffic? Long lines at the grocery store? People that talk too much? A crying baby or a strong-willed child? Do things like misplaced keys, stuck zippers, popped buttons, cold food, spilled milk, interruptions in your day, phone calls, deadlines, and feeling rushed make you impatient? Maybe it's cooking, shopping, cleaning, doing laundry, your in-laws, pulling weeds, flat tires, balancing your checkbook, doing your taxes, waiting for test results from the doctor, or people that rub you the wrong way that make you impatient. The things that cause us to be impatient are so mundane in comparison with what these readers were going through, aren't they? But they are important to our heavenly Father who has numbered the very hairs on our head and cares when a sparrow falls. But this same heavenly Father wants you and me to accept each difficulty from Him as a gift. There are some principles we can learn from the text on this topic of patience, therefore, I have put them in an acrostic—***PATIENT***. Dear readers, you can be patient by doing the following:

Prophet's Example (v 10). Be patient by looking at the example of the prophets and Job. They endured incredible suffering and came through as gold. Go back to the Old Testament and read some of those accounts and be encouraged to remain steadfast.

Arrival of the Lord (v 7). Be patient in view of the Lord's return. He is coming, and we will give an account of our murmuring and impatient attitude.

The end is not yet here (v 11). Be patient by realizing you don't have the big picture—the story hasn't ended yet. The end of what the Lord does in our lives is pretty incredible. Anticipate it and wait for it! Aristotle once said: "Patience is bitter, but its fruits are sweet."

Illustration of the farmer (v 7). The farmer does not get angry at those poor defenseless plants who can do nothing about the lack of rain, and neither should you or I.

Establish your hearts (v 8). Be patient by being steadfast—prop yourself up! Be firm and unwavering.

No murmuring (v 9). Be patient by not murmuring about your difficulty and especially not taking it out on others. Murmuring only further cements the difficulty in your mind and causes you to become a critical person. Thankfulness is a cure for murmuring and complaining. Look for the good that God is doing in the situation.

Tenderhearted is God (v 11). Be patient realizing that God is tenderhearted and merciful. He is not a mean God in heaven wanting to inflict pain. He is tender, and even in the hard times His faithfulness is great and His mercies are new every morning!

Questions to Consider
"The Patience of Job"
James 5:7-11

1. (a) Read James 5 making note of all the words that are repeated three or more times. (b) What is the significance of these repetitions?

2. Memorize James 5:8.

3. (a) Read Matthew 26:47–27:50 noting all the ways our Lord was patient with those who were persecuting Him. (b) How does this compare with your persecutions and with your patience?

4. Read Acts 5:17-42. (a) What were the Apostles doing that was causing them to be persecuted? (b) What was their response?

5. James mentions in verse 10 that we are to look to the prophets as an example of suffering affliction and patience. Pick one prophet from the Old Testament and note the affliction and note the patience. (Some ideas: Jeremiah, Ezekiel, Daniel) What have you learned?

6. How could you use the following verses to help James' readers be patient during the trials they were going through? Romans 5:3-4; 8:25-28; Colossians 1:10-12; 1 Timothy 6:11-12; Hebrews 12:1-2; James 1:3-4.

7. List all the people and/or circumstances that you feel you are being impatient with. Ask the Lord to establish your heart (prop it up) in each one, determine not to murmur about it, and take hope in the examples of those who have gone before us.

8. Has there ever been a time that you suffered persecution for Christ's sake? Did you exhibit patience?

9. Looking back at question 7, how do you think God would have you to respond in this situation? Put it in the form of a prayer request.

22

Being a Woman of Your Word

James 5:12

When I was a little girl, sometimes my friends and I used two foolish phrases to make a vow or to convince someone that we were being truthful—"Cross my heart, hope to die, stick a needle in my eye" and "I swear on a stack of Bibles." Do you remember those? Hopefully as Christian mothers we are training our children not to say such foolish things. As grownups we no longer use those childish expressions, but some of us use similar "grownup" phrases like "I swear to God" or "May God strike me dead if I am lying." We would all agree that, as believers, we should eliminate those phrases from our vocabulary, but even if we do, are we any better off than if we make promises to others that we have no intention of keeping?

Rarely a day or week goes by that we don't make a promise to a friend, or our husband, or our children, but do we keep that promise? For example, we might say to our friend, "I promise I won't tell anyone what you just shared with me," and then you call one of your other friends to tell her the piece of juicy news. Or you promise the kids that you will take them out after school for a special treat, but then you don't fulfill your promise for one reason or another. Or, you tell your friend that you will meet her for lunch at noon, but you don't show until 12:15 or, even worse, you don't show at all! Or you tell your husband that you will iron his shirts while he is at work, but you find something better to do with your time. And we justify these broken promises by saying, "To err is human." But God says to lie is sin.

In the last chapter we saw that James teaches us how to be patient during trials and difficulties by giving us three examples: the patient farmer, the persistent prophet, and the patriarch Job. As we begin to unpack verse 12, you might ask, "What in the world does letting our 'yes' be 'yes' and our 'no' be 'no' have to do with being patient during persecution?" If you have ever been persecuted or if you have ever feared for your life, you will know the answer to that question. In the midst of a trial or difficult situation—such as tornadoes, thunderstorms, earthquakes, or turbulent airplane rides—it is easy to say things you don't mean and make promises to God. We might vow, "God, if you will only get me out of this, I promise to serve You for the rest of my life, and I will clean up my act, too." In times of trial we must guard our speech in case we make rash vows. The practice of oath taking or making rash vows was a logical subject for James to address at this point in his discourse.

> But above all, my brethren, do not swear, either by heaven or by earth or with any other oath. But let your "Yes," be "Yes," and your "No," "No," lest you fall into judgment. (James 5:12)

Two themes emerge from the two sentences in this verse: The *sin* of making rash vows (v 12a) and the *sentence* of making rash vows (v 12b).

The Sin of Making Rash Vows

James 5:12. But above all, my brethren, do not swear

James initiated the sentence with the phrase, "But above all, my brethren." That is to say, "Be especially careful on this point. Whatever else is done, let this not be." This *above all* signifies that James regarded this sin to be of a serious nature, one that in all circumstances was to be avoided by those to whom he was writing. During this particular time of stress and affliction the most frequent sin would be to take the Lord's name in vain by uttering hasty and irreverent oaths. What a wonderful example he had just given them in the person of Job, as we just saw in verse 11. What did Job do during his adversity? He did not sin with his lips (Job 2:10). In all of Job's sufferings he did not make one rash vow. What an example that is for you and me to follow. So James says "above all things my brethren," he says, "do not swear." This phrase is used to affirm or deny something by an oath. This is not the same thing as profanity—even though profane speech is a forbidden as well—but this practice confirms a statement with an oath.

Before we proceed, let me clarify that making oaths or vows were not forbidden but rather encouraged. Deuteronomy 10:20 commands: "You shall fear the LORD your God; you shall serve Him, and to Him you shall hold fast, and *take oaths* in His name" (emphasis mine). God told the prophet Jeremiah that swearing in His name was a sign of spiritual vitality. "And it shall be, if they will learn carefully the ways of My people, to swear by My name, 'As the LORD lives,' ... then they shall be established in the midst of My people" (Jeremiah 12:16). The act of making of a vow was acceptable. The acts of breaking a vow or making rash vows were condemned. The verb *do not swear* is in the present tense, indicating that the swearing was habitual.

James 5:12. Either by heaven or by earth or with any other oath.

James completes this sentence by saying that they should not swear "either by heaven or by earth or with any other oath." What is he talking about? In New Testament times, some rabbis had begun to teach that an oath was not binding if it omitted God's name or did not imply His name. Therefore, they could swear by their own life or someone else's life or by their health or some object such as heaven or earth. But if you avoided using God's name, then you were not bound by it. Today we call that a loophole. The *Mishnah* devotes one whole section to an elaborate discussion of when oaths are binding and when they are not.[63] The results, commentators say, were disgraceful. There was frivolous swearing. Vows were mingled with words like "by your life" or "by my beard." Swearing had become a fine art. Lying was at its peak, especially lying to convince others you were telling the truth by swearing by some object. To tell you how ridiculous it had become, one rabbi taught that if you swore *by* Jerusalem then you were not bound to your oath, but if you swore *towards* Jerusalem, then you were bound because it somehow implied the Divine Name. This is not the first time swearing is mentioned in the Bible. Jesus has already addressed this issue in the Sermon on the Mount.

> Again you have heard that it was said to those of old, 'You shall not swear falsely, but shall perform your oaths to the Lord.' But I say to you, do not swear at all: neither by heaven, for it is God's throne; nor by the earth, for it is His footstool; nor by Jerusalem, for it is the city of the great King. Nor shall you swear by your head, because you cannot make one hair white or black. But let your 'Yes' be 'Yes,' and your 'No,' 'No.' For whatever is more than these is from the evil one (Matthew 5:33-37).

We have observed that the Sermon on the Mount is closely related to James, and here we see it again. Jesus says to them that just because God Himself had not been involved did not mean that their oaths were not binding. He says that they are all binding because they are God's throne, God's footstool and God's city. To swear by these things, therefore, was to treat with irreverence objects that were created by God. Their thinking was really crazy, wasn't it, as God is behind everything? The entire creation is His and you and I can't swear by anything that isn't His anyway.

James 5:12. But let your "Yes," be "Yes," and

---

[63] The first, and basic, part of the *Talmud* and the written basis of religious authority for traditional Judaism. The *Mishnah* contains a written collection of traditional laws (*halakoth*) handed down orally from teacher to student. It was compiled across a period of about 335 years, from 200 B.C. to A.D. 135. For many Jews, the *Mishnah* ranks second only to the canon of the Hebrew Scriptures. Indeed, many Jews consider it part of the Torah. Because it is the core for both the *Jerusalem* and *Babylonian Talmuds*, the *Mishnah* serves as a link between Jews in the land of Israel and Jews scattered around the world. (*Nelson's Illustrated Bible Dictionary,* 1986, Thomas Nelson Publishers)

your "No," "No"

James modeled Jesus' words in the Sermon on the Mount: "But let your 'Yes' be 'Yes,' and your 'No,' 'No.' For whatever is more than these is from the evil one" (Matthew 5:37). Jesus says that all such lying is of the evil one and comes from Satan, "for he is a liar and the father of it" (John 8:44). Consider this sobering passage from Matthew 23:16-22. James' half-brother Jesus warned:

> Woe to you, blind guides, who say, 'Whoever swears by the temple, it is nothing; but whoever swears by the gold of the temple, he is obliged to perform it.' Fools and blind! For which is greater, the gold or the temple that sanctifies the gold? And, 'Whoever swears by the altar, it is nothing; but whoever swears by the gift that is on it, he is obliged to perform it.' Fools and blind! For which is greater, the gift or the altar that sanctifies the gift? Therefore he who swears by the altar, swears by it and by all things on it. He who swears by the temple, swears by it and by Him who dwells in it. And he who swears by heaven, swears by the throne of God and by Him who sits on it.

For some reason, the scribes and Pharisees believed that swearing by the gold in the temple was binding, whereas swearing by the temple that housed the gold was not binding. Jesus calls them fools and blind men and tells them that it is all swearing by God. In Matthew 23:23, He begins to pronounce a series of woes on them for their hypocrisy. Jesus and James are not the only ones to condemn this practice of frivolous swearing. The third commandment says "You shall not take the name of the LORD your God in vain, for the LORD will not hold him guiltless who takes His name in vain" (Exodus 20:7).

In contrast to the way the scribes and Pharisees swore, James warns, "but let your 'Yes, be Yes,' and your 'No, No.'" The word for *yes* here is not *maybe*. It carries a strong affirmation, yes, even so, surely, truth, verily, and yea. And *no* is not *maybe* either. No means no, not, nothing, none, and never. The way to avoid swearing or making rash vows is by being truthful to the letter, right? We must have total honesty as Christians. Women should say what they mean and mean what they say. Don't make promises to the Lord that you don't plan to keep. It is written:

> When you make a vow to the LORD your God, you shall not delay to pay it; for the LORD your God will surely require it of you, and it would be sin to you. But if you abstain from vowing, it shall not be sin to you. That which has gone from your lips you shall keep and perform, for you voluntarily vowed to the LORD your God what you have promised with your mouth. (Deuteronomy 23:21-23)

Ecclesiastes 5:1-7 is another good passage to read on this topic, and the admonition is also good advice when dealing with others as well—"Do not be rash with your mouth, and let not your heart utter anything hastily before God. For God is in heaven, and you on earth; therefore let your words be few" (Ecclesiastes 5:2). Recall when Peter denied Jesus with the oath, "I do not know the Man!" (Matthew 26:72).

There was a time when we were dealing with a businessman (a Christian, I might add). He would commit to get back to us right away, or call us that day, or affirm that a document was on its way, etc. I do not believe that any commitment he ever made to us actually came to pass, so finally we had to get firm with him. What a disgrace his behavior was to his testimony for Jesus Christ as well as his employer. We all know people like that. You can't trust a thing they say. What should be the mindset of a believer when making and keeping commitments? Let us look at what the Apostle Paul wrote:

> Therefore, when I was planning this, did I do it lightly? Or the things I plan, do I plan according to the flesh, that with me there should be Yes, Yes, and No, No? But as God is faithful, our word to you was not Yes and No. For the Son of God, Jesus Christ, who was preached among you by us—by me, Silvanus, and Timothy—was not Yes and No, but in Him was Yes. For all the promises of God in Him are Yes, and in Him Amen, to the glory of God through us. (2 Corinthians 1:17-20)

What Paul is saying is, "Hey, I am not fickle like other men; I do not vacillate in what I mean. My yes is yes and my no is no." Why? Because God's word is yes, yes and no, no, and Paul's ministry was founded upon God's Word. In his letter to the Romans, Paul also says, "I tell the truth in Christ, I am not lying, my conscience also bearing me witness in the Holy Spirit" (Romans 9:1). To the church in Ephesus, he wrote, "Therefore, putting away lying, 'Let each one of you speak truth with his neighbor,' for we are members of one another" (Ephesians 4:25). That should be the mindset of us all. We could study many more Scripture verses about the importance about being truthful with God and with one another, but we'd best move on. There is a reason that James gives us for why our yes should be yes and our no should be no—it is sobering.

The Sentence of Making Rash Vows

James 5:12. Lest you fall into judgment.

The reason James warns us about making an empty oath is "lest you fall into judgment." Failure to heed this demand exposes us to the danger of judgment, because making empty oaths and swearing frivolously is in its essence lying, and we will ultimately give an account for it. By now James has warned us several times that we will give an account to God and will be judged by Him someday. (1) In James 2:12-13, we saw that we will be judged without mercy if we have not been merciful to others. (2) We saw in 3:1 that teachers will receive a stricter judgment for the things that they teach. (3) We saw in 5:9 that we should not murmur against one another lest we be condemned. And just now James has reminded us that the Judge is standing before the door and He is ready to open it. Now he is saying, (4) watch your yes's and your no's because you will be judged. Can you figure out what three out of those four warnings pertain to? They pertain to our speech! By the way, the word for *judgment* does not just mean punishment. It is the Greek word that means *the sentence is pronounced*. This sentence is a decision that has resulted from an investigation. In fact, the Greek translated literally reads like this: "But your the yes, yes, and the no, no, that not into hypocrisy under judgment you may fall." I interpret that to literally mean that if your yes is not yes and your no is not no, then you are on your way to hell, as there are no hypocrites in heaven (Matthew 23:13). Making promises or oaths that you have no intention of fulfilling is just another form of lying. You might say, "Those are strong words, Susan." If you are in the habit of lying, my friend, then you are in serious, I repeat, serious danger. We know that James is a book that tests us to see if we are in the faith. If lying is a habit with you, may I warn you, dear friend, of a few passages? Turn to Revelation 21:8, 27 and Revelation 22:15 and read them carefully.

Summary

How are you, dear readers, in the area of being a woman of your word? When you tell someone you will pray for him or her, do you? When you sign up for a job or a ministry, are you faithful to be there? When you say you will be there at 9:00, are you there at 9:00? When you say you will pay a bill by the fifteenth of the month, do you? When you tell your kids that you will take them out for ice cream after school, do you? If you have ever taken an oath in court, have you told the truth? Are you keeping your marriage vows—"In sickness and in health, being faithful to you and you alone"—and all other vows you made on your wedding day?

If you claim to be a Christian, which, by the way, is a vow and commitment to God, does your life show it? Can your word be trusted? When you say yes, do others know they can count on you? When you say no, do your children know that you mean it? Or does no in your home mean keep pestering me and I will say yes eventually? I am sure many of us can identify with the following quote by George MacDonald:

> I always try—I think I do—to be truthful. All the same I tell a great many petty lies, things that mean one thing to myself though another to other people. But I do not think lightly of it. Where I am more often wrong is in pretending I hear things which I do not, especially jokes and good stories, the point of which I always miss, but seeing everyone laugh, I laugh too, for the sake of not looking a fool. My respect for the world's opinion is my greatest stumbling block, I fear.[64]

These are all forms of lying, and we cannot allow ourselves to shrug our shoulders and continue to say, "to lie is human." It is not human; it is sin. And when you lie to men, you are also lying to the Holy Spirit, as Peter said to Ananias and Sapphira before their death (Acts 5:3, 9).

---

[64] James Hastings, *The Speaker's Bible* (Grand Rapids, MI: Baker, 1971), p. 130.

We all know people whose word is a joke. They are undependable, and everything they say goes in one ear and out the other. They are like the boy who cried, "Wolf!"—they cannot be trusted. On the other hand, there are times when we are unable to keep our word due to unexpected circumstances. That is why I believe it is important to say, "If the Lord wills," as James taught us in chapter 4, verse 15. When our kids were growing up and we made promises to them—promises like family night, or vacations, or this or that—we communicated this principle to them. As preacher's kids, they were very aware that many times emergencies or crises happened which would force a change in plans; but at such times we were honest with them and made up for it later. I am afraid that with some this is not the case, and it boils down to a lack of being faithful, a lack of integrity, and a lack of being a woman of your word. When you do fail in this area, do you seek forgiveness? Or do you rationalize? The world is looking for honesty, and I am afraid they are seeing very little of it represented by believers.

The following are six ways to ensure that your yes remains a yes, and that your no remains a no. They all begin with the word *Be:*

(1) *Be sensitive* to the deception that lying is not sin, especially "little white lies." Not only is it a sin, but a heinous sin. Do not desensitize yourself to the truth. I know people whose habit of lying is to the point they don't even recognize it.

(2) *Be reminded* of Matthew 12:36-37: "But I say to you that for every idle word men may speak, they will give account of it in the day of judgment. For by your words you will be justified, and by your words you will be condemned."

(3) *Be filled* with God's spirit and sensitive to His leading in your life in this area. If you are not walking with the Lord, His spirit has been grieved and His voice is dull.

(4) *Be asking* God to make you aware of the way you deceive yourself and others. You might be surprised how deception plays out in your life. Also ask your husband if he sees any form of lying in your life. One year my husband and I held each other accountable for exaggerations, and that exercise was extremely profitable.

(5) *Be feeding* on the Word of God. When you feed your

mind on the Word—the *Truth*—and obey it, it will produce what God desires, which is truth in the inner woman or man. A truthful inward spirit is bound to produce truthful outward speech.

(6) *Be careful* what you say—think before you speak. If you have said something that is not true, go to the person and correct it. Believe me, after you do that several times, hopefully you will be humbled enough to guard your words more carefully.

There is only one person that I know in the whole universe who has kept every promise He has made, and that is our model, our example, the Lord Jesus. One of the promises that He has made to you and me is that He will return. He will keep His Word, and so must we keep our word as well lest we fall into judgment!

Questions to Consider
"Being a Woman of Your Word"
James 5:12

1. Read James (perhaps take a chapter a day) noting all the times James uses our speech as a test of our faith.

2. Memorize James 5:12.

3. Read Numbers 30. (a) What does this passage specifically teach women about making vows? (b) What principles can you glean for your own life in regard to making vows?

4. (a) What was Jephthah's vow in Judges 11:29-40? (b) What does this teach you about making rash vows?

5. (a) From any portion of the Scripture, write down at least five promises made by our Heavenly Father. (b) How has He kept these promises to you? (c) Would you say that you keep your promises?

6. (a) Is there a promise that you have made to someone but are failing to keep? (b) In what areas of your life are you being untruthful? (c) Would others say you are a woman of your word?

7. Make a promise this week to someone and fulfill it.

8. After reflecting on question 6, what area is God speaking to you about? Write a prayer asking Him for help!

23

Becoming a Woman of Prayer

James 5:13-18

When my daughter, Cindi, was a little girl, we would often listen to a song by Twila Paris, which went like this: "He is exalted, the King is exalted, and I will praise Him ... He is exalted, forever exalted ..." One day my daughter was singing along with Twila, but with a twist. She sang, "He is exhausted, the King is exhausted ..." Of course, it was funny to me then and still is now. But as I reflect upon the actual words that Cindi was singing—"the King is exhausted"—it causes me to think "How sad! Exactly the opposite is true!" Rarely do we even attempt to exhaust the King in prayer. Instead we are the ones who are exhausted because of our failure to seek His face in every area of our life. We have come to six important verses in James dealing with prayer and will attempt to answer such questions as: What should we do when we are sick? Should we really call for the elders? And should they bring anointing oil? What *is* the prayer of faith? What is effectual, earnest prayer? The verses that we will be studying in this chapter contain one of the key biblical passages on sickness and healing. Before we look at these verses on prayer, let me remind you that James is not speaking merely from observation. It was said that James' life was one of prayer. In fact, he spent so much time on his knees in the temple praying for the people that his knees became as hard as camels' knees.

In the previous chapter we unpacked verse 12, which addresses making rash vows and oaths that we have no intention of keeping. At first it may appear that there is no connection between verse 12 and 13, but some have suggested that James is contrasting the wrong way to use God's name—rash vows, oaths, or swearing—with the correct way to use God's name, which is prayer. James wrote:

> Is anyone among you suffering? Let him pray. Is anyone cheerful? Let him sing psalms. ¹⁴Is anyone among you sick? Let him call for the elders of the church, and let them pray over him, anointing him with oil in the name of the Lord. ¹⁵And the prayer of faith will save the sick, and the Lord will raise him up. And if he has committed sins, he will be forgiven. ¹⁶Confess your trespasses to one another, and pray for one another, that you may be healed. The effective, fervent prayer of a righteous man avails much. ¹⁷Elijah was a man with a nature like ours, and he prayed earnestly that it would not rain; and it did not rain on the land for three years and six months. ¹⁸And he prayed again, and the heaven gave rain, and the earth produced its fruit. (James 5:13-18)

From these six verses emerge three major constructs: (1) the *reason* for prayer (vv 13-14); (2) the *result* of prayer (vv 15-16); and the *representation* of prayer (vv 17-18).

The Reason for Prayer

James 5:13. Is anyone among you suffering? Let him pray.

James launches this portion of Scripture on prayer by posing the question: "Is anyone among you suffering?" The Greek word translated as *suffering* means to undergo hardship, to be afflicted, to endure afflictions (hardness), and to suffer trouble.[65]

Suffering refers to various hardships including physical and emotional distresses. We can't imagine the mental, emotional, and physical affliction these persecuted believers were experiencing. They were working without pay. They were being dragged into the courts unjustly. Many were suffering condemnation, and some were

---

[65] *Biblesoft s New Exhaustive Strong s Numbers and Concordance with Expanded Greek-Hebrew Dictionary.* 1994, Biblesoft and International Bible Translators, Inc.

even murdered. In the midst of this adversity, what does James command them to do? Does he command them to gripe? To murmur? To complain? Does he say to rent a movie to forget your sorrows? Hit the bottle? Take antidepressants? No!

He commands them to pray. He asks, "Is anyone among you suffering?" He answers, "Let him pray." In the Greek, the word for *pray* is restricted to sacred use and always refers to prayer to God. That is what affliction should drive us to do—lift our hearts to God. Think about the last time you were afflicted. To whom or what did you lift your heart? Did you turn to your friend, to your food, or to your Heavenly Father? Not only should we pray for deliverance but for the strength to endure. Remember in 2 Corinthians 12:7-9 Paul asked God to remove the thorn in his flesh, but God did not grant Paul's request. Instead He chose to give him the grace to endure the thorn. The Lord replied to him, "My grace is sufficient for you, for My strength is made perfect in [your] weakness."

Prayer may not remove the affliction, but it can certainly change our perspective on it. I am confident that we can all recall times when we have been in deep sorrow over something or have been going through a trial, and we call on the name of the Lord and seek His face for relief. Many times He has chosen not to give us the relief we request, but we find relief in simply communing with Him and casting all our cares upon Him (1 Peter 5:7). "Times like those are bittersweet," as someone once said to me. Even Christ prayed that His cup of suffering might be removed, but it was not. Instead God gave Him the strength He needed to go to the cross and to suffer and die for our sins (Matthew 26). James' command to pray is in stark contrast to making rash vows, as we just saw in verse 12. Instead of making a rash vow in the midst of trouble, they were instructed to turn to God in prayer. As believers in Jesus Christ, we should be in the habit of praying at all times and in all places, especially during affliction. The unbeliever does not have this privilege, so they tend to despair and be without hope during adversity. James is saying to us, "Let trouble drive you to God, and let trouble drive you to prayer." From the topic of affliction, James now moves to another aspect of our lives—joy.

James 5:13. Is anyone cheerful? Let him sing psalms.

Next James asks the question, "Is anyone cheerful?" The word translated as *cheerful* means to be merry and happy. It describes the well being of a soul, the strength and the disposition of the mind. This phrase confirms that our lives are not full of afflictions. Praise the Lord! Did you notice from the meaning of the word that everything doesn't need to be going our way for us to be merry? To be cheerful is an inner state of our mind and heart regardless of what may be happening. "My brethren, count it all joy when you fall into various trials," James told us immediately in chapter 1, verse 2. So what are we to do when we are merry? Are we to party? Celebrate? Forget our sanctification? No!

James says, "Let him sing psalms." To *sing psalms* means to sing songs of praise usually to the accompaniment of the harp. In the New Testament it is confined to the praising of God in sacred music (Ephesians 5:19). James' reminder to them is probably directed to the fact that occasions of merriment can often lead to sensuality and sin, that is, "Let's celebrate! Let's party!" Our perspective is best when we have God at the center of our thoughts. The two conditions here—suffering and cheerfulness—describe the continuum of emotional experience in our life. If we let them, the gloomy valley and the sunny mountaintop can both be instruments used by God in strengthening our relationship to Him. As the old hymn says, "In every joy that crowns my days, in every pain I bear, My heart shall find delight in praise, or seek relief in prayer."

James now moves from general afflictions to a specific affliction—illness. By now most of us have lived long enough to experience illness, accidents, physical disabilities, and even death. These events either affect us personally or someone in our immediate, extended, or spiritual family. So what do we do when we, or someone we love, gets sick? James asks the same question in verse 14.

James 5:14. Is anyone among you sick? Let him call for the elders of the church.

James wants to know if "anyone among you [is] sick." The word translated as *sick* means to be feeble or diseased. This is not just a cold, but a serious condition. It is the same word used to describe Lazarus when he got sick and died. "Now a certain man was *sick*, Lazarus" (John 11:1, emphasis mine). It is used to describe Epaphroditus, whose illness almost caused his death. "For indeed he was *sick* almost unto death" (Philippians 2:27, emphasis mine). From the text here in James, we know that this sickness was serious enough to cause this person to be bedfast, which we infer from the clause "the Lord will raise him up" in verse 15.

So what are we to do when we become sick? Most of us would say, "Call the doctor, honey." But do we ever say, "Honey, call the elders?" James commands us to call for the elders of the church. We do not wait for them to hear about it. The person who is sick takes the initiative. The one who is sick, or someone acting on behalf of the one who is sick, needs to call the elders of the church and let them know. Who exactly is an elder? An elder is a man who is older and an officer of the church, a man who is spiritually mature and experienced in intercessory prayer (Acts 6:4). A man with these attributes is appointed an elder because he meets the necessary biblical qualifications (Titus 1:5-9).

James 5:14. And let them pray over him, anointing him with oil in the name of the Lord.

So the elders are to go to the one who is sick and "pray over him, anointing him with oil in the name of the Lord." When we are sick, sometimes it is difficult to pray for ourselves, and we need someone more spiritually mature to pray for us. While the elders are praying, they also anoint "him [or her] with oil." Olive oil was the type most frequently used, regarded by some as a method of healing. *Anointing* (Greek, *aleipsantes*) means to oil with perfume, to rub with oil. The word translated as *anointing* here is the same word used to describe the anointing of the dead body of Christ by the women. "Now when the Sabbath was past, Mary Magdalene, Mary the mother of James, and Salome bought spices, that they might come and *anoint* Him" (Mark 16:1, emphasis mine). Luke used this word to describe the anointing of the feet of Jesus by the woman in a Pharisee's house. "She kissed His feet and *anointed* them with the fragrant oil" (Luke 7:38-emphasis mine). The verb means to stimulate or to encourage through application of the oil. In ancient times people would rub their bodies with oil after bathing. The Gospel according to Mark records the disciples anointing the sick when Jesus sent them out two by two. "And they ... *anointed* with oil many who were sick, and healed them" (Mark 6:13-emphasis mine). The story of the Good Samaritan is another example of oil used for its healing properties. The Good Samaritan went to the bruised and beaten traveler and "bandaged his wounds, pouring on *oil* and wine" (Luke 10:34, emphasis mine). It is still a common practice in the Middle East to rub the sick with oil.

James is not saying that elders are always required to carry a bottle of olive oil with them to ceremonially anoint the sick, but James is saying that we should exhaust all medicinal resources—including prayer—when we are sick. It might mean the sick one needs an antibiotic or an operation. Or maybe a good rubdown with oil is exactly what is needed. (I would not refuse a good therapeutic massage with oil!) So we should pray and do whatever else necessary to alleviate the person's problem. While the elders are praying and anointing, they are doing so "in the name of the Lord." This utterance demonstrates the elders' total trust and dependence in Christ and His authority. The phrase "in the name of the Lord" does not mean that we are always required to close our prayers that way or "in Jesus' name," but rather it indicates a willingness to pray according to the sovereign purpose and will of God. It is limited to the person of Christ and the work of Christ. Jesus said, "And whatever you ask in My name, that I will do, that the Father may be glorified in the Son (John 14:13). Just as there is no magic in the oil itself, there is no magic in tacking on the phrase "in the name of the Lord" because *the Lord* shall raise him up. In verses 15-16, James writes of the wonderful result of prayer.

The Result of Prayer

James 5:15. And the prayer of faith will save the sick, and the Lord will raise him up.

Verse 15 does not mean that God will answer every prayer of the elders or that all who are prayed over will be healed, and we cannot disregard the phrase "in the name of the Lord" in verse 14. First of all, James says that the "prayer of faith will save the sick." The *prayer of faith* is a prayer offered in faith when we seek the mind of God and pray according to His will. The prayer relates back to the prayer in verse 14 offered by the elders. Faith has motivated the prayer. This is not an ordinary prayer offered on behalf of another person, but a prayer prompted by the Holy Spirit, that it is the Lord's will to heal the one being prayed for. (Recall that James 1:6 says to "ask in faith, with no doubting.) The phrase "will save the sick" means "will restore to physical health." It is interesting to note that the Greek word translated as *sick* is used to describe ailments such as gout and diseases of the eye. After James gives us the outcome of the prayer of faith, he then says, "The Lord will raise him up." It is important to understand that it is the Lord Himself who actually accomplishes the restoration; the Lord will enable the afflicted one to stand on his feet.

Now what do we conclude when our prayers have been offered in faith and all medical resources have been exhausted and the person still dies? When we pray for healing and God does not choose to do so, is it God's fault, or is it because we lacked faith enough to believe? Did we forget to use that magical term "in the name of Jesus?" We must remember that God does answer prayer. He does restore the sick to health—sometimes by prayer alone, sometimes with the use of medicine or surgery, and sometimes by a combination of the two. Sometimes it is not His will to restore the afflicted. However, in this passage it is probable that the afflicted person about whom James is writing is sick as a result of sin, because he says, "If he has committed sins, he will be forgiven." James is not saying that this person has definitely committed sins, but *if* he has committed sins. Physical illness may result from sin, as we see today with sexually transmitted diseases, alcoholism, and substance abuse, just to name a few. The Bible also teaches that God may bring sickness as a discipline for sin (1 Corinthians 11:30). Whenever we fall ill, we should examine ourselves before the Lord to determine if it is due to personal sin. I once had a Christian physician who, during visits, would always ask me about my spiritual life, because he knew a direct correlation exists between sin and sickness. But not all sickness is due to sin.

Sickness is in the world because the world in which we live is fallen. Sometimes we are sick because in some way God desires to be glorified through it. Remember the blind man in John 9? Jesus' disciples asked Him, "'Rabbi, who sinned, this man or his parents, that he was born blind?' Jesus answered, 'Neither this man nor his parents sinned, but that the works of God should be revealed in him'" (John 9:2-3). Not only was this man given his sight, but his eternal soul was also saved as a result. This we know because the man said, "'Lord, I believe!' And he worshiped Him" (Luke 9:38).

James 5:15. And if he has committed sins, he will be forgiven.

Forgiveness pictures sins being sent away so that they are no longer held against us. The word *forgiveness* means to send away, to bid go away, to let go. The promise implies that the afflicted has confessed his sins to God and has determined to turn from them because they are offensive to Him. Remember the account of the man who had an infirmity for thirty-eight years? Jesus told him to "rise, take up your bed and walk." Later Jesus found him in the temple and said, "See, you have been made well. Sin no more, lest a worse thing come upon you" (John 5:5, 8, 14). We infer from Jesus' response that this man was sick as a result of sin, and about the only thing worse than being sick for thirty-eight years is to be eternally lost. Before we go on, may I make three suggestions for you to consider the next time you are sick? (1) When you are sick, examine your heart to see if you are living in any known sin. If you are, confess it and forsake it. (2) You may need to notify the elders or the authorities in your church to come and pray for you. (3) You may need to go to the doctor for appropriate medical care. When you think about it, we do it backwards, don't we? At the first sign of the flu or a suspicious lump or a runny nose, first we go to the doctor, then we ask others to pray, and when all else fails we search our heart for sin. Because we are sinners and do commit sin, we need to confess our sins, not only to God but also to one another. That is why James says next that we are to confess our sins to one another.

James 5:16. Confess your trespasses to one another, and pray for one another, that you may be healed.

This command to "confess your trespasses to one another and pray for one another" seems to be directed to the one who is sick. This one should confess his or her faults to another and pray for one another. Why? So that she "may be healed." This confession of trespasses seems to be related to those committed against other believers. It is impossible for us to worship alongside each other if we have something against a brother or sister, or if the brother or sister has something against us. Jesus said, "If you bring your gift to the altar, and there remember that your brother [or sister] has something against you, leave your gift there before the altar, and go your way. First be reconciled to your brother [or sister], and then come and offer your gift" (Matthew 5:23-24). "Confessing your trespasses," conveys the thought of an open, frank, and full confession. It literally means, "to say the same thing." By confessing our trespasses, we agree to identify it by its true name—sin—and admit that it is sin. We all know people that simply will not admit that they sin. They seem to always have an excuse for their sin, or they blame it on someone else. The Apostle John wrote, "If we say that we have no sin, we deceive ourselves, and the truth is not in us. If we confess our sins, He is faithful and just to forgive us our sins and to cleanse us from all unrighteousness. If we say that we have not sinned, we make Him a liar, and His word is not in us" (1 John 1:8-10). This does not mean that we go around confessing our sins to everyone, but rather to confess specific sins to those whom you have wronged. For example, if I have lied to you, I need to confess that sin to you and to God alone. I don't need to tell everyone I know. However, if I have sinned against a group of individuals, then I need to confess to the group. I also need to give a word of warning here—when confessing sins of a sexual nature, limit the details lest we pollute and defile one another. Paul addressed this particular issue in his letter to the church at Ephesus: "For it is shameful even to speak of those things which are done by them in secret" (Ephesians 5:12).

Not only are we to confess our trespasses to one another, but we are to "pray for one another." Again, the reason we are to confess our faults to each other and pray for each other is so that we may be healed. Prayer should be offered for one another for forgiveness and healing, so that the sick can be restored to physical as well as spiritual health. The concepts of spiritual healing and physical healing are closely related, and many Scripture passages prove that physical suffering can be a result of sin.[66] Modern medicine confirms this, too. Doctors will tell you that bitterness, anger, and hatred cause many diseases and afflictions. Confession must lead to intercession—we must pray for one another. Without prayer, confession may prove to be harmful, but when we secure faithful prayer support

---

[66] For example, the Lord warned the second generation of the nation of Israel: "If you do not carefully observe all the words of this law that are written in this book, that you may fear this glorious and awesome name, THE LORD YOUR GOD, then the LORD will bring upon you and your descendants extraordinary plagues—great and prolonged plagues—and serious and prolonged sicknesses. Moreover He will bring back on you all the diseases of Egypt, of which you were afraid, and they shall cling to you. Also every sickness and every plague, which is not written in the book of this law, will the LORD bring upon you until you are destroyed. You shall be left few in number, whereas you were as the stars of heaven in multitude, because you would not obey the voice of the LORD your God. And it shall be, that just as the LORD rejoiced over you to do you good and multiply you, so the LORD will rejoice over you to destroy you and bring you to nothing; and you shall be plucked from off the land which you go to possess" (Deuteronomy 28:58-63). Another example was Paul's summary to the Corinthian believers about why some of them were sick or had died: "Therefore whoever eats this bread or drinks this cup of the Lord in an unworthy manner will be guilty of the body and blood of the Lord. But let a man examine himself, and so let him eat of the bread and drink of the cup. For he who eats and drinks in an unworthy manner eats and drinks judgment to himself, not discerning the Lord's body. For this reason many are weak and sick among you, and many sleep. For if we would judge ourselves, we would not be judged" (1 Corinthians 11:27-31).

from others, it proves to be of great value in furthering victory and spiritual maturity. I thank God for the people in my life to whom I have been able to reveal my weaknesses knowing that they will pray for me and hold me accountable. Not one person is above accountability; we *all* need it. In his book *Life Together,* Dietrich Bonhoeffer says this about confession:

> Sin demands to have a man by himself. It withdraws him from the community. The more isolated a person is, the more destructive will be the power of sin over him. Confession in the presence of a brother is the profoundest kind of humiliation. It hurts, it cuts a man down, and it is a dreadful blow to pride. To stand there before a brother as a sinner is a disgrace that is almost unbearable. In the confession of concrete sins the old man does a painful, shameful death before the eyes of a brother.[67]

James 5:16. The effective, fervent prayer of a righteous man avails much.

James goes on to say, "The effective fervent prayer of a righteous man avails much." The prayer of a righteous man is very powerful in its operation, and a righteous man's praying has great effect when he prays. *Effective* means energetic or that which has power. It is "much strong." This kind of prayer is not lifeless, indifferent, and cold, but sincere, earnest, and persevering. The effective prayer must be offered by one that is "righteous," a required attribute on which the success of the prayer depends. Dear ladies, it is not talent, smooth words, good looks, rank, or wealth that makes our prayers effective, but being a righteous woman, a godly woman. If you pray earnestly, and if you are a righteous woman, then I have good news for you. Your prayers avail much! They are strong—they prevail! They are effective, and they are capable of producing results. Sir Laurence Shipley said, "Prayer is the arm that moves the world." Do your prayers move the world? Do they avail much? You may reply, "No, my prayers don't avail much. My prayers are ineffective." If that is the case, there may be some underlying reasons.

---

[67] Dietrich Bonhoeffer. *Life Together* (San Francisco: Harper, 1977), pp. 115-116.

(1) You must know the One to Whom you are praying. "If you abide in Me, and My words abide in you, you will ask what you desire, and it shall be done for you" (John 15:7). C. S. Lewis said, "The prayer preceding all prayers is 'may it be the real I who speaks. May it be the real Thou that I speak to.'"

(2) You must have no known sin in your life. Confess your sins. "If I regard iniquity in my heart, the Lord will not hear" (Psalm 66:18). "And whatever we ask we receive from Him, because *we keep His commandments* and do those things that are pleasing in His sight" (1 John 3:22, emphasis mine).

(3) You must pray according to God's will. "And whatever you ask in My name, that I will do, that the Father may be glorified in the Son. If you ask anything in My name, I will do it" (John 14:13-14).

(4) You must not pray for selfish reasons. "You ask and do not receive, because you ask amiss, that you may spend it on your pleasures" (James 4:3).

(5) Maybe it is not God's time. "He has made everything beautiful in its time" (Ecclesiastes 3:11). "'For My thoughts are not your thoughts, nor are your ways My ways,' says the LORD" (Isaiah 55:8).

(6) Maybe God has answered your prayer and you are not willing to accept His answer. It may be no.

The Representation of Prayer

James 5:17. Elijah was a man with a nature like ours, and he prayed earnestly that it would not rain; and it did not rain on the land for three years and six months.

Elijah is the fourth Old Testament example that James uses in his epistle. (The other three are Job, Abraham, and Rahab.) Elijah's name appears thirty times in the New Testament, and he appears as an example in other passages of Scripture as well. Because he was so highly regarded by the Jews, James uses him as an example for prayer here. Many felt that Elijah was the grandest and most romantic character that Israel ever produced. Here are some facts about Elijah that greatly impressed the Jewish people: He fought a life and death battle with idolatrous Ahab and Jezebel (1 Kings 22); he killed the prophets of Baal (1 Kings 18); he raised the dead (1 Kings 17); he feasted in the wilderness at the hands of angels (1 Kings 19); he foretold both the famine and the coming of rain (1 Kings 17); and he vanished from the earth in a chariot of fire (2 Kings 2).

Elijah was also considered the prototype of the prophet who would prepare the way for the coming of the Messiah (Matthew 17:10-13). Elijah was one of the prophets who conversed with Jesus on the Mount of Transfiguration (Mark 9:4). This righteous man, James says, was subject to the same passions we are. This means he had a nature like ours and was subject to weakness and infirmities like us.

James 5:18. And he prayed again, and the heaven gave rain, and the earth produced its fruit.

James says that Elijah "prayed earnestly ... and the earth produced its fruit" (1 Kings 17–18). Wicked King Ahab and Jezebel, the queen, had led Israel away from the Lord and into the worship of Baal, so God punished the nation by withholding the necessary rain. Elijah prayed earnestly for rain to cease, and his prayer brought a drought of three and a half years in Palestine. The nation still did not repent. Next, we see the dramatic account on Mt. Carmel. When Elijah prepared the evening sacrifice and prayed once, fire came down from heaven consuming it, proving Jehovah to be the true God. But the nation still needed rain, so Elijah went to the top of the mountain and fell down before the Lord in prayer. He prayed and sent his servant to look for a rain cloud seven times. Elijah believed in a God who answers prayer and he was intent on looking for the answer. He was persistent in his prayers. He did not give up. He prayed expectantly and looked for the answers. Do you? Do you look intently for how God is working in your life by answering prayer? Do you recognize the ways God is answering prayer in your life in the same way Elijah kept on looking and kept on praying? It was after the seventh prayer that the cloud and rains came and the nation was saved.

Elijah believed not only in prayer but in persistent prayer. He *prayed earnestly*. Translated it literally means "and he prayed in his prayer." Many people do not pray in their prayers. They languish in religious words, but their hearts are not in their prayers. E. M. Bounds said:

> There is neither encouragement nor room in Bible religion for feeble desires, listless efforts, lazy attitudes; all must be strenuous, urgent ardent. Inflames, desires, impassioned unwearied insistence. These delight heaven. God would have His children earnest and persistently bold in their efforts. Heaven is too busy to listen to half-hearted prayers or to respond to pop-call. Our whole being must be in our praying.[68]

The point is clear. God answers prayer when righteous men and women pray. God can and will accomplish His will through His

---

[68] E. M. Bounds, *The Complete Works of E. M. Bounds: Purpose in Prayer* (Baker Book House, 1990), p. 323. Bounds is a good devotional author on prayer from an Armenian perspective, although he doesn't develop his ideas from Scripture itself. His later works on prayer are replete with excellent quotes from a wide range of Christians, that are helpful.

faithful and obedient children. Since Elijah was a man like us, we should not be discouraged as we travel through life. God will answer our prayers as we pray earnestly and live a righteous life.

Summary

How is your physical and spiritual well being this day? Are you sick? Could it be because of sin? What have you done about it? What will you do about it? How is your prayer life? Do you "pray in your prayers" earnestly and fervently, or are your prayers cold and listless, just one-minute calls to God? Do your prayers accomplish much? Do you thank God when the answers come? Do you see the answers? (Keeping a prayer journal acts as a good reminder of your petitions to God and how and when He answers them. A journal also reminds you of the petitions for which you need to be persistent.) Is there someone in your life to whom you are accountable—someone who knows your *real* struggles and is committed to pray for you? As we have seen in this chapter, your prayer life is another test that determines whether your faith is genuine. If you are not a woman of prayer, or if you do not feel a need to commune with our Heavenly Father, then once again, as James would say, your faith is suspect.

Questions to Consider
"Becoming a Woman of Prayer"
James 5:13-18

1. (a) Read James 5, noting all the times we are to pray. (b) Read the story of Elijah in 1 Kings 17 and 18. How was he earnest in his praying?

2. Memorize James 5:16.

3. Compare 2 Chronicles 16:11-14 with 2 Kings 20:1-11. (a) What does this teach you about seeking the face of God when you are sick? (b) Do you think Asa would have lived had he sought the Lord God? (c) Why or why not?

4. Read 1 Corinthians 11:23-34. (a) What does this passage say about coming to the Lord's Table with sin in our lives? (b) What do the words *weak*, *sickly* and *sleep* mean in verse 30? (c) Do you think we take these verses seriously?

5. David wrote both Psalm 32 and 38 when he was suffering because of his sin. Choose one of these psalms and list all the physical, emotional and spiritual sufferings that David experienced because of sin.

6. Read Luke 11:5-13 and 18:1-8. (a) What parables does Jesus tell to illustrate persistent prayer? (b) What does this teach you about persistence in your own prayer life?

7. (a) Do you know of a time when you were sick because of sin in your life? (b) What did you learn during that time?

8. (a) Do you have someone in your life that holds you accountable for spiritual growth? (b) Do you share real struggles and sins? (c) Are you honest and transparent?

9. (a) Analyze your prayers this week. Ask yourself these questions: Do I fervently pray for the needs of others? Are my prayers earnest or listless and cold? Do I confess my sins? Am I sensitive to any sin that might be hindering my prayers? (b) What is your prayer request?

24

A Call to Salvation – Conclusion

James 5:19-20

Many years ago someone gave me a poem that I hung in my closet reminding me of the final two verses that close James' epistle to the twelve tribes scattered abroad. The poem is simply titled "My Friend."

> "My friend, I stand at judgment now,
> And feel that you're to blame somehow,
> On earth I walked with you day by day,
> And never did you point the way.
>
> You knew the Lord in truth and glory,
> But never did you tell the story.
> My knowledge then was very dim;
> You could have led me safe to Him.
>
> Though we lived together on the earth,
> You never told me of the second birth.
> And now I stand this day condemned,
> Because you failed to mention Him.
>
> You told me many things tis true,
> I called you friend and trusted you.
> But I learn now that it's too late,
> You could have kept me from this fate.

> We walked by day and talked by night
> And yet you showed me not the light.
> You let me live, love and die,
> You knew I'd never live on high.
>
> Yes I called you friend in life,
> And trusted you through joy and strife,
> And yet on coming to the end,
> I cannot now call you my friend."
>
> —Dr. D. J. Higgins

The words in the last two verses of James chapter 5 convey the same thought as the words in the poem above. Now readers, God is sovereign in salvation, but that does not negate our responsibility to pursue others as indicated in these last two verses.

> Brethren, if anyone among you wanders from the truth, and someone turns him back, [20]let him know that he who turns a sinner from the error of his way will save a soul from death and cover a multitude of sins. (James 5:19-20)

Two major themes emerge from the two verses: the concluding *charge* (v 19) and the concluding *promise* (v 20).

The Concluding Charge

James 5:19. Brethren, if anyone among you wanders from the truth,

While James has been writing this epistle, he has been giving us tests along the way to see if we are genuinely in the faith, that is, does our faith work? The entire letter has been designed to confront those who profess Christ but perhaps are not saved. James wants to be sure that no one is deceived. He is aware, as are we, that hearers of the Word are not necessarily doers of the Word. In James' closing statement he warns us about the danger of apostasy, the danger of proving to be among the "hearers" only. He also challenges genuine believers to pursue those among us whose faith may be suspect. Essentially he is saying, "Hey you, go and convert these who are proving to be false. Love them enough to warn them." Or as Proverbs 11:30 says, "The fruit of the righteous is a tree of life, and he who wins souls is wise."

This ultimate statement ties it all together by laying the responsibility on the church as well as delivering an encouraging promise. In the first clause of the sentence, James says, "Brethren, if anyone among you wanders from the truth." *Brethren* is the form of address that James has used frequently throughout his epistle, which expresses his love for them. *If anyone among you* refers to those who are members of the readers' local group. If any in your midst are erring from the truth, go after them, convert them. What does James mean to "wander from the truth"? It refers to those who have strayed from the truth of the gospel and its responsibilities. The wanderers need to be brought back to proper conduct. The word translated as *wander* comes from the Greek word for *planet.* The ancients watched the skies and detected the planets wandering from the fixed stars in the heavens. James refers here to one who wanders in the midst of other believers who remain fixed in their devotion to Christ. This is not only a warning against wandering from doctrinal truths, but also a warning against wandering from a godly lifestyle.

The Bible teaches that moral deviation can and often does affect one's doctrine. Paul says, "Demas has forsaken me, [because he] loved this present world" (2 Timothy 4:10). Alexander the metalworker caused Paul great harm because he objected to his doctrine. Of this, Paul writes, "Alexander the coppersmith did me much harm ... for he has greatly resisted our words" (2 Timothy 4:14-15). We see this today as men and women change their beliefs to accommodate their moral behavior—how convenient and how sad! Men in leadership soften their standards and the sheep follow. "'Woe to the shepherds who destroy and scatter the sheep of My pasture!' says the LORD" (Jeremiah 23:1). The object from which they are wandering is the truth, the gospel of Jesus Christ, the person and work of Jesus Christ. It is that same word of truth that James mentions in 1:18: "Of His own will He brought us forth by the *word of truth*, that we might be a kind of firstfruits of His creatures" (emphasis mine). Jesus Himself said, "I am the way, the *truth,* and the life" (John 14:6, emphasis mine). To *wander from the truth* calls to mind the familiar image of sheep wandering away. The Apostle Peter said, "For you were like sheep going astray, but have now returned to the Shepherd and Overseer of your souls" (1 Peter 2:25). A true believer will not wander from the truth of the gospel. They cannot deny it. As the aged-old Apostle John states, "They went out from us, but they were not of us; for if they had been of us, they would have continued with us; but they went out that they might be made manifest, that none of them were of us" (1 John 2:19). So says James, "You see this one who has erred from the truth—now go do something about it!" James tells his readers to go and convert him.

James 5:19. And someone turns him back

In the phrase "and someone turns him back," pay attention to the word *someone*. By using this particular word, James is intending that someone, anyone, everyone, in the congregation pursue and turn the wayward one back. James is saying, "You go. You do it." As a pastor's wife, this makes sense to me because many members of the congregation are far more aware than the pastor of those who have erred and wandered away. The pastor is not always aware of the details in an individual's life. Readers, this wayward one might be your husband or your children or your sibling or a friend at your church. Perhaps you know what is going on behind closed doors, and you are responsible to pursue them. A paraphrase of James' instructions could be: "Go after her whose life is not showing true Christianity. You pursue her."

This is a call for the believer to evangelize in the church. "In the church?" you might ask. "Susan, don't you know that everyone who goes to church is a Christian? What's wrong with your theology?" Jesus reveals what is wrong with our theology in the parable of the weeds. Jesus relates the parable of the tares—a weedy plant that grows in a grain field—among the wheat and how they grow together until harvest time when the tares will be eliminated. Jesus says that there will come a time when one will no longer be able to hide the fact that his or her faith has not worked, and then it will be too late. The tares will be cast into a furnace of fire, and there shall be wailing and gnashing of teeth (Matthew 13:24-30, 36-43). This is a very sobering passage. In fact, three well-known pastors were asked how many people in their church they thought were truly redeemed, and they answered fifty percent. Even Jesus said, "There are *few* who find it" (Matthew 7:14, emphasis mine). *Few* is translated from the Greek word *oligos*, which means puny in extent, degree, or number.

Are there some in your church body whose faith you suspect? Have you lovingly sought them out? If not, James is telling you to go and "turn him back." What does this mean? This means to convert, to return, and to turn about. James does not tell us how this one he mentioned is converted, but we must go, speak, and pray, all the while being empowered by the Holy Spirit. You might say, "I can't do that, I feel inadequate." Good! It was said of Dwight L. Moody that after a service a man came up to him and said, "Sir, you made eighteen grammatical mistakes in your sermon," to which Moody responded, "At least I am using my eighteen grammatical mistakes to the glory of God, what about you?" Would that we were all like the Apostle Paul in our zeal for evangelism, as he said, "Now then, we are ambassadors for Christ, as though God were pleading through us: we implore you on Christ's behalf, be reconciled to God" (2 Corinthians 5:20). To the elders of the church in Ephesus, he wrote, "Therefore watch, and remember that for three years I did not cease to warn everyone night and day with tears" (Acts 20:31). Some of Jesus' final instructions to His disciples were "Go therefore and make disciples of all the nations, baptizing them in the name of the Father and of the Son and of the Holy Spirit, teaching them to observe all things that I have commanded you; and lo, I am with you always, even to the end of the age" (Matthew 28:19-20).

Something is wrong with us if we have no desire to bring sinners into the kingdom, or if we have no desire to tell a deceived brother or sister that we don't see fruit in their life. You might say,

"Well I have pursued those who claim to know Christ and yet they don't respond. What should I do?" If they are a professing sister or brother in sin, then you follow the steps that Jesus sets forth in Matthew 18:15-20. If they just deny the faith and are hardened towards it, then we have to agree with the Apostle John's conclusion: "They went out from us, but they were not of us; for if they had been of us, they would have continued with us; but they went out that they might be made manifest, that none of them were of us" (1 John 2:19).

In my own life I have lost good friends, or those I thought were good friends, because I warned them of what God says in His Word, but I take great comfort in the disciples who were able to go away rejoicing for the Kingdom's sake (Acts 5:41). I also take comfort in the words of the Apostle Peter who said that it is better to suffer for doing what is right than to suffer for doing what is evil (1 Peter 3:17). Even if we are rejected, we should never stop praying for the soul of the one who rejects us, and we must continually live Christ before them. In verse 20, James continues with some encouraging words for those who pursue the wandering one.

The Concluding Promise

James 5:20. Let him know that he who turns a sinner from the error of his way will save a soul from death and cover a multitude of sins.

"Let him know that he who turns a sinner," conveys a personal word of encouragement and assurance for the believer who pursues the sinner. "Be encouraged," James is saying. "This is a good thing you are doing. If you convert this woman—if she turns around and turns to God—this is a great thing!"

Sinner is a word that is often used to describe those outside the kingdom of God. The Apostle John wrote, "Whoever has been born of God does not sin, for His seed remains in him; and he cannot sin, because he has been born of God" (1 John 3:9). Jesus says, "For I did not come to call the righteous, but *sinners*, to repentance"

(Matthew 9:13, emphasis mine). In the parable of the lost sheep, He said, "I say to you that likewise there will be more joy in heaven over one *sinner* who repents than over ninety-nine just persons who need no repentance" (Luke 15:7, emphasis mine). Paul wrote, "God demonstrates His own love toward us, in that while we were still *sinners*, Christ died for us" (Romans 5:8, emphasis mine). To Timothy, Paul wrote, "Christ Jesus came into the world to save *sinners*, of whom I am chief" (1 Timothy 1:15).

Now that James has warned all of the church to pursue sinners, he delineates the benefits of converting a sinner. They are (1) to "save a soul from death" and (2) to "cover a multitude of sins." *Save a soul from death* means to save one from eternal death and punishment. It could also mean a physical death, as one who dies spiritual will certainly die physically. This spiritual death includes eternal separation from God, as He says, "The soul who sins shall die" (Ezekiel 18:4). The verb *save* is used in the sense of eternal salvation.[69] James has already used this term when referring to the implanted word which is able to *save* your souls (James 1:21). In 4:12, he uses it again: "There is one Lawgiver, who is able to *save* and to destroy" (emphasis mine). To participate in saving someone from spiritual death is the greatest act of love that one human being can do for another.

The second benefit of converting a sinner is that it "will cover a multitude of sins." This is not meant in the sense of keeping their sins secret, as in covering them up, but in the sense that you secure their forgiveness. In Psalm 32:1, David says, "Blessed is he whose transgression is forgiven, whose sin is covered." We know that David's sin with Bathsheba was not kept secret, but it was forgiven. Think about Psalm 85:2, which says, "You have forgiven the iniquity of Your people; You have covered all their sin." This verse refers to the nation's captivity and rebellion. It was not a secret—but it was forgiven. The covering is performed by God who covers our sins in such a way that they will not be seen. James describes our

---

[69] John MacArthur comments on this term: "A word used to describe the unregenerate (Proverbs 11:31; 13:6, 22; Matthew 9:13; Luke 7:37, 39; 15:7, 10; 18:13; Romans 5:8; 1 Timothy 1:9, 15; 1 Peter 4:18). James has in mind here those with dead faith (2:14-26), not sinning true believers." John MacArthur, Jr. *The MacArthur Study Bible* (Word Publishing, 1997), p. 1935.

sins as "a multitude of sins," which would denote one's sins in their entirety, which God will forgive to those who believe the gospel truth. This act of mercy on the part of God certainly demonstrates the extent of His forgiveness. Because of God's love, His Son's shed blood covers the multitude of sins. In His grace God hides all our sins. Praise the Lord!

Think back to the time you gave your life to Christ—think of the countless sins that God covered and forgave. They were many, were they not? The person who led you to the truth had a part in that covering of your sins. Salvation is of the Lord, but He uses human instruments as tools for proclaiming the gospel of His Son Jesus Christ (Romans 10:14). I know some who have attempted to use this passage to prove that we are to cover one another's sins in our personal relationships, but that is not what James is speaking of here. He is talking about the covering of our sins because of the shed blood of Christ Jesus. He is plainly speaking of our salvation. There *are* passages which talk about covering others' sins, like "Above all things have fervent love for one another, for 'love will cover a multitude of sins'" (1 Peter 4:8). The notion here is that we hide and cover the sins of those we love and do not expose them unless they are living in unrepentant sin. In that case, we would go to them and follow the principles that Jesus outlined in Matthew 18:15-20.[70] But again, that is not the issue that James is addressing here.

With these clear and practical words James ends his letter, although excluding the customary greeting and closings usually found in the other epistles. The Apostle Paul usually ends his letters with "peace be with you," or "grace be with you," or "greet one another with a holy kiss." But James is practical and to the point.

---

[70] Jesus taught on reproving a brother and the process of discipline in the local church: "Moreover if your brother sins against you, go and tell him his fault between you and him alone. If he hears you, you have gained your brother. But if he will not hear, take with you one or two more, that 'by the mouth of two or three witnesses every word may be established.' And if he refuses to hear them, tell it to the church. But if he refuses even to hear the church, let him be to you like a heathen and a tax collector. Assuredly, I say to you, whatever you bind on earth will be bound in heaven, and whatever you loose on earth will be loosed in heaven. Again I say to you that if two of you agree on earth concerning anything that they ask, it will be done for them by My Father in heaven. For where two or three are gathered together in My name, I am there in the midst of them" (Matthew 18:15-20).

How unusual for him! The abrupt ending keeps with the nature and purpose of the book. James' motive as well as mine is not to condemn you, but to encourage and motivate you to a more committed walk with the Lord, and to make sure that each of you as women have committed your life to the Lordship of Christ. Otherwise, I have failed you and I have failed my Lord. I think we must always be measuring our faith and ourselves by what the Word teaches. James has demonstrated to us that Christian faith is a serious matter—not a creed, but a life-transforming experience that shows itself in action. It is a faith that works!

Questions to Consider
"A Call to Salvation – Conclusion"
James 5:19-20

1. Read the book of James prayerfully asking God what areas still need to be changed in your life.

2. Memorize James 5:19-20.

3. Read Ezekiel 3:16-21 and 33:1-20. (a) What did God tell Ezekiel to do? (b) Why was Ezekiel to do this? (c) Do you think this is a loving thing to do? (d) How does this relate to what James is saying as he concludes his epistle in 5:19-20?

4. We have brought out many times throughout this book that James and the Sermon on the Mount (Matthew 5–7) are similar. Read both the Epistle of James and the Sermon on the Mount, listing as many similarities as you can find.

5. Read Isaiah 53. (a) What did Christ endure on your behalf? (b) What should your response be to this? (Your answer is not in the book of Isaiah, but inside your heart.)

6. (a) Is there someone in your life to whom you need to be witnessing? Will you? (b) Is there someone who is in sin that you need to admonish and warn? Will you? (c) Is there someone who professes Christ but whose faith you doubt? Will you lovingly warn them?

7. After considering these questions, what is your prayer?

Postscript

Since the Epistle of James is a series of tests to test our faith, I will now give you a test—teachers have the prerogative to administer tests, right? I would encourage you to go over the following questions from each of the five chapters of the Epistle of James. Do this in the privacy of your heart with the Lord. If you are married, you might also want to review these with your spouse asking him to honestly evaluate your faith. In addition to evaluating your own faith, think of those closest to you and look to see if their life is bringing forth these fruits. If not, will you go and convert them? Will you honestly share the Good News with them?

> Now may the God of peace who brought up our Lord Jesus from the dead, that great Shepherd of the sheep, through the blood of the everlasting covenant, make you complete in every good work to do His will, working in you what is well pleasing in His sight, through Jesus Christ, to whom be glory forever and ever. Amen. (Hebrews 13:20-21)

Tests of Faith – James 1

1) Do you count your trials with joy? (v 2)
2) Do you see your trials as something that God uses to perfect your faith and develop patience? (v 4)
3) Do you ask God for wisdom in trials, and do you ask in faith? (v 5)
4) If you don't have much money today, are you still joyful in what God has provided? (v 9)
5) If you have an abundance of money today, do you recognize your wealth as a gift from God, and do you see your life as fleeting, regardless of your wealth? (vv 10-11)
6) Do you endure trials? (v 12)
7) Do you blame God for your temptations? (vv 13-14)
8) Do you recognize the many gifts that God has poured out on you and are you grateful? (v 17)

9) Are you swift to hear, slow to speak and slow to get angry at the Word of God, or to those who proclaim it? (v 19)
10) Have you put away all filthiness and wickedness from your life? (v 21)
11) Do you receive the Word with meekness? (v 21)
12) Are you a doer of the Word, or merely a hearer (an auditor)? (vv 22-25)
13) Do you continue in the Word, or are you haphazard in your time with God? (v 25)
14) Do you keep a tight reign on your tongue? (v 26)
15) Do you minister to the orphans and widows? (v 27)
16) Are you keeping yourself unspotted from the world? (v 27)

Tests of Faith – James 2

17) Do you show favoritism to any class of people—poor or rich? (vv 1-10)
18) Do you love your neighbor as yourself? (v 8)
19) Is your life characterized by showing mercy? (vv 13)
20) Does your faith show itself by your works? (vv 14-26)
21) Do you help the destitute brother or sister? (vv 14-17)

Tests of Faith – James 3

22) If you have the gift of teaching, have you rushed into that office? (v 1)
23) If you have the gift of teaching, do you study hard to interpret Scripture accurately, and does your life measure up to what you teach? (v 1)
24) Do you bless God and curse others with the same mouth? (v 10)
25) Does your life manifest a life of wisdom? (vv 13-18)
26) Do you prove yourself to be wise by an upright life? (v 13)
27) Do you have bitterness, envy, or strife in your heart? (vv 14-16)
28) When you speak and give advice, is it pure, peaceable, gentle, willing to yield, full of mercy and good fruits, without partiality and without hypocrisy—or is it earthly, sensual, and demonic? (vv 14-18)
29) Are your fruits of righteousness sown in peace? (v 18)

Tests of Faith – James 4

30) Are you known as a person who argues? Do you always have to have things your way? (vv 1-3)
31) Do you pray for selfish desires? (vv 1-3)
32) Are you a friend of the world? (v 4)
33) Is your life characterized by humility? (v 6)
34) Do you submit to God? (v 7)
35) Do you resist the devil? (v 7)
36) Do you draw near to God? (v 8)
37) Do you weep and mourn over your sins? (v 9)
38) Do you speak evil of others and judge others? (v 11)
39) Do you make plans without consulting the Lord? (vv 13-16)
40) Are you a proud and boastful person? (v 16)
41) When you know that something is right, do you do it? (v 17)

Tests of Faith – James 5

42) Do you live for pleasures on this earth? (v 5)
43) Are you oppressive towards those who are less fortunate than you? (vv 4, 6)
44) Are you patient towards those who afflict you? (v 6)
45) During afflictions, do you establish (prop up) your heart? (v 8)
46) Do you murmur against others during afflictions? (v 9)
47) Does your "yes" mean "yes" and your "no" mean "no"? Can your word be trusted? (v 12)
48) Do you make rash vows? (v 12)
49) Do you pray in affliction? (v 13)
50) Do you sing when you're merry? (v 13)
51) When you're sick, do you call the spiritual leadership to come and pray for you? (v 14)
52) When you are sick, do you search your heart for sin? (v 15)
53) Do you confess your sins to those you have wronged? (v 16)
54) Do you have someone that you are accountable to? Someone to pray with and with whom to share your real struggles? (v 16)
55) Are you a woman of prayer? (vv 17-18)

56) Do you go after the sinner? Do you share your faith? (vv 19-20)

TATE PUBLISHING & *Enterprises*

Tate Publishing is commited to excellence in the publishing industry. Our staff of highly trained professionals, including editors, graphic designers, and marketing personnel, work together to produce the very finest books available. The company reflects the philosophy established by the founders, based on Psalms 68:11,

"THE LORD GAVE THE WORD AND GREAT WAS THE COMPANY OF THOSE WHO PUBLISHED IT."

If you would like further information, please call
1.888.361.9473
or visit our website
www.tatepublishing.com

TATE PUBLISHING & *Enterprises*, LLC
127 E. Trade Center Terrace
Mustang, Oklahoma 73064 USA